J

B

CW00515330

Joy Mawby was born and grew up in Camberley, Surrey. She became a primary school teacher and later head-teacher of three very different schools.

Throughout her career she encouraged children in their writing and in the performing arts. She wrote and produced numerous plays for her students.

On retirement she moved to Anglesey and, at last, had time to give to her own writing. She runs a creative writing group, has had two plays performed on the island and several poems in local publications. Joy has two children, three very creative grandchildren and two dogs, who keep her fit.

FOOTSTEPS TO FREEDOM

JOY MAWBY

FOOTSTEPS TO FREEDOM

AUSTIN & MACAULEY

A CIP catalogue record for this title is available from the British Library.

ISBN 978 1 905609 56 7

www.austinmacauley.com

First Published (2009)
Austin & Macauley Publishers Ltd.
25 Canada Square
Canary Wharf
London
E14 5LB

Printed & Bound in Great Britain

DEDICATION

This book is dedicated to Anna Dzierzek and to my family including those members who live on in our memories.

ACKNOWLEDGEMENTS

I acknowledge my sincere gratitude to:

Anna Dzierzek, the central figure in this amazing story, who handed me her manuscript in 1994

Anna's daughter who trusted me with the re-telling of her mother's story and who has edited the text, with special reference to Polish and Russian names, place names and phrases.

Alexa Sturrock and Kay Middlemiss who edited the text painstakingly and thoroughly and who encouraged me in my endeavour.

The Amlwch Creative Writing Group for their suggestions and encouragement.

The Polish Historical Institute and General Sikorski Museum for allowing me to publish statistics held in their archives.

The original members of the 'Dinner Club' for their help with the cover illustration.

INTRODUCTION

In 1994, an amateur dramatic group with which I was involved, wanted to stage a play about the Second World War. I remembered hearing a little of Anna Dzierżek's story at a dinner party so I phoned her and asked if I could visit her with my tape recorder. She agreed.

We sat in the front room of her house in Tooting and she started to talk. She told me story after story. We ran out of tape but still she had more to tell. Finally, I thanked her very much and, as I was leaving, I said, 'You've had such amazing experiences. You really should write them all down.'

'I have.' She said. 'Would you like to read my memoirs?'

I read into the night. I couldn't put the manuscript down. When I returned it I asked if she'd tried to have it published.

'I did try,' she answered. 'Someone in America wanted to make it into a film but nothing came of it. I wrote it all soon after the war. I needed to get it out of my system before I could get on with the rest of my life. It probably needs a lot of work to make it ready for publication.'

In 2007 Anna's daughter handed the manuscript to me. 'I think I should do something with this,' she said. 'Would you like to take it on as a project?'

Footnote

Apart from members of her own family, Anna changed the name of the people still living at the time she wrote her memoirs. She did this to protect their privacy. I have retained Anna's chapter headings and the title she gave the whole work. I have also sought to find a cover illustration to match one she described to her daughter as appropriate for her story.

PART ONE

CHAPTER 1

Blitzkrieg 1939

The Luftwaffe bombers appeared, without warning, in the blue skies over Krzemieniec. They released their first bombs over the town centre, returning again and again to machine-gun the terrified people in the market square. Anna dashed into a doorway, sick with fear. Across the road she saw a boy, in scout uniform, running towards her. She screamed at him to get flat on the ground but he didn't hear. The bullet hit him as he reached her. He died in her arms a few minutes later, calling for his mother.

This memory was to haunt Anna forever. It was 13th September 1939...

One week earlier, Anna had parted from her mother on the doorstep of their Warsaw home. The Ministry of Foreign Affairs, for whom she worked, was to be evacuated to Krzemieniec, away from the Nazi threat – or so it was thought. Her mother stood pale but composed as she handed Anna a small parcel of provisions for the journey. Then she kissed her and traced the sign of the cross on her forehead. They never saw each other again.

In the courtyard of the Foreign Office, Anna found a corner in a truck laden with personnel and cases of official papers. Above her, fluttered the grey snowflakes of hastily burned documents. Later, at the station, the train was delayed until evening and all over the city, fires lit up the sky. Anna stared at them, blinking back her tears. Loneliness and fear for the safety of her loved ones swept over her.

The week on board the train passed as if in a nightmare. The train had to be replaced several times because of direct hits by enemy fire. The passengers, cramped as they were, were better off than the thousands of panic stricken refugees they saw clogging the roads, which were targets for the Luftwaffe. Villages and hamlets burned. Nowhere was safe.

At last, dirty and tired, Anna's party had arrived in Krzemieniec in the Ukraine. At first glance it seemed peaceful and the shops well stocked but as she and her office colleague, Irena, made their weary way to the Castle of Visnioviec, where they had been told to report, the bombers had swooped in.

Distraught now and with their suitcases lost somewhere during the air raid, they struggled to the castle where they were comforted and fed. Next they washed the grime of the journey away and sank, exhausted, into comfortable, makeshift, beds.

Next day a meeting was called. 'It's been decided,' the senior official told them, 'it will be safer for you and for the Ministry if personnel are dispersed to lodgings throughout this neighbourhood. The castle is an easy target. Some work will be done here and some can be carried out at other venues. You're to be paid three months salary in advance. Ministry officials will be in touch with you very soon.'

Anna and Irena, clutching their few belongings, were dropped off at a large farm several kilometres from the castle. The owner, a Polish woman, met them with a scowl.

'I already have far too many people here,' she complained. 'Refugees arrive every day. We're crowded out. My neighbours hate me because I'm a 'foreign' landowner. All our men are away in the war and three local Polish women have been raped and beaten and their houses and crops burned...'

She was interrupted by a thundering at the door, which burst open to reveal a large Ukrainian woman, swaying drunkenly.

'Lady,' she shouted, 'I have served you and your husband faithfully for many years. I deserve your money and your jewels. The Russians are coming tomorrow so we'll burn your house tonight.'

Anna and Irena stood, transfixed, but the owner jumped at the cook and tried to push her out of the door.

'Help me!' she shrieked. Anna and Irena leapt to help and, between them, they managed to bundle the woman through the doorway, slam and then bolt the door. They listened while her shouts grew fainter as she reeled away, back to the village.

'I'm not staying here for my house to be burnt about my ears or to be taken prisoner by the Russians,' declared the Polish woman. 'I've packed a bag ready. I'll take some food. If any of the refugees wish, they can come with me. We'll make for the nearest town.'

'We should go back to the castle,' Anna whispered to Irena. 'Let's go now, while it's dark.'

They wished the Polish woman luck, went quickly and quietly out across the orchard and through a small wood to reach the main road. They turned towards the castle and walked until the sky began to lighten. With the dawn came thick white mist, enveloping the countryside. Wearily, they rested by the roadside waiting for it to lift. It would be too easy to lose their way and stumble into trouble. They dozed, waking suddenly to blue sky and sunshine. Behind them they saw bombs falling on a hamlet. Hastily eating a little bread they'd brought from the farm and washing it down with a couple of gulps of water, they turned once more towards Visnioviec Castle. By midday it was extremely hot and they were within a mile of their destination.

It was then that Irena gripped Anna's arm.

'What's that?'

It was a band of youths, rushing towards them, brandishing sticks and shouting loudly.'

It was the last straw. Anna's mind raced.

'We've survived the bombs, escaped from the Russians, walked all night and now we're going to be beaten to death by a crowd of angry Ukrainians...there's nowhere to run...'

And then a strange and wonderful thing happened. A car horn sounded and an old fashioned limousine, driven by a military chauffeur, drew up beside them. It was crammed with Polish soldiers and, at the back, sat a young woman, dressed in black. Afterwards, Anna could not imagine how the soldiers managed to squeeze in two more passengers, but manage they did. At the sight of so many armed Polish men, the rabble of Ukrainians melted away.

When Anna told the officer in charge that they were trying to get back to the castle, he looked grave.

'This morning, Russian troops crossed into Poland at hundreds of points,' he explained. 'They're advancing rapidly, we gather. It would be dangerous to return to Visnioviec Castle on your own. If you stay with us we'll take you to Lviv, where we are going to rejoin our units.' Irena and Anna exchanged glances and nodded at each other. They could only accept the offer.

'Perhaps we'll find out what's best for us to do when we get to Lviv.' Irena said softly. They discovered that the young woman in black was Danish and called Helga. The car belonged to her and her husband, a Polish officer who had been killed in an air raid the previous day. She had offered the officer and his men the use of the chauffeur-driven car in exchange for their protection on the journey to Lviv. There, she would try to contact the Danish Consulate.

The occupants of the car shared out what little food and water they had as they drove and then, in the late afternoon, the car stopped.

'Out of petrol,' the driver informed them. 'I wondered how long it would last.'

After the consternation, the officer took charge.

'We must disable the car,' he said. 'We won't leave it for the Russians.' The driver had lifted the bonnet and unholstered his pistol when a second strange and wonderful thing happened. First came an odd rumbling noise, then a cloud of dust and then, from a side road, a diminutive tank – a tanquette. It was driven by a Polish soldier. Four more men sat on top.

'We're out of petrol,' called the officer. 'Can you give us a tow?'

The tanquette halted and the driver called back, 'I'm terribly sorry, sir. We've very little fuel left ourselves. We have to get to Lviv urgently.'

'Drive on then,' answered the officer. 'We'll make our own way there.'

Ruefully, Anna watched the tanquette disappear but almost before anyone could speak it was back beside them.

'We couldn't leave Polish ladies in distress,' announced the driver with a grin. 'We'll tow you as far as the fuel holds out and then decide what to do.'

Joyfully, a rope was found and tied to the limousine and the strange convoy proceeded for six or seven miles. The driver brought it to a halt in the shelter of a small birch wood.

He turned to the officer.

'The petrol's nearly gone, sir,' he said. 'This is the last shelter for some miles. What do you think we should do?'

Before the officer could answer, the third strange and wonderful thing happened – the strangest of all. The bushes at the side of the road parted to reveal an old man, an Orthodox Jew, dressed in a black kaftan and a skullcap.

'Do not draw your pistols, sirs,' he requested quietly. 'Would you gentlemen soldiers like some petrol?'

They could hardly believe their ears.

'Want petrol? We're desperate!' the officer managed.

The man disappeared into the undergrowth for a moment, returning with two cans of fuel. He refused payment.

'Not from our soldiers,' he affirmed with quiet dignity. His grey beard and long side locks trembled as each of the group thanked him and shook his hand.

'Goodbye and Godspeed,' he said and his old eyes were full of tears.

As the car could travel faster than the tanquette, the officer decided his group should part company with their rescuers. Thanking them warmly, they sped towards Lviv. Ahead they saw the sky lit with fire and heard the boom of bombs and sharp crack of machine-gun fire. Twice they were forced to take shelter in ditches at the side of the road. The road became packed with pedestrians, fleeing from the town. Vehicles lay shattered and everywhere there were corpses.

Still they drove on, Irena and Anna silent and fearful. Suddenly the car swerved, almost leaving the road. At the same time, the sound of tearing metal and screams filled the air. Irena lurched into Anna and lay still. The flying shrapnel had hit her in her chest and on her head.

'Irena!' Anna was beside herself. 'Irena. Wake up, wake up!'

The car stopped and the officer leant over the injured girl.

'She's breathing,' he said quickly. 'Driver, there's a field hospital at the edge of Brody, the town just ahead. Get there as fast as possible.'

As they bumped along, Anna offered up a prayer as she held her friend gently in her arms. At the hospital, Irena, now conscious, was taken by the sisters.

'She must stay here,' one said. 'The shrapnel must be removed from the wound and she will need to rest for a week or so.'

Anna and Irena bade each other a tearful farewell.

'We'll try and meet up again in Lviv,' Anna assured Irena. 'We'll find a way out of all of this.' How little she dreamed that this was the last she'd see of Irena.

As they drove the fifty kilometres between Brody and Lviv, the air raids subsided and the roads were thick with refugees. The officer told them what he had learned from the sisters at the hospital.

'The Germans are almost at Lviv,' he reported. 'Our soldiers are just about holding them off. I'm delighted to say that Warsaw has not surrendered but the news from the front is grim. The Germans are advancing rapidly and the Polish divisions are fighting desperately but are being pushed to the East, where the Russians are waiting to capture them.'

'The Russians! A new threat,' Anna thought as they drove into Lviv. It was dusk. She could hardly see the ancient city for the clouds of dust and smoke and she could hear the now familiar artillery fire and sirens.

The streets were crowded with soldiers and civilians but there was no sign of panic. The people of Lviv seemed to be in fighting mood. The chauffeur stopped the car in the main square. Bidding a hasty farewell, the officer and soldiers hurried off to report to the military headquarters.

The chauffeur managed to get a room for the two women in the Hotel George, the biggest hotel in the town.

'You'll be as safe here as anywhere,' he said. 'I'll help you with the luggage – and take this with you.' He produced a loaded revolver and a small box of ammunition from the glove compartment. Anna took them gingerly and pushed them into the middle of her small bundle of belongings. Helga's luggage was soon unloaded into the first floor bedroom. Then the driver departed to report to the military authorities.

Just then another raid commenced. An urgent voice on the landing called, 'Everyone must go to the basement bar for safety.'

Leaving everything, Anna and Helga joined the rush down the two flights of stairs. The bar had been converted into a shelter and first aid post. There, they were given small portions of bread and meat and tea. The place was crowded with frightened but prosperous looking civilians. Helga and Anna found a corner and sat down on the floor. Anna immediately dropped deeply asleep and didn't stir until the bustle of morning awoke her.

Helga had hardly slept and now, exhausted with sorrow and fear, she fell asleep in the bedroom. Anna asked some elderly Polish women to keep an eye on her and went into the hotel's reception hall to see what she could find out. The hall was full of weary and dusty Polish officers and NCOs organising food, hot drinks and first aid for their men in the trenches. In a side room, women were engaged in tearing hotel sheets into strips for bandages and, near the front entrance, a group of girl and boy scouts was preparing to set off with buckets of soup and jugs, cans and kettles containing tea and milk.

'Please can I help. Is there anything I can do?' An officer turned and smiled at Anna's question.

'Certainly, young lady,' he replied. 'Our men are dug in two streets away. They need supplies and you can help.' He handed her a jug, brimming with milk. 'Follow the others...and don't spill it!'

'At last,' Anna thought, 'I can be useful.' She hardly heard the artillery a few streets away. She crossed the square, holding the jug carefully. 'Our soldiers need me and I won't...' The thought was never finished for a German sniper, from the top of a nearby building fired at her, missed, hit the pavement which smashed, sending a piece of concrete shooting upwards into the china jug. It shattered and, in dismay, Anna saw the milk lying in a pool at her feet. Humiliation rather than fear swept over her. How could she face the officer who had trusted her? But when she ran back to the hotel, he only laughed and called her plucky and gave her another jug to carry.

Over the next few days, Anna and the scouts made the hazardous journey between hotel and trenches again and again. The soldiers were so brave, exhausted and many were injured. Somehow they always managed a smile and a joke as they gratefully took the provisions offered. The bodies of the dead could not be cleared fast enough so Anna sometimes had to step over them on her way. The wounded were tended by the townsfolk. Despite desperate circumstances, there was optimism and patriotism in the air.

'You know Lviv's motto,' a woman called to Anna, once; 'Semper Fidelis – Always Faithful – We'll never surrender!'

Everyone Anna met about the town, in the hotel or in the trenches, believed that somehow help would arrive from somewhere. Each day she and everyone else in the hotel huddled round the radio in the hotel lounge. The news from Warsaw was encouraging. Its people were still fighting. Stefan Starzynski, the charismatic and brave Mayor, was leading the civilian volunteers in the stand against the Nazis. Stories of heroism abounded. But in Lviv there was no let-up to the air raids and the fighting.

Then on September 21st, Anna woke to silence. Absent were the distant rumble of guns and drone of warplanes. Eerie stillness filled the air. Anna ran down to the reception hall. For the first time, there were no officers about. People stood around uneasily.

'What's happening?' Anna asked several onlookers. And then, as if in answer to her question, there was the roar of planes and before anyone could dive for cover, leaflets, not bombs, dropped from the sky… thousands of them. They lay like snow on roofs and roads and were thick in the city square. Anna picked one up. It had a black border and was written in very bad Polish.

'To the people of Lviv,' it began. 'The German Command demands that your city surrenders within the next twenty-four hours. Meanwhile, the bombardment will cease. Those wishing to leave the city must take the road leading to the village of Vinniki where Soviet troops will meet them. If your city does not surrender by 11am tomorrow morning (September 23rd) it will be totally destroyed together with the remaining inhabitants.'

Anna rushed back to her room, where Helga was getting dressed.

'What can we do?' Helga cried. 'We'll be killed if we stay but we can't deliver ourselves up to the Russians.' Anna, herself sick with fear, did her best to soothe her friend.

'I'll go and see what I can find out,' she replied. 'You stay here and pack your belongings in case we have to move.' With that, she was gone and, strangely, it calmed her to walk among the people of the city and learn of their plans. She gathered that the City Fathers, with the full support of the population, had decided that they would never surrender. She sent a message to Helga to say she was helping with the effort to supply the Polish soldiers, in defence positions, with food, water and ammunition. That work over, she joined others at church where, all night, masses were said for the living and the dead.

It was morning before Anna returned to the hotel. She was filthy and very tired. She wore the only clothes she possessed – and they were torn and stained. She found a little water in a carafe and washed as well as she could. Then she, Helga and everyone else in the city of Lviv waited.

The promised destruction did not come at 11am, or at noon, 1pm or 2. People crept out of their houses to ask each other what this meant. Anna was watching them from her window when, suddenly, she heard a heavy metallic sound. Tanks were approaching. She watched in horror as the first tank crawled from a side street into the square. It was flying a white flag. More tanks were arriving all the time but these were not German tanks. No black swastikas glistened on the sides of these monsters. Instead, red stars shone in the September sun, shone like splashes of freshly spilt blood.

Lorries full of soldiers followed the tanks. They looked strange to Anna's eyes… mud coloured shabby uniforms, pointed caps, Asiatic faces. They held rifles and bayonets at the ready and looked with sour suspicion on the silent crowd on the pavement.

Next came the cavalry, led by a young officer with a pistol in his hand. A pretty Ukrainian girl, in national costume, stepped out and with a welcoming smile, offered him a bunch of flowers. The officer's horse, alarmed by the sudden movement, reared. The officer aimed his pistol at the girl's breast. There was a single shot, the flowers fell to the ground and the girl, with head bowed, crumpled and disappeared into the throng. Anna turned away, tears streaming. For Helga's sake, she would not break down and when she turned back to the window, the infantry was marching past, row upon row, rank upon rank of hostile soldiers, the red stars bright on their shabby caps.

Anna swung round to Helga.

'There's no time to lose. This is the main hotel and the Russians are bound to requisition it. At any moment it will be inundated by the enemy. Finish packing, I'll make my bundle up but we must get rid of the pistol and ammunition. If they find them, we're dead.' Helga started to cry again, becoming hysterical. She called again and again for her dead husband, for her mother and screamed, 'We'll be raped and murdered... raped and murdered,' until Anna was in despair. She flung the pistol and ammunition on top of the huge old wardrobe, which stood in the corner of the room and, being unable to reason with Helga, pushed her down on to the bed. The woman stopped screaming and stared in surprise.

'Stay there!' Anna ordered. Shocked by her tone, Helga meekly got into bed and pulled the covers about her.

'Just stay there, please,' Anna entreated. 'If the Russians come, we'll say you're ill.'

It was not long before they heard loud Russian voices in the corridor. The door burst open. A Soviet officer and four soldiers walked in. The officer was short and pugnacious.

His burning cigarette stub rested on his lower lip as he surveyed them. 'Do not be afraid, grazhdanki/citizens.' He spoke in Russian and his voice was sharp but polite. 'We Russians are kulturny/cultured people. We have come to save you from the Germans and your cowardly capitalist government. A brilliant future awaits all Polish people under the benevolent guidance of the Soviet Union.' Although Anna was a fluent Russian speaker, she decided to hide this fact, to pretend she didn't understand anything the officer was saying. When she and Helga made no response, he went on. 'This hotel has been chosen as temporary accommodation for the Soviet Command. You will have to leave.' His speech was accompanied by actions, to enable the woman to understand.

Then the men searched the entire luggage in the room. They were much taken with one particularly frilly nightgown belonging to Helga. The officer held it up to the light.

'What a beautiful ball gown!' he exclaimed. 'How my wife would love to wear this.' In spite of the grim situation, Anna gave an inward smile. The officer's next discovery was a bottle of 'White Horse' whisky.

'Polish wine?' he queried. Anna took it from his hand and then offered it back to him, indicating that he could keep it. He shook his head vehemently and answered in Russian.

'I do not accept gifts while I am on duty. Soviet soldiers are not Barbarians like the Germantzy. We do not rob women.' For the first time, it seemed, he noticed Helga's wretchedness. She lay on the bed, sobbing uncontrollably. He became embarrassed and sent his men out of the room.

'Do not distress yourself, madam,' he said, and, producing two pieces of paper, wrote down the women's details on one and handed the other to Anna, saying, 'This is the name of the hotel you can go to until things are put in order.'

He glanced round once more. Anna held her breath. Would he suddenly decide to check the top of the wardrobe? He didn't. Instead, he casually slipped the bottle of whisky into his pocket and without another word strode from the room. It was only then that Anna remembered that he hadn't checked their documents.

She roused Helga by a sudden recollection.

'My parents used to have friends in Lviv, a Mr and Mrs Rylski. They stayed with us when I was a child and we visited them once. Come with me now and we'll try to track them down. I don't think it's safe to put ourselves in Soviet hands, by going to that hotel.

Choose which of your things you really need. We can't manage all your cases.'

Within half an hour, Anna and Helga had slipped out of the hotel and set off towards the Rylski's house. Anna knew she had been right in her doubts about Soviet intentions when, close to the hotel to which they had been told to report, they heard shouting and saw scuffles. Polish people were being forced into trucks and driven away to unknown destinations.

After one or two wrong turns, the two arrived at their destination. Anna was relieved to see signs of habitation. Mrs Rylski was at home. She was astounded to see Anna but was immediately hospitable.

'Come in, my dears. How tired you look. We've lots of people staying here already but we'll make room for you.' Quickly she produced a simple hot meal while Anna explained how she came to be here.

Then Mrs Rylski told them the latest news. She said that the Germans and Russians had agreed to divide Poland and surrounding territories between them. The east, with its rich oilfields would remain in Soviet hands while the Germans had the rest, including the coalmines and steel plants of Silesia. The fighting was still continuing in Warsaw. Some infantry and cavalry divisions were attempting to break through enemy lines to bring help to the stricken capital. Although she was hungry, Anna could eat no more. The faces of her family in Warsaw swam before her. She blinked back tears and, sensing her distress, Mrs Rylski changed the subject and offered Anna a change of clothes.

After a bath and dressed in clean, borrowed, over-large garments, Anna washed those she had worn since leaving Warsaw. Then she set out, with Helga, to the house of a Swiss family known to the Rylskis. These good people said Helga could stay with them and promised to help her obtain an exit permit. Anna and Helga held each other close for a moment.

'Thank you so much. Without you, I would have perished,' whispered Helga.

'It was your car I escaped in,' smiled Anna and, knowing Helga was in good hands, returned to Mrs Rylski. A mattress had been placed, on the floor, in a tiny room. Gratefully, Anna flopped on to it and was soon asleep.

The next morning, after a breakfast of bread and tea, Mrs Rylski advised Anna to destroy her Foreign Office identity card because, if it were found on her, she could be accused of spying. Anna had already decided to burn her Polish passport because it showed she had been born in Kiev. If that were discovered, the Soviet Authorities might choose to treat her as a Soviet citizen – Anna could not bear that thought.

'I'm Polish through and through,' she declared as she made a small bonfire of the papers.

The many refugees, who had lost their documents during their travels, were required to register with the Soviet Authorities in the city. Anna queued all day and, at last, received a new card, stating that she had been born in and was a resident of Warsaw and that she was a student, on holiday.

On her way home from the Soviet Office, Anna witnessed a scene she was never to forget. A long line of Polish officers and soldiers, with grave and sorrowful faces, were filing through the city square. Each stopped for a moment near its centre and threw down his belt, rifle, sabre and ammunition. Soviet officials watched them.

'What's happened?' Anna demanded of a woman nearby.

'Those fiends have ordered the surrender of all our arms,' she muttered. And as Anna turned back and saw the dignity with which the exhausted and defeated men threw their weapons on the growing pile, she wept.

It was September 29th; the day Warsaw fell to the Nazis.

CHAPTER 2

Under the Red Star

October 1939

'So it's decided, is it?' Anna looked eagerly round the group of students. 'We'll aim for England, via Sweden and France?'

Zosia, George and the two other young men Anna had met at Mrs Rylski's house, nodded vigorously. Zosia, said; 'We'll buy tickets just to the next station but stay on the train as far as Luck. Do you think your sister will mind us descending on her for a meal and a night's sleep, Anna?'

'I'm sure she won't,' Anna replied. 'It'll only be for one night then we can catch a train across the border.'

In later years, Anna could not believe they had been so naïve and stupid. They hadn't enough money, proper clothing or the right documents to travel so far. All the frontiers were heavily guarded and many of those trying to escape were summarily shot. But their youthful optimism drove them on and, bidding a grateful farewell to Mrs Rylski, she joined the others at the railway station.

The train arrived. It was full of Soviet soldiers. Anna's group managed to find seats in a compartment in which three rather drunk Russian NCOs were already sitting.

'Where are you off to?' one asked, in broken Polish. Anna thought fast.

'We're returning to our village near Luck,' she answered. 'We wish to work hard on the land for the glory of Socialism.' She wondered if she had gone too far, but, after a moment's silence, the three men burst into cheering and clapping.

'You're right about the glory of Socialism,' one exclaimed. 'But not just Socialism has glory, the mighty Soviet Republic has much, much glory too.' The others joined in, extolling the virtues of their homeland.

'We have everything,' they told Anna and her friends. 'Our factories are the best in the entire world. They can mass produce anything we want.' The young people pretended to be mightily impressed. George winked at the others.

'Surely you can't mass-produce – say Copengaga/Copenhagen he said sceptically.

'Copengaga? Copengaga?' They screamed. 'We have enormous factories which make nothing but Copengaga. There are huge machines and conveyer belts and... chop, chop, chop... out comes the Copengaga. The very gutters are full of the stuff!'

Fortunately the soldiers were too drunk to notice Anna and her friends biting their lips and trying not to laugh.

Later the ticket collector looked in but, after a sharp word from one of the Russians, withdrew and the soldiers fell asleep.

As the journey progressed, Anna began to feel unwell. Her head ached, her throat felt raw and she could not stop shivering. George wrapped his coat round her for her threadbare suit offered no warmth. She had no stockings and her shoes were stuffed with cardboard, where the soles had once been.

At last, the train arrived at Luck. By now, Anna was coughing almost continually and could barely drag herself along. Supported by George and Zosia, she led the way to her sister's house, passing a large church, which had been taken over for billets for Soviet soldiers. Dismayed, they saw the broken stained glass windows, a protruding stove pipe, belching black smoke and even horses inside the sacred building.

They hurried on, worried that they might be stopped, but reached the house without incident. Anna leaned on the gate, coughing but even as she thought, 'Thank God, I've made it,' a woman came out of the neighbouring house.

'Is it Justa you want?' she asked. Anna nodded, fear knotting her stomach.

'She's all right. Don't fret yourself.' The woman had noticed Anna's distress. 'She and the children have been moved out to a labourer's cottage round the corner.' Then, in a low voice, 'A heathen family of Russians needed this superior property.'

Gasping and coughing, but flooded by relief, Anna thanked her for the information and she and her friends moved off in the direction indicated.

'Is it really you, Anna, my darling?' Justa clasped Anna to her.

'I have been so worried about you all. Have you news from Warsaw...' Justa broke off abruptly. Anna had collapsed at her feet.

Anna didn't remember being washed and put to bed. She remembered hearing a man's voice saying softly, 'Influenza. She must stay in bed, have plenty of fluids and be kept warm.' She knew no more until she woke in the night to find Justa beside her.

'Don't worry, little one,' Justa whispered, 'you shall all stay here as long as you like. Drink some water now and then try to sleep again.'

The next day, the fever was less severe but Anna was so weak, she could hardly move from the bed. Zosia came into her room, looking serious.

'Anna, we can't all stay here with your sister until you're well enough to travel. That's some weeks away, the doctor says. Apart from Justa and her three children, eight other refugees are staying in this tiny cottage. It's not fair of us to take advantage of her kindness so I've been sent to tell you that we plan to leave tomorrow.'

In her weakness, Anna allowed the tears to trickle down.

'I know you're right,' she whispered, 'but we had such plans...'

'We've changed those,' Zosia said. 'Now we won't make for Britain. We plan to get to France and join the Polish Army there. When you're well, you can come and find us. We'll all meet again, you'll see.'

The next day the students were gone.

At the end of October, while Anna was still convalescing, elections were held in those parts of Poland currently occupied by the Soviet Union. These elections, it was proclaimed, were to allow the people to decide whether or not the Russian-held areas were to be incorporated into the Soviet Union. Only Communist candidates were allowed to stand. Predictably, in spite of assurances of fair elections and the patently patriotic sentiments of all the Polish inhabitants, the results were declared as being conclusively in favour of incorporation. Behind closed doors, Anna and Justa talked.

'This part of Poland has defended Western Europe from the Muscovite threat for years,' lamented Anna.

'And from the Tartars and the Turks,' added her sister. 'And now it isn't even called Poland any more, but Zapadnaya Ukraina/Western Ukraine – it's an integral part of the USSR.'

Justa was the only member of the household with a work permit. She was employed at her old office in the town hall. She and her children had ration cards, unlike Anna and the refugees who were staying in the house. The family shared what they could but there was never enough to go round and the children had to have priority.

By the start of November, Anna had recovered enough to report to the military office to register as a refugee, living temporarily with relatives. Then she set about trying to obtain some food.

Day after day, while Justa was at work, Anna spent many hours in long queues, trying to buy something, anything, by way of food. She bartered any saleable belongings she could lay her hands on. When she was not queuing, she carried countless buckets of water from the well at the bottom of the garden to the house.

There was an outbreak of typhoid fever in the town, due to bad sanitation and contaminated water. One by one the children and the refugees fell prey to the dread disease. Only Anna and Justa remained well. They did all they could for the stricken and, slowly but miraculously, they all recovered.

As Anna was standing in a long queue for food in early December, she shivered in the bitter wind which penetrated the man's overcoat and holey shawl she was wearing. Her feet were ice cold, in spite of her two pairs of old stockings, boots and snowshoes, fashioned from straw. She looked around.

'We all look more or less the same,' she thought ruefully,

'...same motley selection of clothes, same red noses, pinched faces, blue lips. We look like members of a macabre carnival. We're even moving in unison, stamping feet and beating hands in some outlandish dance.'

Suddenly she became aware of a man, in a new winter coat with fur collar, watching her from the other side of the street.

'Look the other way,' she said to herself. 'Don't make eye contact. Pretend you haven't noticed.'

Just then, the shop opened and Anna shuffled forward with the others. Today was lucky. She came out of the shop with a bag of flour and a bottle of oil.

To her dismay, the man was waiting for her near the corner of the street. He stepped in front of her.

'I remember you,' he said. 'You used to work at the Foreign Office in Warsaw in Marshal Pilsudski Square.' Anna's heart thumped and she almost dropped her basket. She gave the man a hard look and tried to get past.

'You won't remember me madam,' he continued. 'I was a taxi driver in the rank by your office. You took my cab many times to your home in Nowy Swiat Street. My name is Kazio Olszuk.'

'It's some sort of trap!' Anna could feel panic rising. 'He's too well dressed...too well nourished...' She sidestepped smartly, dodged round the man and didn't stop running until she reached home.

She decided not to say anything to her sister about the incident,

'It might be nothing,' she rationalised. But two days later, there was Kazio Olszuk again, watching her as she queued. This time, he came over to her and spoke softly,

'I have something very important to say to you,' he insisted.

Anna's heart lurched. She didn't want to make a scene or to antagonise the man. She swallowed hard and, trying to keep her voice steady, replied, 'I must get food first for my sister's children. After that, I'll allow you to speak to me here, in full view of many people.' He nodded and waited while she moved slowly forward to buy whatever food she could. This time she could not escape him. He stood squarely in front of her and spoke quietly. 'I have a favour to ask of you,' he said. 'My two young sisters are at school and are having great difficulties with their lessons. I know you are a well-educated young lady. I would like it very much if you would act as a tutor to them for two for three hours a week. I can offer a good salary and maybe able to 'organise' some extra food for your sister's children.'

It was very tempting – a chance to earn some money to help Justa, but there were questions she must ask.

'How is it that you can afford to engage a tutor?' she asked. 'How is it that you are so well dressed and obviously eat well when so many of us Poles can barely keep ourselves alive?'

There was a long silence then the man sighed and looked straight at her.

'It's a long story,' he replied, 'but you have a right to ask. I was wounded in the bombardment of Warsaw. I, with many of the injured, was evacuated to the South East. Once I had recovered, I discharged myself from hospital and set off in the direction of my hometown, Luck, where my mother and two sisters live. Along the road, I found a broken down and abandoned car. I managed to fix it and to obtain some petrol. I reached here two days before the Russians did. When they arrived, a Soviet colonel commandeered the car and employed me as chauffeur.'

Anna had listened in silence. Now she said, 'So you are a Soviet employee?' The man flushed.

'I am. In extreme times we all do things we would not do otherwise. If you will do this favour for me, I'll pay you a substantial salary and I'll probably be able to obtain some extra food, from my colonel, for your sister.'

Anna made up her mind. She must do something to earn her keep at Justa's. Here was a golden opportunity.

'I will tutor your sisters. If you tell me where you live, I'll come later today to find out how we get on.'

That evening, Anna met her pupils who were pleasant girls, not very accomplished, but willing to learn. The parents were simple, straightforward and honestly anxious about their daughters' education.

For the next few weeks Anna went every evening to work with the girls. Often she was invited to stay for a meal. She was paid regularly and able to carry home small food parcels for Justa's household. On several occasions, she met young men and women in the house. They stayed a few days and then left, to be replaced by another group. This didn't seem at all strange, as refugees came and went all the time – until, one evening, she met a man called Severyn,

He was about forty, older than the usual visitors and had an air of quiet authority. After supper, the girls, Kazio and their parents went out of the living room, leaving Anna alone with him. He regarded her with his deep-set grey eyes, frowning as he spoke.

'Anna, we have been watching you for some time,' he began. The room seemed to swim before Anna's eyes.

'Is this it?' Her mind raced. 'Have I been lured into some sort of trap?' She stood up and looked at the door. Severyn moved away from her as if to reassure her that he wouldn't stop her going if she so chose.

'Anna, I understand your alarm and suspicion but listen to what I have to say. If it holds no interest for you, you can walk away and carry on with your life just as if this conversation had never happened.' Something in his voice made Anna sit down again, look straight at him and listen.

'We've been watching you,' Severyn continued. 'We know of your background at the Foreign Office. Kazio and others I have spoken to vouch for your loyalty and patriotic spirit. We invite you to join our ranks – the ranks of the Polish Resistance.'

CHAPTER 3

A soldier in mufti 1939 – 1940

For a moment, Anna couldn't reply. She was almost overwhelmed by a mixture of pride, joy and relief. At last, she was able to say, 'Thank you. It's a great honour to be asked.'

'Are you absolutely sure?'

'Absolutely.'

'Then raise your right hand.' Anna obeyed and, under Severyn's guidance, swore a solemn oath of allegiance and became a member of the Polish Resistance.

Life, for Anna, continued much as normal until two days before Christmas. It was late in the evening when one of Kazio's sisters appeared at Justa's house, asking for Anna.

'Please come to my home quickly,' she begged. 'My brother needs to talk to you.'

When Anna arrived at the house, she learned that Kazio was ill and in bed. She was taken straight to his room where she found him with a high fever but able to talk rationally.

'Downstairs there is a young Polish pilot,' he told her. 'During September, his plane crashed. Both of his arms are fractured. Somehow he's managed to avoid being caught by the Russians, who are still looking for him. His injuries will not heal without proper medical care. He's in terrible pain and tonight I was to have taken him, in the colonel's car, to Kovel, where he can be treated. I am too ill to drive, I'm afraid and you are his only hope. Tonight you must drive him there. My wife will give you the address.'

He sank back on his pillow, exhausted with the effort of talking and he waved Anna away when she protested.

'But, Kazio, I've only had a couple of lessons, I'm not very good at changing gear yet.

Kovel is 40 kilometres away… It's minus twelve degrees outside. The roads are icy…'

'There's no-one else,' he whispered. Anna thought of her oath of loyalty and knew that she must do her best.

She went downstairs into the living room, where Kazio's wife handed her the address in Kovel. A young man, wrapped in a sheepskin blanket, lay on the couch. He didn't open his eyes when Anna entered the room. His face had a greenish tinge and he gave an occasional gasp of pain.

At midnight, the car, an Opel, which had been pushed from the colonel's garage, stood outside the house. The young pilot was helped into the back and Anna drove away. Later, she could not imagine how she managed to get through the dark and narrow streets without mishap. The road ran through dense pine forest. The car kept stalling and skidding on the icy surface. The poor pilot groaned and swore and condemned all women drivers. Anna bit her lip and didn't reply, reserving her angry words for the gears, the erratic engine and the ice.

They arrived at their destination at 3am. Both were exhausted. The pilot was immediately carried inside and Anna invited in for a hot drink and something to eat. She was sorely tempted, but, 'Thank you, but I'd better not,' she answered. 'I'll fall asleep if I get warm and I'll never have the courage to get back into the car. I'll go straight back.'

Almost before she'd finished speaking, a mug of hot soup and a hunk of bread were placed in her hands. So, sitting in the car, she had this simple meal and felt her strength returning. Then, as she started the engine, a woman ran from the house, carrying a large fish – a carp – wrapped in newspaper.

'A Christmas present for our brave little driver,' she laughed as she handed it to Anna. 'My husband has only just caught it. He had just hit it on the head with a hammer, when you arrived.' Thanking the woman, and wishing everyone a happy Christmas, Anna started the return journey.

Now there was even more ice about and the car, lighter without the passenger, seemed to dance and glide all over the road. Anna gripped the steering wheel, crying with fear and frustration. Suddenly, the carp, revived, it seemed by the warmth, flapped inside the newspaper and leapt out of it, in its own 'Danse Macabre.' Thoroughly unnerved, Anna screamed, skidded to a halt, opened the door and flung the fish into the frozen ditch. She sat, for a moment, head in hands, trembling. Then the faces of her three hungry nieces rose before her and, pulling herself together, she scrambled out of the car, knelt in the ice by the ditch and retrieved the now immobile carp.

The car would not re-start. In despair, Anna decided she must abandon it and walk the remaining 5 kilometres. As she reached inside for the fish, she heard the sound of hooves and a herd of cows emerged from a lane. Two Ukrainian herdsmen drove them. Anna saw a chance. She summoned her best Russian, swore at them and shouted that they must push the car. They obeyed without question, the Opel stuttered into life and Anna arrived on the outskirts of Luck at 5.45am. She left the car at a pre-arranged spot, removed the carp and reported back to Kazio's house.

It was 7.30am before she arrived home. Justa was in the kitchen, preparing a meagre breakfast. Anna couldn't tell her of her adventures because she had been sworn to secrecy – she must tell no one at all about her membership of the Polish Resistance. Justa regarded Anna and the fish suspiciously but said nothing. That evening, when the fish was served for supper, Anna could think only of its final dance and surprised everyone by refusing to eat any of it.

That winter was a hard one. Anna learned of many elderly people and children who died of cold and hunger. People began to disappear after being arrested on trumped-up charges and the queue outside the prison was as long as the ones outside shops. As bitter night followed bitter night, families huddled together in unheated rooms, dreading the sound of a Soviet lorry stopping outside, followed by a hammering on the door by Russian soldiers. Hundreds of families, Polish, Jewish and Ukrainian, were deported, deep into the USSR, to work in labour camps. Their homes and livestock were confiscated. Russian officials and their families arrived to take them over – well fed, warmly clad people who were openly hostile to the remaining residents.

It was in this tense atmosphere that Anna laboured, alongside her fellow Resistance workers, producing leaflets and news bulletins on a printing press, hidden away in a cellar. She was fluent in French, Russian, Ukrainian and English so was particularly useful in translating radio reports from the Allies. Every day and all day, and even at night, the Soviet loud speakers blared propaganda from street corners and squares. Private possession of a radio was forbidden so the underground news bulletins were particularly welcome to the people of Luck.

Anna also helped to organise the teams of couriers who carried orders and accompanied under-cover workers across German-occupied Poland and through the mountains into Hungary and beyond. Co-operation between the regional resistance groups grew and, although many people were arrested, tortured and killed, there were always others prepared to take their places.

Spring arrived and with it, disaster struck. As she was walking towards Kazio's house one evening, she saw Severyn hurrying towards her. She was about to greet him, but without looking at her, he shook his head. His face was ashen and grim. Anna walked past the house, where, to her dismay, she saw a Soviet soldier, posted outside the front door. She hurried home, sick with fear.

She waited, in trepidation, unable to eat or sleep. It was three days before a note came from Severyn. She was to meet him in a bar on the far side of town and there she learned the terrible news from a Severyn who seemed to have aged twenty years.

'Danka, was intercepted by the NKVD' (Narodnoi Komissariat Vnutrennikh Del/ Soviet Secret Police) he said in a low voice. 'She was just leaving the town when she was picked up. She was taken to the police station and tortured until she broke down and told the whereabouts of the press.' Anna gasped.

'Poor little thing,' Severyn went on. 'She was only fifteen…'

'Was?' Anna interrupted. 'She's not dead is she?'

'Killed herself in her cell.' Severyn was silent for a moment while Anna took in the tragic news. 'And that's not the worst of it. Kazio, Stefan and Adam were at the press when the NKVD burst in. They have all been arrested and are in prison. Their families have already been transported by cattle truck – east bound.'

Anna sat quite still, letting the news wash over her. In her mind, she saw Kazio, the taxi driver, his pretty wife, Stefan and Adam, the eager young students, Kazio's generous parents and the girls, his sisters, heads bent over their school books. She knew she would never see any of them again. She wanted to wail aloud, to let the tears flow but instead, with a pale face and tight lips, she asked, 'What are we going to do? How can we make sure no more of our people are arrested here, in Luck?'

Severyn leant forward and spoke quickly. 'The announcement has just been made that the Germans will allow all Polish refugees, who come from Western Poland and are currently living in German held territory, to return home. Similarly, repatriation will be permissible in the opposite direction. The exchange of refugees will take place in Przemysl and Vlodzimierz Volynski, which are right on the frontier of Russian/German-held land. I think we should take advantage of the big movement of refugees and get away from here. I have contacts in Vlodzimierz Volynski. We can join them and begin our work anew. Are you with us?'

Anna nodded her head. In spite of her sorrow at what had happened, she felt a surge of excitement.

'I am. I just want to get on with our work. When are we going?'

'The day after tomorrow, I'll meet you at the station at 7.30 am. Don't speak to me but try to stay near.' And then he was gone.

At the station, eager crowds of refugees, carrying bundles and battered suitcases, stood waiting for the train. Anna couldn't see Severyn at first, but finally recognised the dirty, unshaven man, sitting on an old fibre suitcase, tied with string – an excellent disguise. She stood near; talking to some women she'd met in the food queues. The day before, she had told Justa that she had decided to return to Warsaw. She remained firm, in spite of tears and pleas but had wept as her little nieces begged her to stay. In her heart she knew that by going, she removed the possibility of a dreadful fate falling on the household. Justa had insisted on giving her a warm coat, much too big for her, a thick skirt, a blouse and a sturdy pair of walking shoes. In a small holdall, she carried a clean set of underwear, two pairs of much-darned stockings, some bread and a bottle of water. Now, as she waited for hours on the scorching platform, she felt faint from the heat.

At last the train arrived. She fought her way on, where the dense crowd bore her along until she came to a standstill in a corner of the corridor. There she stood, pressed hard against the others, all night. She was grateful to be near an open window but she couldn't see Severyn.

Early next morning, they arrived at Vlodzimierz Volynski. The platform was crowded and, as Anna forced herself through and out into the street, it was obvious that the town had been taken over by refugees. They were camped in shop doorways, at the side of the street – anywhere there was a little space. Suddenly, to her delight, she saw Severyn beckoning her through the crowd. When she got to him he said, 'Come on, I've found a space in the churchyard where we can stay out of sight. You can rest there while I try to make contact.'

It was there, between two tombs, that Anna had to wait for three days. Severyn's last words to her as he set out on his first foray, were, 'Don't talk to anyone, if you can avoid it. You never know who they are. There are plenty of Soviet and German agents about.'

From her vantage point, she had her first glimpse of the Germans – the German Repatriation Committee – in their well-cut grey uniforms, shiny boots and peaked caps. Beside them, the Russians soldiers looked unkempt and shabby.

On one of his brief visits to the churchyard, Severyn described the scenes he had witnessed in the town. 'When the refugees saw the Germans, they rushed forward, begging to be sent home. They were brutally kicked and shoved aside by the soldiers, who clearly held them in contempt.'

'It's a good job we're not relying on the Germans to take us anywhere, then,' Anna replied wryly.

'Absolutely,' Severyn continued. 'The evacuation has begun. Several trains have already left. They were packed with happy and expectant people, all delighted to be going home. There were Poles, Jews, Ukrainians... but I don't trust the Germans.'

By the end of the third day, Anna was close to collapse. Long ago she had finished her water and bread and there was no more to be had. Severyn returned, dressed as a railway worker, to find her propped against the wall of a tomb, weak, drowsy and barely conscious. He was exhausted and bad tempered.

'Come on, Anna. I've made contact and found a safe place to hide. Pull yourself together.' He propelled her through the churchyard gate, where an elderly man, also dressed as a railway worker, met them.

He led them to the small cottage where he lived with his tiny, silver haired wife, who immediately took pity on Anna and sat her down in front of a bowl of soup.

'No talking until you've eaten,' she ordered. Anna didn't need to be told twice. When she was replete, she washed and changed into clean clothes. Then she sat in the little kitchen and, with Severyn, learned about their hosts. Olek was an engine driver. He and his wife, Ela, were both members of the resistance and well aware of the penalties attached to the crime of 'harbouring enemies of the people.' They had heard nothing of their two sons, mobilised at the beginning of the war, and had no idea what had become of them. Later Anna discovered that Olek had served in the Polish army, under Marshal Jozef Pilsudski in 1920, and had been decorated for bravery.

Anna was shown to the attic where a bed had been prepared for her. It was clean and sweet smelling and she fell asleep immediately.

It was noon the next day before she awoke. She watched the dust motes, dancing in the sun's rays, which shone through the gaps in the shutters. She felt rested and peaceful as she lay wondering what the next few days would bring forth.

Downstairs, the old lady was alone in the kitchen.

'Our men have gone into town to find out what is going on,' she smiled as she placed a mug of milk, fresh bread, butter and honey in front of Anna. Severyn and Olek returned as she finished eating.

'The Germans have gone – they left on the last train yesterday, with the last batch of refugees,' Olek said.

'They've said they'll return soon and continue with the repatriation.' Severyn added.

Nothing happened for two days. Anna helped Ela with the household chores and Severyn went about the town, checking on contacts, gathering information. On the second evening, Olek hurried in from work, his expression disturbed.

'A long train of cattle trucks has arrived at the station,' he said quickly. 'It's facing east. There's a lot of activity at Soviet Headquarters. There are also army lorries and armoured cars parked near the station. My 'railway connections' have told me that the Germans have no intention of returning. They have agreed with the Russians that all remaining refugees should be evacuated to the USSR.'

'There's no time to lose, then,' Ela spoke calmly. 'We're all prepared. Come both of you and I'll show you where you'll be safe in the event of the Russians searching our house for refugees.'

Originally, it had been a storeroom for milk churns, butter and cheese in the hot summer weather. Now Anna and Severyn, with their belongings and some food and water made themselves as comfortable as they could, secured the door, with planks, from inside, and settled down to wait.

'If the worst comes to the worst, Anna,' Severyn's voice was serious, 'we will pretend we don't know anything about each other and that we just stumbled upon this dugout. We must not incriminate Olek and Ela.' Anna nodded, a tight knot of fear gripping her stomach.

The uproar started a couple of hours later. Lorries revved and drove to and fro. There were shouts, shots and screams.

'Oh God,' breathed Severyn. 'Those poor wretched refugees are being forced on to the train, just as Olek said.' At 3 a.m., the noise ceased. It became uncannily quiet. Anna was very cold and covered in heavy dew.

'We'll give it an hour,' Severyn said, 'If all's quiet then, we'll go back to the house.'

It remained quiet so, hardly daring to breathe, they crept towards the house, just as the sky was lightening in the east and the first birds began to sing. There was no sign of life at the cottage. The shutters were closed.

'Let's not disturb them,' Anna whispered. 'Look, let's go up there.' She pointed to a ladder against the wall of an out building. Severyn nodded and, climbing up first, beckoned to her It was a hayloft, full of fragrant hay. Silently they burrowed into it and fell asleep.

She woke with a start. Anna opened her eyes to see a pair of black boots. She could smell the tar on them – the smell of the Russian army. And the boots were inches from her face. She looked up. A Soviet official, wearing an NKVD cap was aiming a revolver straight at her.

CHAPTER 4

Enemy of the People 1940

The officer laughed as she gave a scream.

'Get up golouboushka/little dove. It's time to go.'

Anna scrambled to her feet, still muzzy from sleep.

'Where are we going?' she stammered.

Her head swam. She looked round for Severyn. He was standing, hands above his head, against the chimneystack. A Russian soldier, long thin bayonet attached to his rifle, stood beside him. Anna affected surprise at seeing another prisoner in the loft, but said nothing.

In the cottage kitchen, Ela and Olek denied all knowledge of the captives. There were more soldiers there. One, a young Jew, moved forward to help Anna when she stumbled. She shook him off angrily.

'I will show no weakness,' she resolved. So she didn't ask for a mug of water, although she was desperately thirsty, nor did she betray the dread that gripped her. She and Severyn were bundled into the back of a waiting lorry, already full of frightened detainees. As the lorry drove away, she looked back at the cottage. Ela was standing in the doorway, tracing the sign of the cross in the air and, in spite of her resolve, Anna felt tears course down her cheeks as she remembered another hand raised in blessing so long ago, in Warsaw.

The lorry finally stopped in front of a large building, decorated with red banners and Russian slogans.

'Quickly, out of there!' came the command and everyone scrambled out of the lorry. They were hurried into a large hall, with barred windows, more banners and slogans and a huge picture of Stalin on one of its walls. It was the first of hundreds that Anna was to see over the coming year.

Men and women were immediately separated and the men led away, to the cries and wails of many of the wives and mothers. With a sinking heart, she saw Severyn leave, without looking at her.

'Now I'm really alone,' she thought. 'Please God, help me to be strong.' She was tired and thirsty. She stood, with the other women, waiting for – they knew not what.

After almost an hour, Anna and four other woman were led through a dimly lit corridor, with doors along each side. One by one, the women were pushed roughly through one or the other of the doors. Anna was last. Her door was at the end of the corridor.

She blinked as she entered a small, brightly lit room. Five women were already sitting on a bench along one wall. Two were Polish, mother and teenaged daughter, clinging to each other. The other three were Ukrainians. Anna sat next to the Polish woman but nobody spoke. Then the Ukrainians began to whisper among themselves until they were sharply ordered, by a guard, to be silent. There were trestle tables along the opposite wall, with chairs behind them and another portrait of Stalin on the wall.

Anna lost count of time. She could think only of her thirst. It threatened to overwhelm her. At last, two men and a woman entered. They took absolutely no notice of the detainees. They laughed and joked and drank black tea from tall glasses.

When the tea was finished, a man called Anna to the table. He was young, good looking and seemed concerned about Anna who stood, swaying, her face drawn and grey.

'Sit down,' he said, in Russian. Anna remained standing and replied, in Polish.

'I am sorry, I do not speak Russian.'

He repeated the invitation, in broken Polish and Anna sat down in front of him.

'Tell me your name.'

'Anna Grzymala Siedlecka.'

'How old are you?'

'Twenty'

'Place of birth?'

'Warsaw.'

'Where were you educated?'

'Warsaw.'

'What is your occupation?'

'I am a student. I have been studying domestic science in Warsaw. I was visiting relations when the war broke out.'

The questions went on and on – names and occupations of parents and grandparents, their whereabouts, nationality and social status. As the man's Polish was poor and he had to write everything down, Anna had to repeat her answers many times. He didn't mention the circumstances of her arrest but, finally asked, 'Tell me, why are you in Vlodzimierz?' Her throat was so dry, she could hardly answer.

'I am homesick and very worried about my family in Warsaw. I came here because I want to be repatriated to Warsaw.'

'If you have answered all my questions honestly, you will soon be released from here,' he assured her. 'Then you will be sent home. Would you like a cigarette?'

Anna was taken by surprise by this kind gesture. She knew she could not go on without a drink, so she replied, 'Thank you very much for your offer but I don't smoke. Instead, would it be possible for me to have a drink of water, please?'

Her interrogator called to a guard to bring some tea, which Anna sipped gratefully. She thought nothing had ever tasted so good. The man slowly read her statement, in Polish, and asked her to sign it. When she obeyed he gave her a wide smile saying,

'I hope you will soon be re-united with your family.' She did not believe him, but as she was escorted from the room and into a waiting police van, she felt a wave of gratitude that her first brush with the NKVD had not been as bad as she had expected.

The inside of the van was dark, crowded and stank of terrified humanity. The doors were slammed and locked and they were on the move. Some people were whispering and others sobbing or moaning. Anna sat still, up against the rear door and, almost numb with tiredness and hunger, waiting to see what would happen.

Before long, the van stopped and its human cargo disgorged into a crowded prison yard. Men were herded to one side, women to the other. Anna was relieved to spot Severyn among the men. He saw her and tried to smile but his face was bruised and swollen. Clearly his treatment had been much worse than hers and her heart went out to him.

Almost immediately, she was taken, with a small group of

women, through the forbidding doorway of the stark, grey prison, into a room where several Soviet soldiers stood and an NCO sat behind a table. He scrutinised their documents and confiscated their jewellery and watches.

'Search them,' he called to the thickset woman who had brought them in. She took them into a side room and told them to undress.

Anna spoke up for all of them.

'Please would you close the door? The men can see us.' The guard laughed loudly, showing an array of large, steel capped teeth.

'Nitchevo! / It doesn't matter!' And throughout the humiliation of the women, she exchanged crude jokes and flirtatious comments with the men in the other room as they enjoyed the spectacle. All buttons and suspenders were torn off, elastic removed from pants and laces from shoes. Then the guard threw all the clothes in a heap on the floor in the middle of the room so that each woman had to bend down and sort through, to retrieve what was hers and dress, as best she could. Finally, the ordeal over, they were marched away by a soldier, depleted bundles under their arms, 'Just like a parade of scarecrows,' Anna thought, forcing back the tears. Two of the women, close to the soldier, begged that they be allowed to use the lavatory, as they hadn't been permitted all day. Grumbling, he stopped outside a door and pushed it open. The stench made Anna retch. Inside were a couple of filthy cubicles, without doors and containing blocked and overflowing lavatories. There was no water supply. The soldier kept shouting at them to hurry. As she stood, waiting her turn, she noticed that the damp and dirty walls were covered with names, dates and inscriptions, relating to prisoners who had been here before her. Strangely, this comforted her.

'I am not really on my own,' she mused. 'All these people…' She was rudely interrupted by a push from the soldier's rifle butt.

When everyone was ready, and to the accompaniment of swearing and jostling from the soldier, the women trailed up some stone steps and along a dim corridor with doors on each side, each with a spy hole. Twice, they were ordered to stop and face the wall while other groups of prisoners were marched past them. Anna was dizzy and her head ached. She infuriated the soldier because she kept tripping in her unlaced shoes. He poked and pushed her, until, at last, they were ordered to stop in front of a strong metal door. He unlocked it and flung it open.

Screams, foul language and a stench as powerful as that in the lavatory met them. Anna saw a cell, crammed with dishevelled, half naked harridans. She stood, helpless and terrified, clutching her bundle, not daring to move. The soldier pushed her and the others forward, with an oath, withdrew and slammed the door.

Anna stood still, listening to the babble of voices, Polish, Ukrainian, Yiddish, and Russian. Only a small fly blown bulb, encased in wire mesh in the centre, lighted the cell. She could see very little but, eventually, moved cautiously along a wall, trying not to tread on the women on the floor. She reached a small, empty space and bent down to touch the slimy floor, which stank of urine and excrement. She sank down, clutching her bundle. There was no ventilation. The air was not only foetid but also full of fumes from the cheap tobacco many women were smoking. The heat was almost unbearable and the noise constant – cries, quarrels, groans and hysterical laughter. She quickly realised why this particular space had been empty. It was very close to the parashka/slop bucket, which was overflowing and in constant use. Anna could never remember whether or not she slept on that first night. She sank into a sort of torpor.

She came to, with a start, very early the next morning. The pale light of dawn was filtering through slats, which were nailed across the high, barred windows. Shakily, she got up and looked round. She reckoned there were about sixty women in the cell. There were a few beds without mattresses, covered in rags. Each of these was occupied by at least two people. Everyone else slept on the floor. Absent-mindedly, she scratched her head, then her leg. Then, 'I'm infested,' she cried inwardly. 'I've been bitten all over by bugs or lice or both!'

Somehow this was the last straw and later she was to tell people, 'If, at that moment, two people had not waved and called to me from the other side of the cell, I think I would have given up there and then.'

It was the Polish woman and her daughter, whom Anna had seen in the interrogation room the previous day. She pushed her way towards them and was received with kindness.

'Come and share our space, my dear,' invited the woman, Mrs Piotrowska. 'We haven't got anything else to give but you're very welcome to stay here with us.'

The space had been made as clean as possible. Some rags were spread over the floor and bundles of clothes doubled as seats and pillows.'

Anna was touched by their willingness to share their meagre possessions with a stranger. She sat beside them, with clamour and filth all around and learned a little of their stories.

'We arrived here just before you,' said Mrs Piotrowska, 'and met these two friends, who have been here for a couple of weeks and who know the ropes. They took us in and – well, we couldn't leave you all on your own, could we?' Anna smiled gratefully as the woman went on. 'This is my daughter, Irka. We have always lived in Vlodzimierz Volynski but my husband is away, in the army, with the Polish Frontier Guards, near the Russian border.' Tears filled her eyes and she took a deep breath. 'We have not heard from him for four months. I don't know what has happened to him. A neighbour of ours, who we have known for years, denounced us to the Russians, to save his own skin, when he was caught with black market goods. So, here we are.'

Just then, a rough looking Ukrainian woman pushed past, swearing loudly. She looked at them and shouted, 'Hi, bieloroutchki /white hands. You Polish ladies, your Poland is kaput now and for ever.'

'She must be one of the criminal inmates, I should think,' commented Irka and when Anna looked puzzled, Mrs Piotrowska explained.

'This is a typical cell in a Soviet prison. It contains both political prisoners, known as 'politicals' and criminals, thieves and such like, known as 'regulars.'

'Yes, and there are black marketeers, prostitutes, perverts, alcoholics and even murderers,' one of her friends added. 'Some of them have pre-war records and seem quite at home here. They get preferential treatment over us 'politicals'. They seem to know how to get tobacco, sugar and even soap, which they barter for clothes. The two groups don't mix, generally. And all the Ukrainians hate us Poles. They shout abuse all the time.'

Suddenly, there was a commotion near the door. It was unlocked and two guards led the way to the washroom. Anna's eyes began to water as soon as she entered the large, dim room. The concrete floor had been covered in chlorine. There was no time to be lost. Everyone had to wash, use the lavatory, and be out of the washroom in twenty minutes, when the next cell full would arrive. Along one wall stood a trough with four or five cold-water taps. At the other end of the room were three gaping holes in the concrete – the latrine.

'Hurry up,' shouted the guard and Anna was caught up in the rush for the taps. She watched the first women strip and wash as thoroughly and as quickly as possible. Some even attempted to wash underwear and stockings or fill a mug with water to take back to the cell. All the time there was pushing and grumbling. Anna managed the merest of washes before she was shoved aside. In the other corner, a fight had broken out as each one of a crowd of desperate woman tried to get to one of the three holes in the ground.

Anna rested her head against the damp, filthy wall and closed her eyes.

'This is a dream,' she told herself. 'I shall soon wake up.' But when she opened her eyes, she was still there among the noise, stench, the naked bodies and the nauseating chlorine. Then she saw them again, in front of her, all over the wall, names – men's names, women's names...

'Marta, Jola, Bugaj...' she read. She searched frantically for Severyn's name... he might have left it as a message to her. But it was not there. The guard pushed her roughly into line with the others and they were marched back to the cell. Then breakfast was served. A woman, a sort of prefect, known as the 'Starosta' elected by the inmates, collected a wooden tray from the guard. She gave Anna and the other new arrivals a wooden spoon, tin bowl and mug. Then she painstakingly divided the soggy bread into sixty portions, watched critically by the hungry women. Next, she distributed a matchbox full of sugar to each person, warning that this must last all day. Finally, she filled the mugs with very weak but hot tea. Anna drank this with relish.

Breakfast over, two guards enter ordered everyone to stand up to be counted, recounted nted again. There was constant crude banter betwe he 'regulars'. At last it was over and it was tim her, as Anna thought, 'Time to shift th brooms, cleaning materials or ev worst job was cleaning arou ka on that first day, a

After this,

'You m

hands be

who d

sev

the

laugh

keeping h

great park ne

Too soon, it wa re oppressive after the litt sisted of thin millet gruel, dishe tarosta'. Anna spent the free time talk ing around their 'quarters' and waging a lo and bed bugs. One more visit to the lavatory wa the last meal of gruel was served, among squabbles an . An hour or so later, the noise abated a little as everyone settle sleep. And so ended her first day as a prisoner and 'Enemy of the People.'

She was surprised at how quickly the shock of that first day passed. She settled into the routine, accepted the unacceptable and began to feel like an experienced prisoner.

A week passed. Anna had not been called for further interrogation. As she lay in her space, at night, she tried to prepare herself for what lay ahead. On many occasions she heard cries and screams of terror and pain, in the darkness.

'Please God, don't let that be Severyn,' she prayed and even the most hardened of the women in the cell were silent when the torture was in progress.

On the seventh day, just after the midday meal, a guard opened the door.

'Anna Grzymala Siedlecka,' he shouted. 'Pick up your belongings and follow me.'

'This is it,' thought Anna, scrambling to obey. 'I shall never see my friends again.' Suddenly the filthy cell seemed safe, was home, in the face of the unknown.

'Come on, come on,' barked the guard, with an oath. Anna stumbled after him, calling goodbye to those who had taken her in on her first day.

The guard stopped outside a small room and pushed her inside.

'Stand over there,' he ordered. 'Stand still' He took her photograph and then her fingerprints. 'Now, follow me.' He led her down a long corridor, stopping outside the door at the end. He unlocked the door and, propelling her inside, went out and relocked the door.

Anna looked round. This cell was smaller, cleaner and less crowded than the first. There were three beds with straw-filled mattresses and more mattresses on the floor. There was even a small table, on which stood a water jug and, in the corner, was the inevitable parashka. A young woman stepped forward with a smile.

'Hello, my name is Ola,' she said.

'Mine's Anna.'

'We're all 'politicals' in here,' said Ola and she introduced Anna to the others. Five were Polish, four Jewish and there was one Ukrainian. Ola pointed out the free mattress and Anna put her bundle on it. One of the Polish women, much older than the rest, lay moaning quietly on one of the beds.

'We've got two rules,' Renia, one of the other Poles, told Anna. 'First, we may say what we are accused of but that is all. We never reveal any real information to each other. This is for two reasons. What we do not know, we cannot tell under duress. Also, we can never be sure that spies and informers will not be planted among us.

Best to say nothing. Second, we don't give details of the 'questioning' by the Soviets. We help each other after a session, if we need to, but that is all. That's for our sanity.'

On that first day in the cell, Anna learned that the elderly Polish woman was demented with grief. Her husband had been killed in the September Campaign and her two sons killed, while trying to cross the border to Romania. She could not believe her loved ones were dead and sat, knees drawn up, lips moving, oblivious of all around her. The others cared for her as well as they could.

'All four of us are teachers,' explained Renia, indicating the younger Polish women. 'We are accused of belonging to a resistance movement and spreading anti Soviet propaganda among our pupils.'

'And we,' said Esther, one of the Jewish girls, 'are also suspected of anti Soviet, pro Polish activities.'

The Ukrainian woman said nothing. She was to remain silent for almost all of the time Anna was in the cell. Later, Ola told her, 'She hardly ever speaks to us. She gets interrogated nearly every night. We think she's accused of belonging to a fiercely nationalistic Ukrainian group, involved in working against the Russians.'

That evening, Anna's name was called and she was led away for questioning. She felt faint with apprehension as she was pushed into the interrogation room. A squat NKVD officer sat behind the desk, his face pale and flat. Anna could see the reflection of his shiny, shaven head on the glossed ceiling above. He spoke to her in Russian.

'Before we begin, I should tell you that I loathe and despise liars. Bear this in mind and everything will be fine.'

'I'm afraid I don't speak Russian.' Anna brought out her stock phrase.

'Nitchevo / It doesn't matter. We will give you a few lessons and you will soon learn.' Anna heard the menace in his voice and shivered. The officer continued to speak in Russian, but more slowly and he interspersed it with Polish words and phrases.

'Are you a member of the Polish Resistance?'
'No.'
'Have you ever taken part in any acts of sabotage or subversion?'
'No.'

He went on to mention the names of some of the people Anna had known in Luck. She tried to keep her face blank.

'Do you know any of these people?'

'No.'

'Where is your permanent residence?'

All the questions from Anna's first interrogation were repeated three or four times.

'We know you are a spy!' he shouted at last, exasperated, for her story never deviated. He got up, walked round the table and hit her hard on the face. She reeled back and he hit her again.

'We know,' he was furious, 'we know that you remained in Western Ukraine just to make mischief.'

Anna's face burned and her head ached but she remained adamant.

'I have nothing more to tell you. I have told you the truth.'

'Take her away!' he screamed. As she was led away, he called after her.

'I haven't finished with you. You'd better reconsider all the lies you have told me. Next time, I will be less friendly.'

Anna was shaking as she was taken back to the cell, not just with shock and pain but also with anger at the complete lack of common humanity she had been shown. Her cellmates were waiting, with towels soaked in cold water, words of comfort and touches of compassion. They washed her swollen face, undressed her and put her to bed, where she was left, undisturbed until morning.

Anna was to discover that all of the women were regularly interrogated. Each, in her turn, went through panic and despair and was often near breaking point. It was only the selfless comradeship of each towards the others that helped them to survive.

Once more, Anna settled into the prison routine. Each of the inmates was self-disciplined and strove to retain her dignity. The cell was cleaned thoroughly every day and all clothes deloused and mended.

'Doing these simple things is our only defence against our oppressors,' thought Anna.

The guards treated them with a certain amount of respect, although this brought no concessions.

Anna noticed that discipline, in the exercise yard, was less strict than at first. The bored guards were disinclined to rouse themselves or take action against the determined 'regulars', who seemed to organise business deals on a daily basis. She saw goods and money change hands and heard hard bargains being driven. She realised that, if careful, one could exchange a word or two with another prisoner or pass a note. Messages from the men's side of the prison could be found in the cracks of the walls. Anna longed for news of Severyn but didn't know who to ask and wasn't even sure if he were using his own name. She searched for a sign from him and, once, came upon the half obliterated word 'Sev...' But that was all.

A few days after her arrival in the cell, the elderly Polish woman collapsed and was removed to the prison hospital. A guard told them, later, that she had had a stroke and had died the next day. They stood in silence for a couple of minutes after he had gone, remembering their friend and finding comfort in the knowledge that her suffering was over.

To replace her, a very young Ukrainian woman was moved into the cell.

'My parents died when I was a child and I grew up in a Roman Catholic orphanage near Lviv,' she told the others. 'When the Russians came the nuns and children were deported, but I managed to escape and was taken in by a wonderful Polish family. One night, we were gathered, secretly, for worship. The Russians burst in and we were all arrested and accused of subversive activities. That's why I'm here.'

Anna could not put her finger on it, but there was something about this girl, she did not like. She was too timid, too self-effacing but too eager to ask all sorts of dangerous questions. Every morning and evening she knelt by the window, eyes raised, hands folded or moving on a rosary, fashioned from stale bread, her lips moving as if in prayer. She was taken out for interrogation and returned, each time in tears, but she never appeared to be hurt, physically. One day, she drove even the patient and kind Ola to anger. It was after the midday meal when the girl suddenly said, 'We can all trust each other here can't we?'

'We do,' answered Ola, 'and we help each other.'

'We're on our own,' the girl continued. 'No one's about to hear. Let's tell our real stories to each other. Let's trust each other enough to say what we have really done.'

Ola stood up.

'That's enough!' she cried. 'We've asked and asked you to be discreet, to respect our privacy. Why do you take no notice? What are you after?'

The girl burst into tears and begged our forgiveness. Next day she was moved out.

'To spy in another cell, no doubt,' remarked Renia. 'Let's hope the inmates won't be taken in by our little orphan.'

A common pastime, in the boring routine of cell life, was the making of rosaries, models and even chess sets out of small pieces of dry bread. If they were found, during one of the regular cell searches, they were destroyed, only to be replaced in a short time.

To alleviate the boredom, Anna and her friends played chess, recited poetry to each other and told stories. They related episodes from favourite films and books but the favourite occupation, for everyone, was inventing incredible and lavish menus for the first feast 'after release.'

Anna had frequent interviews with the squat NKVD officer. They followed the same pattern as the first. Occasionally, he hit her but she was never badly beaten or tortured.

One evening, she became ill. She developed persistent and crippling stomach cramps. She lay on her bed, unable even to drink the proffered water. Suddenly the door was flung open and her name was called. She struggled up, out of the cell and along the corridor. When she entered the interrogation room, she saw, at once, a revolver lying on a pile of papers on the desk. Next, she noticed the thunderous expression on the squat officer's face. He began to shout the usual questions at her, stamping his feet and banging the flat of his hand on the desk with every one. Through her pain, Anna saw the revolver slowly sliding off the pile of papers with every bang on the desktop. Anna repeated her story, as usual, several times and then the pain overtook her, she gasped and cried out, as the room swam around her, 'I'm ill. I'm in terrible pain. Please may I sit down?'

The officer's face was purple with fury. He clicked his fingers at a guard, who placed a stool behind Anna. She turned to look and realised he had put it upside down, its thick wooden legs sticking into the air. She said nothing but, knowing she would collapse if she didn't sit, sat gingerly down on one of the legs.

'What is your real name? Where do you live…?' He was shouting the questions at her but she couldn't hear them. They came from too far away. She could not speak.

The officer came from behind his desk and, with calm deliberation, kicked the stool away from under Anna so that she crashed, face downwards, on to the floor. Something about this fall galvanised her, made her forget her pain. She was on her feet in a moment, facing her tormentor. Never before had she felt such blinding hatred and rage. She screamed at him, in Polish, 'How dare you! How dare you, you peasant…. you oaf….' She was cut off there because the man had grabbed his revolver and hit her across the face with its butt. He hit her again and again. Everything around her seemed to explode and she knew no more.

It was not until after midnight that Anna recovered consciousness. She lay, sore all over, unable to open her blackened eyes, aware of broken teeth and blood oozing from her mouth and nose. The cramps in her stomach had not abated.

'Just let me die,' she thought but she said nothing. Her friends took it in turns to sit with her through the night, doing everything they could for her. In the morning, they called the guard and she was transferred to the hospital.

When she returned three days later, she could still hardly move without help. Her cellmates washed and fed her. One of them was always at her side. Later, when she was able, they helped her into the exercise yard. She never forgot their kindness and compassion. Even the Ukrainian woman would sit by her, patting her hand and smiling sadly, silent as ever.

For a week, she was left in peace, gradually healing but still shocked. Then one morning, the door opened and her name was called. Shakily she got to her feet and, unable to think clearly, left the cell, without a backward glance. In the empty corridor, the guard stopped, put his hand on Anna's shoulder, and said quietly, 'Don't be too proud, girl. They will break you.' It was a human touch, but Anna daren't respond to it. She made no answer, but turned and looked deep into his eyes. Embarrassed, he turned away, but when they arrived at the door of the interrogation room, he touched her shoulder softly once more.

In surprise, Anna saw a different officer behind the desk. He was wearing a smart civilian suit and had a bronzed, attractive face.

'Nevertheless,' she told herself, 'he's still a Soviet official, albeit a civilian one.'

'Sit down,' he said quietly. Anna forced herself to sit, without wincing. The man smiled, as if he appreciated her effort. She was painfully conscious of her bruised and battered face and missing teeth. It was a strain to keep her chin up and look straight at him, but her hurt pride and growing anger stiffened her resolve and her neck.

The officer indicated another man, sitting near him.

'I was told that you insist on speaking Polish so I have an interpreter here.'

'I understand a little Russian if it is spoken slowly,' Anna replied. 'But I cannot speak it.'

'I am in a similar situation,' the man smiled, 'I understand your language but find the pronunciation very difficult. I am sure we will manage with the help of the interpreter.' He stopped for a moment, as if observing her carefully, and then spoke, again, still quietly.

'I want you to forget what has happened to you so far. We will start again, you and I. Please tell me your story right from the beginning.'

Once more, Anna repeated what she had told so many times. When she had finished, the officer raised his eyebrows and leant forward.

'Ah, but you have forgotten the part about your anti-Soviet

activities and your work in the secret organisation. That's what I want to discuss with you.'

'I am truly sorry,' Anna answered, looking straight into his eyes. 'I do not know what you are talking about.'

The officer raised his voice slightly and spoke sternly.

'Why do you persist in this nonsense? You are an intelligent, well-educated young woman. You must know that your lies are not acceptable to us. Why do you refuse to co-operate?'

Anna continued to look at him, but remained silent.

'Very well,' the officer gave a great sigh. 'You may go now. We will speak again tomorrow.'

Anna tossed and turned all night, on her straw mattress. She had learned not to trust any of the Soviet officials, even if they were softly spoken and appeared sympathetic. She decided that the fear of what might happen was worse than the ill treatment itself. With this thought in mind, she fell into a fitful sleep.

The same man sat behind the desk when she was led in, the next day. Another officer, in uniform, sat next to him. The interpreter was in the corner. Anna was not invited to sit down. The civilian spoke first, in a flat voice, giving no indication that they had met before. 'Tell us your story, from beginning to end.'

Anna did so, in Polish.

'Have you nothing else to tell us,' the civilian asked.

'Nothing.' Anna replied, bracing herself for an outburst of rage and violence. It didn't come. The officer continued speaking, but his voice was cold. 'I was hoping that you would come to your senses and change your attitude. Alas, I see you are not only dishonest but also stubborn and stupid. Therefore, I have nothing more to say to you.' He pulled back his chair, turned away and lit a cigarette. The uniformed officer slowly lifted his head to stare into Anna's face. He wore thick glasses and stared, without speaking for a full minute.

Anna fixed her eyes on the shining metal bridge of his spectacles and stared until his face became blurred.

'I will not break,' she told herself. 'I will not be intimidated.'

At last the man spoke.

'We have proof that, while pretending to be a refugee from the west, you abused Soviet hospitality by taking part in subversive activities,' Anna heard him say. 'We have discovered that you are the daughter of a rich landowner, a member of the Polish bourgeoisie and a spy. You hate communism and the proletariat.

'As an enemy of the people, you will be tried and sentenced under paragraph 54/12 of our constitution. You will serve at least ten years hard labour.' He paused but Anna did not speak. She had realised that all the accusations were vague – that they had no hard proof of anything. Even her 'hatred of the proletariat' could be attributed to her calling the squat interrogator a 'peasant' and an 'oaf'. Anna looked down at the dirty floor, still silent. She could see shapes of faces and animals in the grime. She waited for what would come next. On the table, in front of her, the officer placed a sheet of paper, covered with Russian characters. He spoke now in a confidential, almost fatherly tone, 'Come now, I am not a cruel man. I understand that you are young and inexperienced. Unscrupulous criminals have led you astray. You will have to be punished but if you sign this paper and promise not to behave foolishly again, the punishment will not be so harsh. I have had this paper prepared for you to sign. It can be translated for you if you wish.' He pushed the paper and a black fountain pen nearer to Anna. She refocused her eyes, so that she looked into his.

'I cannot sign,' she said.

The officer narrowed his eyes. His voice became menacing.

'You will sign in the end,' he snarled. She thought he was going to strike her but he only shouted,

'Take her away!'

CHAPTER 5

Trans-Siberian Express

An NKVD officer fired several shots into the air. Another sprang into a railway truck, holding his revolver ready. He swore at the mass of refugees.

'I'll shoot anyone who disregards orders,' he shouted. 'Get into this train in an orderly fashion.'

The three hundred or so, ragged, hungry people, Anna among them, obeyed.

It was two days since her interview with the two officers and during that time a rumour had been rife in the exercise yard and washroom. 'Soon we'll all be going to hunt polar bears.' Anna had heard this again and again and had learned that it was code for 'Soon we'll all be going to a Siberian labour camp.' She had taken little notice, assuming that she would be put on trial first, but she was to be proved wrong.

That morning, breakfast had been different. There was soup as well as tea and small pieces of bread for everyone. Afterwards, they were hurried to the washroom, but when they asked the guard what was afoot, he only swore and shouted at them to hurry. Back in the cell two guards counted then searched them, before ordering them to pick up their belongings and file out into the yard.

There, several lorries were parked and about three hundred prisoners, clutching their miserable bundles were counted and recounted. Anna searched the lines of men for Severyn but couldn't see him.

At last the lorries were loaded with their human cargo. The tarpaulins were tightly tied, the lorries moved off, away from the prison, but, try as she might, Anna could not shift the canvas and gain a glimpse of the free world outside.

Very soon her lorry stopped, the tarpaulin was lifted and Anna recognised the railway station.

'It seems a lifetime since Severyn and I arrived here,' she thought. The station had changed. All notices were now in Russian and red banners with pictures of Stalin adorned its walls. There were no passengers on the platform.

'Out, everyone,' shouted a guard. Anna scrambled out with the others and lined up to be counted again. A long train stood in the station. She thought there were about forty trucks – cattle trucks.

It was when the order was given to get on to the train that the near riot had happened. Women glimpsed their men or their sons and visa versa. Families, desperate to travel together tried to meet up. People were trampled underfoot. One guard was knocked over. It was at this point that the NKVD officer had fired his rifle.

Anna was pushed into a truck. The door was slammed and locked behind her. In total darkness she stood hemmed in on all sides by frightened men and women. At first, she was afraid to move lest she trod on someone. The heat was intense. There were cries and moans – all the sounds of misery. As Anna's eyes became accustomed to the dark she could make out two shelves, one above the other, at each end of the truck. These shelves had already been taken, as resting places, by any of the first comers who were energetic enough to clamber on to them. The less agile sheltered beneath the shelves, while everyone else squatted or lay in whatever space they could find. In the centre of the floor, a hole, about a foot square, had been cut in the boards, to serve as a latrine. This was covered with strands of barbed wire to discourage any attempt at escape.

As Anna had been one of the last aboard, the only space she could find was next to the door. The keyhole was tiny, but she hoped that when the train moved, she would get a whisp of fresh air and that, whenever the door was opened, she would get a glimpse of the 'outside'. Then she discovered a minute crack in a plank of the door, through which a delicious stream of air reached her.

'It's my invisible thread, linking me to freedom, outside,' she told herself.

Finally, with a jolt, which bumped Anna against the man next to her, the train moved, not forwards but backward. There were further jolts and crashes and it came to rest, evidently in a siding. The sound of the engine subsided, there were a few shouts from men outside and then silence, stillness.

'We must be staying here for the night.' A man spoke from the darkness.

'Without food or water?' a woman asked.

'It seems so,' said the man and silence fell once more.

Sleep would not come to Anna. She was hungry and very, very thirsty. The bed she had contrived from her dirty, threadbare coat, offered little protection from the wooden floor. Her whole body ached, her face, still bruised and swollen, throbbed mercilessly and she was itching from the bloodthirsty insects she could feel crawling inside her clothes. She felt utterly alone, among this crowd of strangers. The tears came until, utterly spent, she fell asleep at last.

She was woken, next morning, by a fearful banging from the outside of the wagon. She learned, later, that the walls, undercarriage and wheel axles were being tested. Each plank and metal plate was systematically struck with a sledge hammer, to see if all were properly secure and that no-one had tried to escape. This procedure was to be carried out after every stop on the long journey. This first experience was very frightening. From all parts of the train, voices cried out for air and water. Nobody answered. The doors remained locked as the sun rose and beat down on the trucks.

The hole in the floor had been in constant use, for there were about sixty people in Anna's truck. A dreadful stench emanated from underneath and swarms of flies buzzed round. Several people fainted, while others became hysterical.

Anna sat in her little space, trying to distance herself from the chaos. She allowed her mind to wander and suddenly she remembered a book of her father's she had once read. She couldn't remember the title, but it was about yoga and was by a man called

Krishna Murti. Squatting in the filthy wagon, on her makeshift bed, she felt, all at once, that the name 'Krishna Murti' was a sort of mantra. She started to repeat it again and again, simultaneously trying to erase all other thoughts from her head.

'Krishna Murti, Krishna Murti, Krishna Murti...' on and on. She didn't know how long she crouched there, chanting softly to herself, but there she was, surrounded by screams and moans, endlessly repeating the name of an unknown Hindu. Gradually a calm descended on her. She could never explain it, even to herself, but it seemed as if the awful present, with its hunger, thirst, exhaustion and fears, together with the terrors of an unknown future, receded and she felt a new inner strength and a certainty of winning through.

The sliding door was, at last, thrown back and Anna was almost hurled from the truck by the impact of the rush for the door. Outside, soldiers were ready for this, with rifles pointing at the prisoners.

'Sit down! Now, quickly, choose a Starosta/leader to organise collection of food and water.'

After some bickering, Mr Kozlowski, a Polish land owner was chosen. He looked strong and determined and spoke fluent Russian.

'You will also be responsible for distributing food and water to these people and for the discipline in this wagon,' the soldier told him. 'Now, choose four people to help you and follow me.'

Everyone wanted to be chosen. There was another push towards the door. This time Anna lost her footing and was propelled through the doorway. She was caught by one of the soldiers before she hit the ground. He laughed and held her in the air, by the scruff of the neck, like a puppy.

'This can be one of them,' he grinned and three others soon joined her, with Mr Kozlowski.

Anna's new sense of well-being lasted as they were marched to the canteen, where four buckets were issued. Two were filled with water, one (Anna's) with kasha/millet porridge and one with tea. Mr Kozlowski was given a baker's tray full of course rye bread.

At only five feet tall and weak from lack of food, Anna struggled to carry the brimming, hot bucket back to the truck without spilling any of the precious food. She was carrying it in front of her, gripping it with both hands, when a man's voice spoke

'Wait, dievotchka/little girl, I will help you.' Anna looked up and saw a friendly Russian face looking down. It was the soldier who had broken her fall from the truck.

She felt an onrush of warmth and gratitude for his kind words. Her eyes filled with tears.

'Thank you,' she whispered.

'Nitchevo, nitchevo/it's nothing, it's nothing,' he responded, his round face pink. And so the porridge arrived at the truck without a single drop being spilt.

Mr Kozlowski quickly organised the distribution. The contents of the buckets and the bread did not allow much for each individual but, at least, everything was fairly divided. Anna noticed how the Starosta's inborn authority and tact worked on prisoners and soldiers alike. He negotiated the leaving of the door ajar to let in some fresh air and even persuaded some of the 'regulars' who had taken possession of the coveted top shelves, to allow some sick and weak people to sit there, near the windows for a while.

For the first time, Anna had a chance to look round the wagon.

'We look like a crowd of bedraggled and exhausted coalminers,' she thought, for fine coal dust was ingrained into sweaty faces and limbs and clung to all the clothes.

'The wagon must have been used for transporting coal as well as cattle.' Her closest neighbour, sitting propped against the door frame, was an orthodox Jew, very old and emaciated. Wrapped in a threadbare prayer shawl, he seemed oblivious to the noise and clamour. He rocked, endlessly, back and forth, muttering incantations or prayers. When his rations were handed to him, he lifted his pale, red rimmed, vacant eyes and smiled timidly. Anna was pleased to have such an inoffensive neighbour until she saw the lice in his hair and beard and the colonies of bedbugs in his torn eiderdown.

Her other neighbour, on the far side of the door, was a grotesquely fat middle aged woman who suffered from asthma. Her face was puffy and purple and she wheezed and coughed incessantly. She was, however, good hearted. Her bundle bulged with mysterious 'treasures' – some pieces of bread and biscuits, a few apples and even some chocolate. Now she passed a biscuit to Anna, with a wink. Anna mouthed,

'Thank you.' She gathered the woman's name was Mrs Tosiak, and dubbed her, in her mind, 'Mama Tosiak.'

Two more buckets of water were supplied in the early evening and the door locked. Then the diabolical banging and clanging told them that testing was underway. That over, the train lurched into motion. The journey continued and the occupants of the cattle trucks slept.

When Anna woke next morning, the train was still moving and the air felt fresher. Someone had managed to remove a few slats from each of the windows, allowing the early morning air to rush in. Then another improvement was put in hand. A makeshift screen was erected round the latrine, to give a semblance of privacy. Mr Kozlowski organised a roster of lookouts so that these modifications would not be discovered.

At about noon, the sound of the wheels changed, the train seemed to be slowing and the lookouts reported signs that they were approaching a large station. Immediately the slats were replaced, the screen removed and Anna realised how hungry and thirsty she was.

The train stopped outside the station and new volunteers went with Mr Kozlowski for food and water. Anna sat in the doorway, legs swinging, watching the 'normal' world outside the barbed wire fence which ran parallel to the track. There were workmen, mending a road, a schoolboy leaning on a bicycle, watching the train, a woman, carrying a small child.

She was contemplating how on earth this every day life could go on just over there, apparently untouched by the misery around her, when a voice said, 'Zdrastvujtie, dievochka/Greetings, little girl.' She looked down to see the smiling face of her soldier helper of yesterday. He was standing with his back to the truck, his broad, pleasant face level with her blackened knees. Although he was not visible to her fellow passengers, Anna was nervous lest she should be accused of fraternising with the enemy. She started to move back into the shelter of the truck and he must have seen the doubt on her face, for he said, 'Don't go. I just wanted to know how you are.'

'I'll survive,' muttered Anna ungraciously. Then, feeling sorry as his face fell, she added, 'Thank you. Have you any idea where we are? Or are you not allowed to tell me?'

'We're at a place called Luck,' he replied.

'Luck, Luck!' Anna could not believe her ears. Memories of her sister, her nieces and the high hopes she and the others had had as they set out from this very station, swept over her. Suddenly she felt full of bitterness and despair. She rested her head on her knees and burst into tears. She heard the soldier's voice, full of compassion,

'Is this your home, dievochka? Does your family live here?'

Unable to speak, Anna nodded.

'Don't cry,' he said quietly. 'The train will remain here for more than three hours. Give me your family's address and I will try to tell them you are here.' He handed her a small piece of crumpled paper and a stub of pencil. Anna hesitated and looked round to see if anyone had noticed. All were engaged in their own affairs, getting ready to receive food and water, tidying their spaces. No-one was looking at her – except for the old Jew, who suddenly smiled at her and nodded his head.

The soldier anticipated her underlying fear – that of betraying her family.

'Dievochka,' he whispered, 'I promise that I will not look at what you write on that paper. I'll give it to that boy, with the bicycle, and ask him to deliver it. Then we will have to wait and hope. Will you trust me?' With tears streaming down her face, she scribbled her sister's address and a short message on the paper and gave it to the soldier. She watched him stroll casually over to the boy, say something, hand him the note and a coin and then stroll back to the train, without looking at her. The boy disappeared in a cloud of dust.

Later food was given out and when everyone had eaten, the ritual banging took place. Then came the sound of slamming doors. Anna gave up hope of a reply to her note.

'The boy probably didn't deliver it... the soldier just pretended to ask him to deliver it...' she thought bitterly. The door by Anna began to close but it was opened again by the young soldier.

'Give me your bucket,' he called to Mr Kozlowski. 'I'll fill it with water.' While another man was filling the bucket, the soldier's voice spoke, too softly for anyone else to hear.

'Look, dievochka, but do not wave.'

Anna stood up in the doorway and, for a few short moments, she saw her sister, standing the other side of the barbed wire. She thought Justa saw her, too, because her hand moved very slightly and she pressed her white handkerchief to her face. A bucket of water appeared in the doorway and, as eager hands took it in, the soldier passed her a small parcel, wrapped in a familiar woollen scarf. She stifled a sob.

'God bless you, soldier,' she said quietly. 'Tell me your name, so that I can include you in my prayers.'

His face was scarlet.

'My name's Grisha. No-one has ever prayed for me before.'

The door was slammed shut and the train began to move.

Anna clutched her precious parcel as she tried to recapture the moment of seeing Justa. In her mind, she saw the dear face, the movement of the hand, the white handkerchief. She put her head on the parcel, smelling the freshness of the newly washed woollen scarf, and letting her tears flow, she fell asleep.

It was morning and the train was stationary when Anna awoke. The parcel under her head showed she had not dreamed the brief glimpse of her sister. Now, she sat up in her small space and carefully unwrapped it, her fingers trembling. What riches! Apart from the scarf, there was a small piece of bacon, a tiny pot of homemade raspberry jam, a few ounces of home grown tobacco and some woollen stockings. Each item had been carefully wrapped in a clean handkerchief, with loving care. Tears started to Anna's eyes as she realised the sacrifice her family had made to get together such a parcel as this. She rewrapped everything carefully, leaving out a small amount of tobacco wrapped in a handkerchief, to give to Grisha at the earliest opportunity.

The train began to move, with no water or rations taken on board. Through the slit in the boards, Anna saw the station's name – Kovel. The dreadful icy journey with the wounded airman and the dancing fish flashed through her mind. It had happened in another life, she felt. It was stifling in the truck. Several people, including Mama Tosiak had fainted. Anna helped to drag her to an upper shelf, where a little air from the window revived her.

'Don't move about or talk unnecessarily,' Mr Kozlowki advised everyone. 'Try to conserve your strength.' His quiet, sensible words had a calming effect and Anna found herself drifting in and out of sleep throughout the day, as the train rattled on relentlessly.

It kept going throughout the night and in the early hours of morning Anna decided to try to enlarge the crack between the boards of the door so that she could lie with her face against a stream of fresh air. She remembered she had a large metal, cloth-covered button in her pocket – one that had come off her coat a few days before. She retrieved it, painfully removed every shred of cloth and started to shave the wood away, slowly. The noise of the train covered the scratching sound and she was relieved to feel minute pieces of soft and somewhat rotten wood crumbling away under the pressure of her tool.

After about an hour and in spite of a splinter and a blister, the crack was wide enough for Anna to feel a current of air brushing her face. Delighted, but exhausted by hunger, thirst and exertion, she fell asleep once more.

The journey continued without respite. By midday, the situation in the truck was grimmer than ever. Anna, sitting up near her stream of air, saw that several people were unconscious, the old Jew looked dead and Mama Tosiak's face had turned purple. She was gasping and rasping loudly. Mr Kozlowski helped Anna to pull her over to the crack in the door, where the life giving stream of air revived her a little.

Then, the croaky voice of the lookout, announced that they were arriving at a station. The train stopped. The door opened.

This time, there was no rush. Most people were too weak to move. Nevertheless, the guard ordered Mr Kozlowski to get volunteers to carry food and water. As the small group moved away, Anna heard an angry exchange between the Starosta and a Russian soldier. He had asked for help for the sick and was being refused in no uncertain terms.

Suddenly, Grisha was at the door of the wagon. His face was hard and he pointed at Anna.

'Here, you,' he barked, 'come down. We need more people to help with the food.' When she hesitated, he pointed his gun at her. 'Hurry up, damn you!'

Anna was hurt and surprised. She climbed down and walked beside him, noting the name of the station, 'Sarny'. She knew this was a town just on the Polish side of the Polish/Russian border. They reached the platform, leading to the main railway building, and approached a little wicket gate. It stood open and lead to a sunlit and deserted street.

'Udirai!/Run!' hissed Grisha, who was one step behind Anna. Astonished, she stopped, her mind racing.

'Is it a trap? Will he shoot if I run through the gate?' His face told her otherwise. 'But where will I run to? No documents, battered face, filthy rags.' She clenched her fists and the moment had gone. They had passed the gate and she hurried to join the rest of her group.

'Doura! Doura!/Stupid! Stupid!' Anna heard him mutter under his breath.

Two hour later, and everyone had been transferred to another train. The truck was identical and, this time, Mr Kozlowski organised the seating arrangements, giving priority to the old and sick. Anna managed to secure a position near the door again. She could hear Mama Tosiak wheezing somewhere nearby but there was no sign of the old Jew. He had disappeared in the upheaval at the station – possibly pushed into another group or, Anna thought grimly, 'Taken away dead.'

The train began to move and, as she lay in the darkness, the voice of the look-out shouted, 'We're almost at the Soviet border. I can see the frontier post… It's down… We're in the Soviet Union now!'

Anna felt a great wave of sorrow sweep over her.

'Will I ever return? Will I ever see my family, my home again?' she thought. Around her others wept and she wept as well.

The train journey lasted eleven days. Afterwards, Anna could not imagine how she and all in her truck had survived. Sometimes there was no break for food and water for two days. During the day, the heat was almost unendurable, while, at night, the temperatures plummeted and everyone shivered with cold. One night, someone in the truck suffered an epileptic fit. Panic and hysteria ensued until Mr Kozlowski managed to restore order and tend the sick woman.

Passengers waiting at stations and workmen, too, averted their eyes from the tattered prisoners, pretending they could not see them. They, themselves, wore drab clothes and seemed cowed by the strutting, blue capped, militia men. Huge portraits of Stalin were posted on every conceivable surface.

It was agreed that at each stop, half a bucket of water should be saved to wash the latrine hole. The barbed wire mesh covering the hole and the planks around were encrusted with faeces. Hundreds of flies had gathered round it and spread out into the truck. Someone offered a broken spoon as a tool and everyone, who was able, took a turn. It was a sickening job. There was little water left over for hand washing but the very fact that attempts were being made to keep the environment clean boosted everyone's self respect.

As the train travelled eastwards, the look-outs reported the names of some of the stations. Kurs, Voronezh, Penza, Kazan all lay behind. Anna knew they were approaching the Ural Mountains, which separated Europe from Asia. Everyone agreed that their destination was Siberia.

At last the train stopped, the door opened and the Urals, glowing in the setting sun, were before them.

'Stay where you are,' shouted a guard. 'No-one is to leave the train.'

Anna noticed that a new detachment of guards had arrived. The ones that had escorted them from Poland were preparing to leave. Suddenly Grisha was at the door.

'Farewell, dievochka,' he said quietly. 'I wish you luck.'

'And God be with you, Grisha, I will always remember you and your kindness,' whispered Anna as she pressed the handkerchief containing the tobacco, into his hand. Then the door was shut and they were all in darkness again.

Three more stops, Sverdlovsk, Petropavlovsk, Omsk and then, on the twelfth day – Novosibirsk.

'All men with their baggage out. All women remain in the train!' came the order. The male prisoners, were marshalled on the station and marched away. Women began to cry, fearing the worst. As Mr Kozlowski disappeared, Anna realised what an important part he had played in all their lives, since the nightmare journey began.

'They wouldn't have fed us all and brought us all this way if they were just going to kill us now,' she reasoned and hoped that she would meet the remarkable starosta again.

Two hours dragged by, then a shout.

'Right, the rest of you. All out, with your baggage!'

They scrambled stiffly out, clutching bundles, an untidy, dirty, pathetic group.

'Into ranks now. If any one of you steps out of line, you will be shot dead. Do not look to right or left. Look straight ahead, eyes down. Now, quick march!'

They shambled out of the station and on through the town, the fitter convicts supporting the sick, old and infirm.

'What's happened to the men?' Anna wondered 'and... what new horrors lie ahead?' She could not resist a quick glance to the side. The townspeople were going about their normal business and they were not looking, deliberately *not* looking at the prisoners. They hurried past the ragged troop, with averted eyes.

At last they were halted outside a large red brick building. They were herded into a hall and, for an hour, counted and re-counted.

'And now,' shouted the NCO in charge, with a smirk, 'you are very lucky because you are going to have a bath. Take your clothes off and stand in a queue for de-lousing.'

There was uproar among the women. Some of the 'regulars' protested loudly but the guards became menacing.

'We'll rip your clothes off if you don't do as you're told,' they bellowed, brandishing guns. There was nothing to do but obey.

Anna attempted to close her mind to what was happening. She took off her clothes but didn't look round. She heard the crude jokes from the guards but tried not to register them. She clutched her bundle of clothes to her. Then she realised that the older women were trying, with their wasted bodies, to make a barrier to shield the younger ones from the stares and taunts of the soldiers.

Anna arrived at a counter, where an old man took her clothes and pushed them through an aperture in the wall for delousing.

'Through there,' he said, indicating a door. In the next room an even older man, in greasy trousers, stood by a long wooden table on which were scissors and a bowl of dirty water. In one hand he held a rusty razor.

'Come on. Up on the table,' he wheezed. Anna was shaking with anger.

'How dare they treat us like this,' she was thinking. The man mistook her hesitation for embarrassment.

'Don't worry, little girl,' he croaked, slapping her thigh, playfully. 'I have seen so many women that it doesn't interest me any more.' Without a word, Anna climbed on the table, closed her eyes and let him do his job with the blunt razor. When she climbed down, all the hair from her head and body had been removed.

At last it was time for the bath. The bath house was huge and full of steam. The concrete floor was covered with wooden slats and there were several hot water taps. Anna found a wooden bucket which she and several others used as a wash basin. There was no soap but, forgetting the recent indignities, she scrubbed herself all over with a sort of frenzy. Eventually, exhausted and clean, she leaned

75

against a wall and surveyed the scene. Many women had festering sores and blotched skin from insect bites. Those who had once been fat, now had unsightly flaps of yellowish skin hanging from their bodies. Some women were so emaciated that it was surprising they could still stand upright, while the younger girls sparkled from their ablutions. Many still looked remarkably pretty.

Too soon the guards called them from the wash room and, dripping, they went in search of their clothes. They found them piled on the floor in the entrance hall, in a crumpled and pungent heap. Once more they suffered the indignity of trying to sort out what belonged to whom, chivvied all the time by the impatient guards.

Within an hour and a half, they were back on the train without food and water. The train moved off. This time it contained only women.

'We have never been more vulnerable,' thought Anna.

CHAPTER 6

Poyma

The NKVD officer stepped forward, hands on hips, glaring at the group with almost colourless eyes.

'You scum, you despicable counter revolutionary saboteurs, thieves and whores. I have been given the disgusting task of re-educating you and seeing that you atone for the crimes you have committed against the Soviet Union. You will work hard and I will be watching you. If you don't work, you don't eat. If you don't eat, you die. But there are many people in our country and there will always be someone to replace you.' He paused for breath, his face pink and blotchy, his hair, eyebrows and lashes pale yellow. He fingered the large revolver, hanging from his belt, as he went on. 'Anyone who disobeys orders will be punished harshly. Disobedience is sabotage. The penalty for sabotage is death. I shall have no pity on vermin such as yourselves.' He clicked his fingers and the big beige Alsatian dog which had been sitting by his side, stood and followed him out of the square.

It was the next day and Anna, along with the rest of the women, had arrived at their final railway destination some hours earlier and been transported by lorry to Poyma Labour Camp. There, at last, they were given soup, bread and water and issued with prison clothes.

Anna tried, unsuccessfully, to glimpse herself in the glass of an office window. Her new apparel comprised a long coarse grey shift, a pair of under pants of the same material, a blue quilted jacket or fufayka and a pair of shapeless blue padded trousers. To complete the outfit, there were padded knee length socks, and shoes fashioned from rubber tyres and bits of wire. All garments were worn and patched but freshly laundered and deloused. With relief, she discarded her

77

filthy, stinking rags, although she felt a pang as she realised that another link with her old world had gone. The women had then been marched to the main square, where the Camp Commandant, Major Kondrashkin had addressed them briefly and had then handed over to Tovarishch Byeriosov, the NKVD officer who was the Politruk/Political Officer for the camp.

Now, the women were divided into groups and separated to march to different billets. Anna counted forty wooden huts, constructed of tree trunks and built on platforms. The huts were spaced evenly around the main square. The connecting paths and even the main road, leading to the gate, were paved with logs. There were other, larger huts behind the living quarters, which must be offices, canteens – and she glimpsed a bath house. The perimeter was fenced with high barbed wire and guarded by armed soldiers in tall watch towers. Outside the camp, she saw a small estate of huts, with children playing around some of them – the officers quarters, undoubtedly. Beyond that, was primeval forest, the taiga, stretching for hundreds of miles in all directions. As her group halted outside a barbed wire enclosure which separated the women's quarters from the rest of the camp, Anna realised how over-heated and thirsty she was. It was the end of July, the middle of the scorching Siberian summer, and the warm hot air was heavy with the scent of pines.

Her group was pushed into one of the huts by the officer. Anna blinked as her eyes adjusted to the gloom. The hut was long, with two tiers of rough wooden shelves, about six feet wide, built on each side. The shelves were divided by rough planks into narrow bunks, with no space between. The six small windows, high up, were shut tightly in spite of the hot weather. There was a door at each end of the hut. In the middle space, stood two large iron stoves, their chimneys sticking through the roof. A long trestle table stood between them. Anna had just taken all this in when a large Russian woman, who had been standing just inside the door spoke.

'I'm the Starosta for this hut. My name is Lyuba and it is my job to settle you in and tell you about the routine here. I can speak to the guards on your behalf so come to me if you are worried about anything. The rest of the women, who live here, are at work at the moment. I was allowed to stay behind today because you were expected. I'll show you your bunks and give you a few minutes to settle your bundles there and have a drink of water. She indicated a large jug and some mugs on the table. 'Then I'll tell you what you can expect while you are living here.'

Lyuba smiled at Anna, the smallest and youngest of the new arrivals. 'Your bunk is over there, quite close to mine.' Anna felt grateful to the woman, who had an almost motherly look about her as she spoke.

'Thank you,' she said, and then, 'What are all those dark brown smudges on the walls by the bunks? They look a bit like dried blood.'

Lyuba laughed.

'That's exactly what they are! Don't look so horrified. They are only squashed khlapy/bedbugs.' Anna shuddered, but said no more.

Fifteen minutes later the group was gathered around Lyuba, again, listening carefully to all she had to tell them.

'This camp is here so that its inmates – that's us – can work in the timber industry. All strong men and women are organised into work brigades of lumberjacks who fell trees in the taiga. Each brigade is in charge of a 'brigadier', who is usually a 'regular'. He is expected to maximise output. Older prisoners work in the saw mills about five kilometres from here. The weak and the sick have jobs inside the camp, carrying water to the kitchens, cleaning latrines and doing other menial tasks. The most sought-after positions, say, in the cook houses, bakeries and clothing stores are occupied by privileged inmates, usually 'regulars'. The working day starts at 5am and lasts 14 hours, with half a day free every fourteen days and a full day free on the anniversary of the October Revolution.

'Food is distributed in direct relation to the amount of work done. The norma/expected output is very high and difficult to achieve. Prisoners who manage it, receive first grade rations, consisting of good soup with meat or fish, one kilogram of bread, kasha/thick millet porridge per day and a weekly ration of a few spoons of sugar, a hundred grams of sunflower oil and a small packet of low grade tobacco. Workers who fall below the norma receive approximately fifty percent of what I have just told you and the rest, the sick and infirm, receive about a third. Apart from the main meal, each of us get three quarters of a litre of hot tchay/'tea', an infusion of pressed and dried apple cores in the morning and, in the evening, you have the same brew and a bowl of thin soup or gruel.

'Don't trust anyone! Take great care of all your belongings. Desperate people cannot afford to have morals. I'm a 'regular' but I'm an exception. I get on well with everyone – 'politicals' and 'regulars' alike. Most 'regulars' will rob and persecute 'politicals' as soon as look at them. They consider them stuck up, proud and over-educated. The guards encourage such discrimination and will simply laugh if you complain. There is just one exception to the 'take what you can get' rule and that is the daily ration of bread. There is an unwritten law here. The theft of another's bread is punishable by death. I have seen it happen. Only last week, a man was found stealing bread from a fellow prisoner. He was beaten and battered to death by his hut mates and the guards looked the other way. It was horrible. He screamed and begged for mercy but to no avail. He died – he was executed... and it'll be some time before anyone else here commits the same crime.' There was a short silence while everyone took in this gruesome and salutary tale and then Lyuba went on. 'We do all get a small amount of money each month, in proportion to the amount of work we do. However, by the time money is taken for our keep, only those who have achieved the full norma have a few roubles over for luxuries such as makhorka/coarse tobacco, small bars of soap, and occasionally watery ice cream.'

There was a sound at the door. The guard had arrived to escort the women to the dining hut, where they were given soup and bread. After the meal, they were taken back to the hut.

'Try to get some rest,' Lyuba advised. Anna needed no second invitation. She flung herself on to her bunk. It was rough and splintery. She had no mattress and only a thin blanket and pillow case. Yet within a minute, she was fast asleep.

She woke, with a start and heard the sound of the women convicts returning from work. Anna lay still, trying to get her bearings. It was dark outside and the hut was lit by four small electric bulbs, hanging from the rafters. Grey, ragged figures milled about, swearing, shouting and pushing each other, endeavouring to get to their bunks. She heard many languages – Lithuanian, Latvian, Russian and Polish. Everyone seemed tired and irritable after a long day at work.

Lyuba came over.

'New prisoners, over here.' She led them out and into the square, where the old hands were lined up behind their brigadiers.

'You'll have to join this queue, I'm afraid,' said Lyuba. 'It's the third grade one. You'll receive the same rations as the no-hopers until you get jobs and join a brigade.' The whole camp was now brightly floodlit. Anna's group was called into the canteen. Anna turned to Lyuba, in dismay.

'We haven't got bowls or spoons. How can we eat?' Somehow Lyuba managed to borrow some and the newcomers were soon seated on a greasy bench, eating thin soup and bread.

In spite of everything, Anna looked round with curiosity. There were women of all ages and many nationalities, all wearing the same prison garb. They sat on benches or the floor, with backs resting against the wall, eating, dozing or simply staring blankly into space, absorbed in their own thoughts. Some were obviously sick, some were old and a few were weeping.

As soon as they had finished eating, the group was accompanied to the latrines and then back to the hut.

'We have about an hour now,' Lyuba told them. 'This is the time we are allowed to visit women in other huts if we want to or we can stand outside and smoke and talk.' Anna propped herself up against the wall of the hut, breathing deeply the fresh pine air. Her thoughts drifted home. She wondered about her family. She thought of Severyn. Where was he? Was he still alive?

Too soon the guards arrived. Everyone was ordered inside and into bunks. Anna noticed that no-one had the bourgeois habit of undressing for bed so she followed suit, taking off her outer garments only and using them as a mattress. Within five minutes, the hut lights were extinguished and the two doors closed and locked.

In spite of her exhaustion, Anna was still awake two hours later. The air in the hut was hot and foetid. The pungent smell of one hundred sweating, unwashed bodies blended with the odour of dirty, damp clothing and four parashas/slop buckets, well remembered from former prison days. There were snores, moans, whispers and scuffling sounds and, finally the creeping crawling sensation of bed bugs all over her body. She felt as if she were being attacked by thousands if red hot pins. Roused by the darkness, the heat and the stench, millions of bloodthirsty bedbugs had left their hiding places to feast on the recumbent women.

At first, Anna could do nothing but lie still and endure. She was afraid to make any noise and wake her neighbours. When she could bear it no longer, she sat up, cautiously, and tried to brush off the horrible creatures, although it was very difficult in the dark. Some were the size of peas, fat and soft. When, accidentally, she squashed one, it smelt of blood and kerosene. The baby bugs were the worst. They were impossible to detect in the darkness and stung viciously. Nauseated and shuddering with disgust, Anna could not sleep, dropping into a light doze only a short time before reveille sounded at 4am.

There was just time to slop out, visit the latrines and wash in cold water from a bucket by the well, before breakfast of tchay and bread. At 5am, all work parties marched away under armed guard and the new arrivals were taken to the square.

On the far side, Anna saw Mrs Piotrowska, Irka, two of the Polish teachers and also some of the women who had been in her wagon. She longed to speak to them and hoped that they would end up in the same brigade.

Politruk Byeriosov arrived, accompanied by his dog, four armed guards and four prisoners, two men and two women. He pointed to these and then gave the assembled company a scornful look.

'These prisoners have been chosen to lead your new work brigades. Their food allowance is entirely dependent on your work output. Be assured, they will do their best to retain their first grade rations. They will report to me, personally, any attempt at sabotage or criminal negligence and I will find an appropriate punishment for the culprit. Your re-education begins from this moment. Male brigadiers, choose the women you want to work with you on the timbers.' He turned his back and lit a cigarette.

The new arrivals were standing in rows of thirty. The two men walked slowly along each row, examining each woman, as they would cattle, in a market. They chose those who looked strong and healthy. Anna, as one of the smallest and thinnest was sure she would not be chosen and so was greatly surprised when one of the men pointed at her and pulled her over to join his group.

The two women brigadiers herded those not chosen by the men and marched them away to the clothing repair shops and wash houses. In despair, Anna saw that none of the women she knew were to go to the timber works. She couldn't understand why she had been chosen. She felt lonely and very frightened that she would be the one to spoil her brigade's chances and so bring down its united wrath on her head.

Anna's brigadier was tall and fair haired. He spoke Russian with a slight accent which she could not place but his voice was pleasant, educated. When the two brigades were lined up, Byeriosov looked at them scornfully, swore, spat on the ground and stalked off, followed by his dog.

Two armed guards stood by each brigade.
'If any of you dares to move one step out of the formation, you'll be shot,' they were warned.
The road led directly into the taiga and the trees gave welcome shade. Anna looked around in wonder. The forest floor was thickly carpeted with pine needles and overgrown with vivid bushes. Clumps of bright flowers, orchids she thought, grew by the roadside.

The air was balmy and the scent of pines filled her nostrils. Suddenly, she was shocked to reality by crude Ukrainian voices.

'Hey Polish Lady! Stop gaping. This isn't your bloody estate.' They pushed her forward, laughing. 'Your Poland is kaput for ever. You'll die here. You'll never see your beloved Poland again, you filthy bloodsucking capitalist!' A couple of Polish women, nearby, came to Anna's defence and a heated argument ensued. It was overheard by the brigadier.

'Stop that!' he shouted. 'There are no capitalists here. We're all workers and equals. Anyone starting a quarrel will be reported and severely punished. Go back to your places. March!' And mumbling under their breath, the Ukrainians could only obey.

At last, after almost an hour and a half's march, the group arrived at a large clearing, containing piles of felled tree trunks. About two hundred prisoners were engaged on a variety of tasks, watched by armed guards. Some were sawing off the thickest branches, some collected the sawn off wood, others sawed this into standard lengths while yet others piled the pieces neatly, ready for collection by truck. Tally men measured the completed stacks and the strongest of the men, pushed the denuded tree trunks to the side of the clearing for transportation to the saw mills.

Anna's group was ordered to collect all the broken and smaller branches and make a pile of them. By now the sun was high in the sky. It was back-breaking and thirsty work but no break was allowed until 4pm, when a ten minute rest was announced. Anna collapsed where she stood. Every muscle in her body ached with the unaccustomed exercise and she was weak from lack of food, water and sleep. Somehow she managed to drag herself up after the ten minutes and continue to work but it was on that day that she decided to become a smoker. She discovered that all smokers, guards and prisoners alike, were allowed a five minute perekourka/smoking break every two hours, whereas non-smokers had to work throughout the whole day, with only a short time given, at midday, for eating. She was also advised by one of the women that smoking would quell some of her hunger pangs.

Afterwards, she had no recollection of the march back to camp. When she got there, she flung herself on her bunk and refused to go to supper. Only when Lyuba threatened her with a bucket of cold water, did she limp to the canteen and return to the hut with a can of thin, tepid soup. She fell asleep while trying to eat it but Lyuba woke her and spooned it into her mouth. Then Anna knew no more until reveille. Not even the bedbugs could keep her awake.

Anna survived the next ten days in the taiga only because of the help she received from Lyuba and Ninka and Zosia, two Polish women in the hut. They fed her, washed her cut and bruised hands and feet and encouraged her in any way possible. Lyuba, particularly, was like a mother to her. She had been in prison for three years, was a respected starosta, noted for her honesty and strength of character and had influential friends. When she was crossed or suspected that someone was cheating, she would lash out with her tongue, using oaths and swear words that Anna had never heard before.

One day, a group of male prisoners made some crude remarks about Anna and a couple of others as they returned to the hut after work. They stood, looking through the wire fence and jeering. Lyuba, eyes blazing, was up to the fence in an instant.

'You sons of mangey bitches,' she shrieked, 'you misbegotten devil's spawn, you uncultured, perverted sons of syphilitic whores! Hold your rotten tongues when women are around...' The men retreated, abashed and Lyuba returned to the hut, dishevelled but victorious.

She spoke of her past life only once to Anna. It was night and Anna couldn't sleep because of the pain in her back. Lyuba sat beside her, on the bunk, and told her that she was serving ten years for stealing money from state farm funds. She made no excuses, but turning away, said, bitterly, 'My husband and two sons disowned me after the trial. I am better off here, where I am someone. I have nothing to go out for.' Anna could say nothing for a moment. She rested her head on Lyuba's shoulder then said quietly, 'You've certainly been a mother to me since I arrived. Thank you.'

At last the free half day arrived. In the morning, Anna helped to clean the hut. She mended her trousers and jacket and then it was time to go to the banyas/bath house. Prisoners took it in turns to carry buckets of water from the well and to stoke the log fire which heated an iron grid set on boulders in the main room. There were rows of slatted shelves round the walls and when Anna she entered, she could think only of Dante's Inferno. The heat was intense and she would have fainted had not Lyuba poured cold water over her head. She perched, self consciously on a lower shelf and watched the women birching themselves and each other and pouring water over their heads. Perspiration, carrying ingrained grime, oozed from her every pore and gathered in muddy puddles round her filthy feet. She wished she had not come. Then, suddenly, the whole macabre scene dissolved in a thick billowing cloud of steam. Someone had poured a bucket of water over the hot boulders. The dry heat changed to the tropics. Anna relaxed and lay still on her shelf.

Five minutes later she moved to the second room, where there was cold water. There were scoops and buckets. And she scrubbed every inch of herself and, moving into the last room, found her freshly laundered, slightly damp clothes. Exhilarated, she returned to the hut.

The main meal was at midday on half day holidays and after that came Anna's first official taste of 're-education'. The doors to the largest hut on camp – the 'theatre' – were opened at 1.30p.m. Five hundred prisoners filed in and sat on low wooden benches, facing a dais, over which hung the inevitable picture of Stalin. A red wooden star, with gold hammer and sickle, were suspended from the ceiling. Strips of discoloured red crepe paper stretched from them and were fastened to the walls. The whole resembled a dusty spider's web, Anna thought.

When the prisoners were settled, the door near the dais opened to admit the Camp Commandant, Major Kondrashkin, another officer and Politruk Byeriosov, followed by three civilians in ill-fitting suits. They were all smiling but Anna noticed that Byeriosev's smile didn't reach his eyes. He scanned each row of prisoners, on the lookout for any uncalled for movement or expression. The Commandant spoke first.

'Good afternoon,' he began, benignly. 'It is my great pleasure to introduce Tovarishch Yefimov who is an expert statistician, specialising in the production of timber.' He clapped, everyone clapped – even Yefimov clapped, dropping his papers and almost tripping as he made his way to the front of the platform. Anna bit her lip. She knew she mustn't laugh. She put her head down and clapped even harder.

When, at last, the applause died away, the short plump man, swelling with importance, read incomprehensible lists of statistics in a patronising tone, stopping now and again and looking up to make sure everyone was attending. When, at last, he stopped, the applause was tumultuous. Anna clapped along with the others, glad for an opportunity to move her hands and feet and for the fact that the statistics had come to an end. But the other two lectures were equally tedious. The first on cotton production in Uzbekistan and the next on the development and benefits of collectivisation.

'Now,' thought Anna, 'surely we can go.' She was wrong. Byeriosov got to his feet.

'I would like to thank all three lecturers on behalf of us all for their lucid and interesting talks.' He stuck his hands into his belt and gave a sardonic smile. 'These subjects are important to every patriot of our glorious country.' His voice began to rise. 'But there is another subject, one of great importance, which I wish to discuss with you. It's the very serious matter of sabotage, criminal negligence and espionage. There are those among you who would bite off the Soviet hand which is outstretched in friendship to all oppressed nations of the world.' Here he became agitated, white flakes of saliva flecking the corners of his mouth. 'We know who you are!' he shouted. 'We have the means, we will crush you mercilessly, like the disgusting, filthy vermin you are!' He continued in this vein for almost an hour. When he finished, he returned to his chair, sweating, wiping his blotched face. There was silence in the hall. No-one clapped. No-one moved.

The Commandant rose to his feet and Anna thought there was a hint of weariness in his voice.

'I would like to thank all our guests and, of course, our esteemed political officer. He is an ever vigilant patriot. I'm sure everyone here has learned something this afternoon.' With this, he began to clap. The spell was broken. Everyone clapped until the platform party had left.

It was time for the evening tchay. Anna left the hall and joined the queue at the canteen. She found herself next to a Polish woman from her hut. They began to talk about the re-education lectures, mimicking Byeriosov and laughing.

'Hold your tongues, stupid girls. You never know who's listening to your idiotic babbling,' hissed a Russian voice from behind. They spun round. There was only an old dirty, ragged convict standing there, staring vacantly ahead. His must have been the voice but he gave no sign.

'That's a lesson for us,' muttered Anna. 'From now on, no loose talk!'

Over the next few weeks, Anna gained in strength and stamina. Lyuba contrived to get extra food for her, she gained weight and her dark, wavy hair began to grow. Even her gums healed, her front teeth stopped wobbling although the left side of her jaw still gave pain, occasionally. Her only real concern was that her periods had stopped since her arrest. She was reassured when finally, she found the courage to mention this to a Russian woman doctor, who lived in the next hut.

'Don't worry,' she said 'this will not be permanent. Almost all the women here are experiencing the same. It's part of the body's way of coping with the conditions in prison. It's a recognised phenomenon.'

Some scratchy pens, watery ink and a stack of postcards were brought to the hut one evening.

'Every six months, everyone may write one of these cards to someone they know, who lives within the borders of the Soviet Union,' announced the officer. 'Write your names on the card, a short greeting and any request you have, for instance, for a food parcel. The cards must be written in block capitals and must be in Russian.'

Anna wrote a short message to her sister in Luck, although she admitted to herself that she had no great hopes of receiving a reply.

CHAPTER 7

The Chulym Interlude

Lyuba held Anna by the shoulders and shook her until her teeth rattled. She swore loudly and then,

'You stupid, stupid, ignorant girl. How could you be so foolish as to agree to go. You'll be raped and probably murdered too and your body will be thrown in the river or left in the forest for the wolves to devour. You stupid, stupid....' She tailed off, with another oath and burst into tears, as she added, 'If you must go, if you are determined, then, please, please let me come with you to protect you!' Anna freed herself from Lyuba's grasp.

'Lyuba,' she said consolingly. 'It's not my place to choose who comes with me and Avgust Gustavich Ounapu has given me his word that I will be absolutely safe.'

Two weeks previously, Anna's brigade had been transferred from the forest to work in the saw mill. Anna was delighted. The place buzzed with activity, people seemed less gloomy and the sweet small of pine resin filled her nostrils. The big snag was that the position of the mill, next to the river meant that great clouds of midges and mosquitoes attacked any bare flesh. They would congregate round eyes and mouths, biting viciously and causing itchy swellings, which turned septic. After a few days, linen hoods were issued, with eye holes, covered in netting. These, tucked into collars protected faces but there was no respite for hands and ankles.

It was the beginning of September. It was still warm in the day but nights were noticeably cooler. Prisoners came back from the forest, every day, laden with wood to add to fuel piles which stood by each of the barrack huts.

It was a golden September day, with a light breeze, which kept the insects away. Anna settled down in a secluded spot by a timber pile, to eat her midday bread. She had found a sprig of wild mint and added it to her mug of hot water. She was sipping this, with relish, when she was startled to hear a voice behind her. She turned to see her brigadier. He was smiling.

'Forgive me for interrupting your rest, mademoiselle,' he said. 'I would like to introduce myself. I am Avgust Gustvich Ounapu, ex-captain of the Soviet forces.' He bowed and held out his hand. Anna shook it and then began to laugh. How ludicrous that she should be shaking the hand of the man who had been watching her and chivvying her all these weeks. How ridiculous that he should be bowing to her! He was looking puzzled and a little hurt.

'It's very nice to meet you properly,' she said solemnly, 'and to know your name.' She offered him the remainder of the mint tea, which he drank, gratefully.

'I am a trained engineer,' he explained 'and I have been selected to accompany a civilian engineer, Nikolaev, on a topographical expedition to examine the safety of the banks of the River Chulym. It's been reported that last spring's heavy rainfall has caused parts of the banks to subside. This means floods around the river but shallow water in the riverbed, causing jams, damage to timber and non-arrival, at the saw mill, of many consignments. I've been asked to select eleven male prisoners to accompany the expedition and four women, who will do the cooking. I have been watching your work. You are always conscientious and you never make trouble. I would like you to be one of the women… if you wish it.'

Anna was astonished and gratified. How good it would be to have a break in the dreary routine. She didn't hesitate.

'Thank you very much for considering me,' she replied. 'I will be happy to come.'

The brigadier looked pleased.

'You may choose three friends to accompany you,' he added. 'There will be armed guards and dogs, of course, so you'll be cooking for quite a large number. We'll be camping in tents and I promise you – you have my word – that you and your friends will be as safe under my protection as you would be in your own huts.'

Anna thought how difficult it would be to make a choice about which other women should go with her. Jealousy was rife in the tight knit community. She spoke quickly.

'It is very kind of you to say I may choose who comes with me.

However, I feel this would be presumptuous of me. I would prefer someone older and wiser to choose.' The brigadier smiled.

'You are very diplomatic. We will leave the Commandant to make that decision.'

That evening, she told Lyuba of this conversation. It was this that had produced the outburst. Anna did her best to calm the older woman, promising not to allow herself to be alone with any of the men and to relate every detail when she returned.

Early the next morning, Anna was called to the main office.

'Ah, Anna Grzymala Siedlecka,' the Commandant was smiling, 'I gather you are happy to go on the expedition. You'll will be in charge of the cooking but I understand that you have said that you wish me to choose the other women to accompany you.'

'Yes, please, sir.'

'I see you are not equipped for life in the forest,' he said, taking in Anna's worn jacket and shoes, which were tied with string. He scribbled something on a scrap of paper and handed it to a guard, saying, 'Go with this woman to the clothing store.' Turning to Anna, he added 'Good luck in the forest. The workers will rely on you for nourishment.'

Equipped with a pair of strong leather boots and a warm bushlat/padded jacket, Anna returned to the empty hut, feeling very pleased. Then she reported for camp duties, which occupied her until the workers returned from the forest.

Just before bed time, Lyuba came up to Anna and, patting her gently on the head said,

'I know it's too late to argue with you, you stupid, ungrateful girl. But if anyone tries anything on with you, just tell Lyuba and she will skin him alive!' Very moved, Anna hugged the big woman, who had become so important to her.

Early next morning, Anna was in the back of a lorry, which was laden with the two engineers, eleven male convicts, four females, four armed guards, with dogs, precious engineering equipment, pick axes, spades and shovels, cooking pots and provisions. She smiled shyly at the other three women, who were Russian, They smiled back.

The lorry drove very fast for about two hours. It soon passed the saw mill, bouncing over ruts and potholes, throwing the passengers from side to side. At last it stopped near the river bank. Most items were unloaded then all the men, except for one guard, drove off to start the reconstruction work, carrying bread for their midday meal. The women were left to light a fire, put up the tents and prepare the supper.

After erecting the tents, they filled the cauldron with crystal clear water from the river and put dried fish, millet and vegetables into it to make soup. While this was simmering, they went, one by one, to the river for a thorough wash, braving the clouds of mosquitoes. The guard took no notice but dozed by the fire.

On her way back from the river, Anna spotted some smorodina/wild black currants. They were delicious and soon the women had collected a sack full. They prepared some batter, and using a pot lid as a skillet, cooked a pile of pancakes, which they wrapped in a cloth, to be filled with the berries later.

When the men returned, muddy and tired, they were more than ready for their meal and delighted with the unexpected desert. Even the guards became mellow as everyone relaxed around the fire, stomachs full. Suddenly one of the convicts started to hum and then to sing a sad old Russian song and the rest joined in, in perfect harmony. One song after another rang through the taiga, prisoners, engineer, guards, singing together, their voices sweet. Anna joined in with gusto. She had always loved Russian folk songs.

'How strange,' she thought, 'I feel happy, really happy… how can that be? I'm a prisoner.' And she sang on until the songs ran out and it was time for bed.

When she woke, day was breaking and the birds were singing. The fire had been stoked during the night so the women quickly prepared millet porridge and tchay.

The men emerged, bleary eyed and stiff to eat breakfast and then set out for work once more.

A different guard was on duty at the camp. As the women busied themselves with the chores, the atmosphere was friendly and relaxed. Then the three Russian women started flirting with the guard. He, in turn, laughed and chased them, slapping their behinds at every opportunity. Anna was worried. She was in charge of the women and things were getting out of hand.

'Laughter can so easily turn sour,' she told herself. 'This could all end in trouble.' She called the women aside and, feeling very small and young, but taking a deep breath, she said firmly,

'I am not a prude. I, too, like laughter and jokes but this stupid flirting must stop.' The women looked at her blankly. 'This sort of behaviour could spoil the smooth running of the expedition,' she went on. 'You're giving the wrong message. This man will think you are loose women. He'll tell his friends this and you won't be safe. If you don't stop immediately, I'll ask for you to be sent back to camp and I'll have to give my reasons.'

The women said nothing. They looked frightened and sulky. But after that, they avoided the advances of the guard who, surprised at first, soon gave up and dozed near the fire, his rifle by his side.

There was no sing-song that night. The women were subdued and retired to bed early. Anna soon joined them. Niura, the eldest of the three spoke.

'We want to thank you, Anna for not reporting us to the brigadier. We're not bad or loose women – just thoughtless. You were right in what you said. In future we'll try to behave with more dignity.' Anna smiled at them.

'It's all forgotten,' she replied.

Camp routine continued for three more days. Anna found some wild strawberries as a change from the black currants. Avgust Gustavich congratulated her on the way she was managing the food.

'Delicious,' he said. 'We won't want to go back to canteen cooking.' Engineer Nikolaev nodded his head.

'Nearly as good as my wife's, which is saying a lot,' he smiled. Anna decided to be brave and voice something she'd been thinking ever since their arrival in the taiga.

'I wonder, sir,' she began 'whether it would be possible for me to join your work team tomorrow, please. I'm very interested in your project. I'd love to help with it. My father's an architect and so I even know how to use a theodolite.'

The engineer laughed.

'I certainly wouldn't let you any where near my precious theodolite, but if the other women can manage the cooking without you, and your brigadier is in agreement, you can certainly come. Another pair of hands would be welcome.'

Avgust Gustavich made no objection and arranged for Niura to take charge of the cooking.

The next morning, Anna, carrying, over her shoulder, a three meter plank, marked as a measure, followed the men into the taiga. She had to pick her way carefully over the tree roots, hidden dips and bumps and through the thick undergrowth. The group reached the bank of the River Ob, which they climbed. An awesome sight met their eyes.

Great chunks of the bank had collapsed and fallen into the water, carrying with them, living trees and bushes. These had made a dam, reaching the middle of the river. Hundreds of felled trunks, meant to float easily down stream to the sawmills, were piled high on top of the dam. Unable to flow as it should, the river had breached the opposite bank and flooded a large expanse of taiga. More than a hundred convicts were working on both sides of the dam. They were using long poles, tipped with steel hooks, to drag tree trunks from the piles in an attempt to get them into the water downstream of the dam. The operation was extremely dangerous. Prisoners were jumping from log to log, pulling, pushing, slipping, often ending in the water. Armed guards stood safely on top of the bank, shouting instructions and swearing.

'We'll start our survey here,' said Engineer Nikolaev. 'Anna, you'll walk ahead of me and stop when I say. We'll work together, you with the scale and me with the theodolite. Avgust Gustavich, you take the other prisoners and divide them into two groups. One group must go along the top of the bank and the other walk at water level. Mark all signs of subsidence with the tall wooden stakes. Don't forget to mark their tops with red paint.' Avgust led his men away and Anna and the Engineer started their work. Soon Anna was filthy and perspiring, crawling along the bank, through bushes and over rocks, determined not to complain or fall.

It was dark when they returned to camp. Anna was exhausted

but wouldn't admit it and accepted the invitation to join in the surveying again the next day.

'Molodietz dievochka!'/'Plucky girl!' laughed Nikolaev.

The same routine was followed throughout the next morning. Then a fire was lit on the edge of the forest and Anna cooked porridge and made tchay for everyone.

'We'll rest for an hour,' declared Nikolaev afterwards 'and then we'll work until nightfall.' He went over to one of the guards and spoke to him. The man nodded and got to his feet. Then he called Avgust Gustavich and Anna.

'Come,' he said, smiling at their puzzled faces, 'we're going for a walk. The guard will have to come with us.'

Anna couldn't imagine why he would take them walking. Nor was she pleased. She'd needed that hour's rest. Preceded by the guard, they walked up river for about fifteen minutes, then climbed the bank, to see a wide flat area of land between the false bank along which they'd been walking and the true bank of the river, which rose on the far side. A group of people were sitting round a fire, over which a large cauldron was suspended. Fishing nets were spread out to dry and a small rowing boat was lying nearby. Children were playing, laughing noisily. Anna thought what a long time it was since she had heard such a sound.

The group round the fire suddenly realised they were being watched. They were silent and stared fearfully at the armed guard. Nikolaev put up his hand in greeting and, signalling the others to stand still, moved slowly forward, speaking quietly.

'Who are these people?' Anna whispered to Avgust.

'They're Sibiryak fishermen,' he replied.

Nikolaev called the other three over.

'They've invited us to share their meal,' he said. Anna smiled as she was beckoned by a young woman to sit by her. The woman passed her a bowl of fish and potato stew and some crisp, lightly salted gherkins.

The food was delicious, the more so because it was unexpected. Afterwards, Nikolaev gave the woman some sugar and passed round makhorka/black tobacco, for the men, who rolled cigarettes in strips of old newspaper and smoked, contentedly. The woman said something softly to Nikolaev and Avgust, who nodded and looked at Anna.

'She wants to show you her zyemlanka/earth house,' said Avgust and, looking at the guard, 'Is that all right?'

'OK' the man answered. He had enjoyed the meal too and was obviously feeling mellow.

Anna followed the young woman into a large rectangular cave, which had been dug in the high false bank. The front wall was of thick, rough planks, out of which four squares had been cut for windows, which were glazed. Inside, the walls were covered in smoother planks. There were long wooden benches, covered in sheepskins along two walls and a scrubbed table in the centre. Next to that was a cast iron stove, its pipe disappearing through a hole in the ceiling. The whole place was clean and neat. Anna turned to the woman.

'It's lovely,' she said. 'You've made it cosy and welcoming. I have never seen a house like this before. I do like it.'

The woman looked pleased. Then she followed Anna's glance to a shelf in a corner, on which there was a small icon, in a silver frame, under which shone a tiny red oil lamp. She whispered,

'Are you a Christian?'

'Yes,'

At this reply, the woman crossed herself three times, with the thumb and first two fingers of her right hand, in the Greek Orthodox manner. Anna followed her example. It was a moment of intimacy that she never forgot.

Later, as they walked back to the rest of the party, Anna spoke to Nikolaev.

'Thank you very much for introducing me to these people,' and then, curious, 'Why did you do it?'

He smiled, Anna thought, a little sadly.

'I, too am a Sibiryak/native of Siberia – possibly a descendant of a convict or exile – and very proud of my country. I wanted our little foreigner to learn something of our ways and customs. Many

Siberian peasants live all summer in such hamlets of zyemlankas by big rivers. They grow vegetables on the banks, fish and collect wild honey and berries. In the winter they move into log cabins and work as trappers and hunters.'

Anna worked even more conscientiously for the rest of that and the next day, to show her gratitude to Nikolaev. That evening, she asked him if she could return to normal cooking duties for the rest of the trip.

'I don't want the others to think you favour me,' she explained.

The last couple of days flew by. The final supper was sumptuous for all the stores could be used up. There was rich bean and pork soup with noodles, fruit pancakes and, finally Nikolaev produced some real tea for everyone to enjoy. They all sang Russian songs round the fire until midnight.

'Thank you all,' Nikolaev said 'for your very hard work. We have finished a day ahead of schedule, thanks to your dedication.'

The next morning, the party returned to Poyma. Suddenly, Anna felt rebellious as she saw the familiar watchtowers and prisoners patiently waiting for their meager rations. The stench in the hut hit her anew, the stained walls and narrow bunks revolted her. But when her Polish friends, Ninka and Zosia, rushed to welcome her as if she were a long lost sister, she felt ashamed and hugged each in turn. Lyuba looked at her searchingly.

'Did any of those men try anything on with you?' she asked.

'Nobody would have dared,' Anna assured her, laughing. 'Not when everyone knows I have such a powerful friend as you!'

'Well,' the older woman retorted, 'I don't altogether trust that blue eyed Brigadier of yours. I think he's in love with you. And what about you?' She regarded Anna suspiciously. 'Have you fallen for him?'

Anna laughed again.

'Lyuba, this is no place to fall in love. What kind of future could we have? We'd have to snatch clandestine meetings behind bushes and piles of timber. That's not going to be my sort of love. When all this is over, I shall have a proper romance!'

'I'm glad to hear it.' responded Lyuba, 'but you are a pigheaded, reckless girl, or you never would have gone into the wilds with all those men. You just take care. I have my eye on you.' Then she gave Anna a big hug and a mug of tchay.

CHAPTER 8

Winter Scene

Next day, Anna returned to her normal work under the supervision of Avgust Gustavich. She felt stronger and healthier after her time in the forest, where there had been fresh air, exercise and excellent food.

As the winter approached, the days shortened so that it was dark when she left for the sawmill and dark when she returned. Temperatures dropped below freezing and the morale of the workers dropped too. Clothes and shoes were worn out and offered little protection from the biting cold. Three people in the hut died and many were ill. On many nights, Anna was unable to sleep because of the coughing of those around her.

Her work was heavy and the quota seemed impossible to achieve. Anna struggled with bundles of fruit box kits, tearing her hands on the brittle wire as she tried to tie them together. The brigade had been split into smaller groups and she found herself working with the four tall, well built Ukrainian women, who had taunted her on her first walk to the saw mill. They were angry that Anna could not work faster, carry more boxes, achieve the quota because this affected their rations as well. By now, her fingers were chilblained, cut and blistered and she had bleeding chilblains on her feet too. The women cursed Anna, threatened to beat her and, finally reported her to the brigadier.

'You stupid girl,' he shouted. 'Your pride will be the death of you. Go to the rest hut. I'll deal with you later.' Pacified by this outburst, the women went back to work. Mortified, Anna did as she was told.

She was unable to hold back her tears as she reached the hut. The old convict, in charge of the stove there, took pity on her, helped her to clean her aching fingers and offered her a mug of tchay. When Avgust Gustavich arrived, he was apologetic.

'I'm sorry, Anna, for shouting at you,' he said. 'I had to satisfy those women, somehow. However, I do think you behaved foolishly. In future, you must come to me if you run into trouble with your work colleagues and you must try not to antagonise them. Tomorrow we will find an easier job for you.'

That evening, Anna went to see the lekpom/untrained first aider, who swabbed her hands and feet with iodine and declared her fit for work.

Her new job was inside a large shed, where a mechanical saw cut tree trunks into planks, which were dropped on to a conveyor belt. Syeriozha, the prisoner in charge of the operation instructed Anna.

'Here's a tin of green paint. You'll find a stick with a piece of rag wrapped round the end over there.' He went on to show Anna how to recognise the different types of timber. 'Now all you have to do, is dab the planks with paint as they go along the belt. One dab for pine, two for spruce, three for larch.' The planks came along at great speed. At first, Anna worked conscientiously but, after a while, frantically dabbed on the paint, almost randomly. She was amazed, at the end of the day, when her supervisor said,

'Congratulations, you've done very well.'
'Thank you, but I'm a bit worried that I've marked some planks wrongly,' admitted Anna. 'They came along so quickly that…' she tailed off feeling awkward.

'Nitchevo/It's nothing,' and Syeriozha laughed. Nobody cares as long as the work quota is achieved.'

Anna quite enjoyed her 'artistic' job. She liked Syeriozha, her cut hands healed and because she was achieving 65% of her quota, her rations improved. Her chilblains still bothered her – but everyone had chilblains. The first snow fell at the beginning of October and the temperature dropped to -18 degrees centigrade. Thanks to Avgust Gustavich, she was given a pair of rather large and worn valenki/knee length boots, moulded out of thick felt. Stuffed inside a pair of galoshes, they were wonderfully warm.

The guards at the mill weren't strict. They left prisoners to their own devices and huddled round the stove in their special hut. As

Anna wasn't part of a work team, she was free, at the midday break, to join various groups of prisoners in their different rest huts. She enjoyed the company of one group in particular. They were all 'politicals', highly educated members of the Polish aristocracy. There were writers, poets, scientists, doctors and teachers, all sentenced to hard labour for political deviation and criticism of the Party. One elderly man she met, a Russian Orthodox archimandrite, had been in prison for twenty years. He was frail but his manner was gentle and his smile serene. Even the guards treated him with respect. Anna would sit in a corner of the hut, listening to the learned conversation and feel privileged.

Her downfall came when she found some pieces of charred birch twigs, near the stove in the mill. She picked them up and realised they were similar to the charcoal she had used, at home, for sketching.

'I must draw.'

The urge was so strong that it took her by surprise. She looked round and found a small, smooth flat plank. She heard voices and quickly hid her treasure and went back to work. She waited impatiently for the break, retrieved her tools the settled down in a secluded corner. She was out of practice and her fingers were stiff with cold but, eventually, she achieved a recognisable portrait of Seriozha.

'Not bad,' she thought. 'I'll collect more thin light planks and birch twigs. I'll practice every day.'

By the end of the week, she had done ten drawings, her technique improving every day. One day she chose her three best sketches and took them to the rest hut where she had spent so much time.

Everyone admired them but Dr Godlevski cautioned her.

'Be very careful, Anna. They're wonderful drawings. You have a great gift but it's dangerous to be an individualist in our situation. You could be accused of drawing things which are anti Soviet. Take care, take care.'

But Anna couldn't stop drawing. She became obsessed by it and although she destroyed most of her sketches, she kept the best, well hidden. She drew throughout each break, often forgetting to eat, sitting behind the hut, shielded by a stack of timber. But eventually, as the doctor had predicted, she was caught by a guard as she was completing a picture of a peasant woman, carrying a small baby.

The guard snatched the board away.

'You filthy Polish convict,' he shouted 'you're drawing an icon. That is an anti Soviet act and you will be severely punished.'

'It's not a holy picture,' Anna protested, though she could feel her heart pumping. 'It's an ordinary woman with her baby.' He wouldn't listen but locked her in a shed until it was time to return to camp. She was very scared. She knew the authorities came down very heavily on anyone who was found practising religion of any sort. She huddled in the corner, wondering if she could persuade the Commandant that the people in the picture were ordinary local peasants she had seen on her way to work, and if she couldn't, what her punishment would be.

On the trek back to the prison, Anna was made to walk behind the main group, on her own. She was taken straight to the main office, where she had to face the Commandant and Politruk Byeriosov. They were both angry and would listen to none of Anna's protests.

'How dare you!' Byeriosov shouted. 'You were given undemanding and easy work to do and this is the way you repay us. What is this icon? Which branch of pernicious religion does it refer to? Tell us or it will be the worse for you…'

'It is the picture of a mother and her baby I saw this morning on my way to the mill…' Anna started.

'Don't lie to us, you wretched girl. We know you set out to sabotage our glorious timber industry…' The interview went on in this way for almost two hours. She gave up trying to justify herself and waited, trembling, for it to end. Finally, came the declaration of her punishment.

'You will spend three days in solitary confinement,' Byeriosov finished. 'You'll have time to contemplate your behaviour, to repent and to determine to be better in future.'

Solitary confinement in the 'calf pen!' Anna's heart sank lower. The solitary confinement cell, dubbed the 'calf pen' by prisoners was a small, dark, unheated hut, with no windows and a narrow bunk. There was no mattress and one thin, cotton blanket. She was marched straight to the hut and pushed inside.

'No food tonight,' said the guard. 'Tchay in the morning, gruel at midday and a slice of black bread in the evening.' And he was gone. Anna stumbled over the slop bucket, felt her way to the bunk and lay down.

'Blank your mind to all this,' she urged herself. 'Think of wonderful things, of sunshine and home.'

But she found it difficult to be positive when the slop bucket froze in the night and she shivered uncontrollably on the hard bunk. Nevertheless, she knew that she would keep on drawing.

'I'll just have to be more careful,' she determined.

The three days and nights dragged by but, at last, she was released to return to her barracks. She was moved by her reception. Lyuba, Ninka and Zosia hugged her.

'Here, my little Anna,' said Lyuba, 'we've saved some bread and a little sugar for you. They're to show you that everyone in this hut loves you.' Others gathered round and Anna felt a warm glow of affection for these women with whom she had developed such close relationships. Her bunk seemed luxurious after the one on which she'd been sleeping. She sank on to it and fell asleep immediately but not for long. She woke with a raging fever. Every bone ached and she became delirious. She started to cough and shake. The next morning, she was unable to rise from her bunk. Ninka ran to the next hut as soon as the door was unlocked. She brought the Polish doctor back with her, a tired looking woman, with a gentle manner. She asked Anna to open her mouth wide and, peering in exclaimed,

'It's bright red and covered in white spots – tonsillitis. You must notify the lekpom. Your temperature is very high.' The lekpom came and confirmed that her temperature was 105 degrees Fahrenheit.

'It's high enough for her to go to the hospital,' the woman said.

Anna floated in and out of consciousness as her friends carried her to the hospital hut. She knew very little of the first two days except that she was dosed regularly with some sort of medicine. When she felt well enough to sit up and look round, she saw that the place was reasonably clean. It was divided into three sections. There were separate wards for men and women and the remaining part was the living space for the lekpom. There were straw palliasses on the beds and course linen sheets and pillowcases. Two women prisoners nursed the sick. Both had been trained as doctors but were not allowed to practice medicine at the camp. They had to accept orders from the untrained lepkom, who, nevertheless relied on them a great deal for advice on treatment and nourishment for the patients. The doctors were kept in their place by being sent, regularly, to do menial tasks about the prison, such as cleaning the bath houses or working in the laundry.

Anna spent five days in the hospital. Once more she was greeted joyfully by her friends and then was summoned to the main office.

'Enter,' came the command, when the guard knocked the door. This time, Byeriosov was sitting behind the desk, on his own except for his large Alsatian dog, lying near his feet. He didn't look up as Anna entered. She took a couple of steps towards him. His head shot up.

'Stop!' he shouted. 'How dare you approach my desk without permission?' He said something to the dog, that Anna didn't catch. The big animal stood up, bared its teeth and walked slowly towards her, growling viciously.

'Dobry piesek/Good doggy,' the words were out before she could stop them, also she gave a simultaneous click of her fingers. She had never been afraid of dogs. At one time there had been ten, including two Alsatians, at her family's country house. The animal stopped growling, stood still and looked expectantly at its master, who was staring at Anna, in astonishment. Then he laughed and called the dog back to him.

'I see you have recovered sufficiently to resume your work at the sawmill,' he said.

Anna, relief sweeping over her answered, 'Yes sir.'

'However,' he continued, 'The Commandant and I are compassionate men and realise you are not strong enough yet to resume your normal duties so we have found something else for you to do. Something that will suit you very well. As from today, you will be the camp sign writer. You will repaint all the numbers on the barracks, rewrite the lists of rules on the boards and execute any other work on signs that may be necessary. You will report to the sub-office every morning to collect your daily work schedule, paint and brushes and you'll return everything there each evening, for inspection.'

He nodded Anna's dismissal so, thanking him, she left the room.

The next morning, Anna discovered that her new supervisor and tally-man was Gavsiuk, an unpopular prisoner, in charge of the offices and inmates who worked there.

'Be very careful.' one of the office workers warned her. 'We think he is a collaborator. Keep your head down and tell him nothing.' Anna was given two paint brushes, a ruler, a pencil, a tin of black paint and a stack of boards from the sawmill.

'You can work in that corner of the hut,' said Gavsiuk. 'Your future depends on me, you know. If you please me you'll be OK but if you don't, you'll live to regret it.'

Anna was angry.

'I don't know what you mean,' she snapped. 'I shall work as hard as I always have. The Commandant gave me this job and I'm responsible to him. If you have a problem with that, please take it up with him – or we could go together to see him.' There was a moment's silence and then Gavsiuk answered.

'That won't be necessary. I'm sure we will get on very well.' He walked away and Anna had no more trouble with him.

It was very cold and snow was falling. She was given a corner of one of the office huts, in which to work. She had a table and pieces of wood, cut to the correct size, a flat carpenter's pencil and a straight narrow plank, to serve as a ruler as well as the paint brush and tin of black oil paint.

There was an unexpectedly large amount of sign writing work required on the camp and Anna enjoyed the challenge. She longed, all the time, to paint pictures instead of notices such as, 'DO NOT DROP LITTER' and 'DO NOT SWEAR' but, for the time being, she resisted the temptation. By the end of the first week she managed to achieve seventy five percent of her work quota. Sometimes the Commandant and Politruk stopped on their way past, to inspect her work. Once the Commandant said,

'Well done,' when he noticed that Anna had cut out stencils from thin wood, to expedite her task. She suspected that Gavsiuk had been told to report on her behaviour so she endeavoured to give him no excuse to complain.

At the beginning of November, Anna was called into the main office, where Major Kondrashkin greeted her with a smile.

'I'm pleased to see that your work is going well,' he said. 'Perhaps one day it will be possible to talk to you about your future. If you behave in an exemplary way, it might even be possible to reduce your sentence. We Russians are cultured people and appreciate art, music and literature. You're very young and you're talented. If you were to accept Russian citizenship, it might be possible for you to go to Moscow and study painting and drawing in one of our excellent schools.' Not wanting to antagonise the Commandant, Anna remained silent.

'But this is not what I wanted to talk to you about. As you know, the anniversary of the Russian Revolution will be celebrated in a week's time. I want you to paint a new portrait of Voshd/Leader Stalin for our theatre. We'll provide all the materials and you'll start tomorrow. You may go now.'

Anna walked from the room, her face flaming.

'How can I spend hours painting that hated face?' she asked herself. 'I can't, I won't – but how can I get out of it?' She went back to work, her thoughts racing.

'Shall I cut my right hand? Shall I fall over and land on my right arm so that I can't paint?' she still hadn't resolved the problem when she queued for supper that evening but fate took a hand. As she reached the cauldron, she tripped and fell, submerging her right arm in the boiling gruel. She screamed loudly and fainted. Her friends carried her back to the hut and lay her on her bunk.

The pain was excruciating, as the padded sleeve of her jacket was cut away and her arm bandaged. Anna got little sleep that night. Her arm throbbed unmercifully and she was anxious about the reaction of the Commandant to her accident. Her heart beat furiously as she presented herself to him the next morning. Kondrashkin rose from his desk, walked over to her and slapped her face hard. He said nothing until he was re-seated at his desk. Then his voice was cold.

'What a disappointment you are to me, Anna Grzymala Siedlecka. You can't paint now so you'll join the group of latrine cleaners. Count yourself lucky that Tovarishch Byeriosov is away for a few days. His discipline is harsher than mine. Now go. Gavsiuk will show you where to go.'

For the next week, Anna was part of a team of old, weak and sick prisoners who had the unenviable task of cleaning the latrines. For fourteen hours a day, she hacked frozen excrement from the platforms and floors of the huts, shovelling it into wheelbarrows and wheeling it to a distant corner of the camp, where it was tipped on to ever growing heaps.

'What will happen when the thaw comes and the flies return in their millions?' Anna asked an old woman who limped beside her on the way to the dump. The poor thing gave a hopeless shrug and replied,

'I don't think I'll be here to see.' Anna said no more.

Food rations for latrine cleaners were pitifully small. Added to that, they all stank at the end of each day's work. Anna tried desperately to keep herself clean but even her good friends, in the hut, who shared their rations with her, moved away when she sat down.

At last, the long promised work-free day, to celebrate the Russian Revolution, arrived. All day long, small concerts and singing parties were held around the camp. Anna was surprised to see how proud and sincerely moved most of the Russian prisoners were, when talking of the 'Glorious Revolution'.

Excitement reached its peak after an unusually tasty evening meal. A show, prepared by some of the convicts and attended by

Russians officials took place in the camp theatre. As some of Anna's Russian friends from the hut were involved, she and Lyuba decided to support them and joined the five hundred strong audience. At first, Anna enjoyed the amusing sketches but when these were followed by loud, patriotic songs about the invincible Red Army, she slipped outside into the cold, clear night. The snow crunched under her feet and, as she breathed the freezing air, she looked up at the star-spangled sky.

'Where is it?' she asked herself, remembering the special star, the middle one of the descending stroke of the T in the Orion constellation. Once, a lifetime ago, she, her mother and brother had promised to look for this star when they were apart, and whenever they found it to think of each other.

'There it is,' she whispered as she found it at last. A terrible homesickness swept over her and the tears came, unbidden.

'Anna Grzymala Siedlecka, I have been looking everywhere for you.' It was Avgust Gustavitch. Anna only wanted to be alone but, conscious of the kindness he had shown when she had been in his brigade, she turned towards him.

'What's wrong? Are you ill?' he asked, noticing her distress.

'I'm fine, thank you,' Anna replied shortly. 'The cold has made my eyes run. That's all.' He paused for a moment, then went on,

'I've heard about your being in trouble again. You're a silly reckless young woman. For your own sake, don't antagonise these people unnecessarily. Do try to be sensible.' Anna was cross. How dare this man patronise her in this way?

'I don't wish to discuss my problems with you, thank you,' she retorted and began to move away.

'Don't go, please,' he pleaded. 'I didn't mean to upset you. I have respect for you and I wish you well. I thought you'd like to know that a group of Poles arrived at this camp today. I know you're anxious about someone you used to know. If you tell me his name, I'll try to find out if he is one of the group.' Anna turned to face Avgust Gustavitch.

'I'm sorry I was abrupt just now,' she said. 'My only excuse is that I'm in trouble and my scalded arm's throbbing. Yes, please do make enquiries about the new arrivals. My friend is called Severyn.

I'd be so relieved to know he's safe. You're one of my very few true friends in this wilderness. Thank you for offering to help me.'

At that moment, the audience streamed out of the theatre and as Lubya spied Avgust Gustavitch and Anna together.

'Leave the child alone, brigadier!' she shouted at once. 'Can't you see she is unwell?'

Early next morning, Anna found herself, once more, in the Commandant's office. He was seated behind his desk, writing. Politruk Byeriosov was standing at the side of the room and it was he who now shouted at Anna.

'I've heard disturbing reports about you. You stand accused of insolence, a brazen disregard for camp rules and, worst of all, of sabotage. You've had plenty of warnings about the penalties for such behaviour, yet you persist.'

'Back to the calf pen,' Anna thought with dread but, eyes downcast, she said nothing. Byeriosov lowered his voice a fraction but his tone was still hectoring. 'Fortunately for you, the Commandant believes you have a spark of humanity in your corrupted mind and that it might be possible to make you understand just how stupid your behaviour has been. But be warned, for the last time. If there is one more complaint about you, it will be my turn to re-educate you and it won't be a pleasant experience.' Red faced and perspiring, he sat down.

Major Krondrashkin looked up. 'Be grateful to Comrade Byeriosov for his forbearance, Anna Grzymata Siedlecka,' he said. 'Now you will report immediately to Gavsiuk and resume your sign writing duties. I sincerely hope you'll repay my trust in you and that you won't cause any more trouble.'

Anna murmured her thanks and left the office, relief sweeping over her.

Back under Gavsiuk's supervision, she found that there was plenty to do. Her work output was slow because her arm was still sore but she strove for the highest quality she could manage. She was grateful that she had not been sent back to the saw mill.

It was heartbreaking to see the pitiful crowd of half frozen inadequately clad prisoners returning to camp each evening in temperatures of -40 degrees centigrade. With their faces pinched and blue, their hands and feet wrapped in rags, they queued silently outside the kitchen huts to collect their daily ration of bread, their only respite a few hours sleep in overcrowded and infested barracks.

A few days after Anna had returned to work, Wanda, a young Polish woman who worked in the sewing room approached her.

'A group of us who are lucky enough to work on camp, are planning to rescue those poor souls who work at the mill or in the forest.' she explained. 'We are stealing small pieces of material and kapok and cotton waste. Some women in the kitchen are sneaking old linen food bags. We are going to meet every evening an hour before lights out, to sew garments for the outside workers. We are also going to cook, for them, on the hut stove, anything the kitchen women can manage to steal to give extra nourishment and keep out the cold. Will you help?'

So it was that it became customary for Anna to spend an hour each evening, helping to produce quilted mittens, socks and waistcoats or stirring a pot of fish bones, vegetable peelings and sweepings of millet. While she and the others were engaged thus, they swapped stories of their pasts and planned for the future – particularly what they would choose to eat when this nightmare was over.

One evening, when it was Anna's turn to speak, she told the group of women, seated on the ground around her bunk, of Poland, it's history and culture, the beauties of the countryside and the happiness of family life. When it was bedtime, the women, mainly Russian and Ukrainian, begged for more.

'Tell us more stories, Anuita, You lie so beautifully.' And nothing Anna said would convince them that she had told only the truth.

By the end of two weeks, Anna had finished all her allotted signs.

'Go and help him fix them in the appropriate places around the camp,' Gavsiuk ordered, indicating a newcomer, an extremely tall, gaunt old man who was stacking boards at the other end of the room.

'Gavsiuk has sent me to help you,' Anna said as she approached him. He didn't answer, simply picked up, without effort, a ladder and six large boards and went out of the room. Anna followed with a tin of bent and rusty nails and a large hammer. These she carried all day, trailing after him, holding the ladder and handing him a nail and the hammer when he looked down at her. They didn't exchange one word. She had plenty of time to observe his shaggy grey-streaked red beard and hair, his enormous hands and feet, his deeply lined and pock-marked face and his deep set wild grey eyes. She was intrigued by his strangeness and silence. When she was next alone with Gavsiuk she asked him,

'Who is this new man, the one I worked with today?'

'His name is Nikita Krivosheyev,' he replied. 'He is a murderer. He killed his wife and his mother-in-law with an axe. You watch out. He is a dangerous madman. He hates everyone and women in particular. You'd better be careful!'

The next day, Anna started on a new batch of painted boards. She was immersed in her work, when Gavsiuk came over to her.

'The Politruk wants to see you in his office, straight away,' he said curiously. 'Not in more trouble, are you?' Anna didn't answer but her heart beat faster.

'What on earth can this be about?' she asked herself. 'I've worked hard, kept myself to myself except... the story telling! Perhaps someone's reported me for telling tales of Poland. Could that be seen as treachery?' By now she was at the office. She knocked and was told to enter.

Byeriosov was sitting alone at the desk, bareheaded, his NKVD peaked hat placed beside him on a pile of papers. He was grinning.

'Close the door,' he commanded. I hope you've been behaving yourself.' He gave a laugh. Anna had never seen him in a jocular mood before. She didn't answer and stood warily, a little way from him.

'Come here, come here,' he almost sang the words. He was holding up a small photograph of a young woman. Anna moved over to the desk and looked at it. 'This is my wife,' he continued. 'Could you draw a picture from it. She's prettier than this in real life. I'd like to present her with a pencil sketch of herself for her birthday.'

Anna gazed down at the face of a smiling woman, plump and attractive. She had large dark eyes and a warm smile. Anna simply couldn't imagine the two of them together, this pretty woman and the cruel, harsh faced Byeriosov.

'Well, can you do it or not?' he demanded impatiently.

'I can,' Anna answered, 'but I'll need some pencils and two or three sheets of good quality cartridge paper.'

With a flourish, the Politruk produced, from his desk drawer, four squares of thick, cream paper and a box of coloured pencils.

'Will these do?'

Anna stroked the paper almost reverently. She'd seen nothing like it since before the war. She looked up at Byeriosov.

'I'm afraid it will take me some time to do,' she said. 'There's not much time after work and the light fades so quickly.'

'You can have three afternoons off work to complete the task,' he responded. 'Now, off with you. I hope the drawing will be good and do my wife justice. Send Gavsiuk to me straight away.'

Three days later, Anna presented herself at the office with the portrait. This time, Major Kondrashkin was there too. The two men bent over the paper together while Anna waited anxiously for the verdict. She had taken great pains over the picture, relishing every moment as she worked. She'd enhance the beauty of her subject and, using a special technique, had made the dark eyes appear to look straight into the eyes of anyone looking at the portrait. At last, Byeriosov raised his head. He was smiling broadly.

'Well done, Anna Grzymala Siedlecka. This is excellent. My wife will be very pleased. Thank you for taking such care and doing such a good job.'

'It's a fine picture. You're a gifted artist,' added Major Kondrashkin.

'Thank you,' murmured Anna and, with regret, held the pencils and unused paper out towards Byeriosov. He hesitated, then said,

'No, no. You keep them – but no more silly icons, remember.' He scribbled something on a piece of paper. 'Take this to the camp shop and they'll give you a loaf of white bread as payment for your labours. Off you go now.'

Elated, Anna carried the paper and pencils to Gavsiuk.

'Please lock these safely away for me,' she requested. Then, in case he should be tempted to steal them and exchange them for food, she added, 'They really belong to Politrik Byeriosov. I am looking after them for him. I've done a drawing for him and may do some more.'

Impressed by Anna's sudden rise to fame, Gavsiuk regarded her with new respect and complied with her request.

The next day, at midday break, Anna claimed her loaf of 'wages' from the camp shop. She hadn't told her friends of her good fortune. She wanted to surprise them with the fresh, fragrant loaf which they could all share. As she ran back to the barracks, she heard someone moaning and crying out. She stopped by a shed where garden equipment was stored and looked inside.

Curled into a ball, on the floor, lay old Nikita Krivosheyev, his face contorted with pain. Anna quickly knelt beside him and touched his arm.

'What is it, Krivoshevev?' she cried. 'What's wrong with you? Can I help?'

He grabbed her hand in his two huge ones and started to weep.

'Lady, it's my belly! I can't keep my food down and my belly is on fire. It hurts! It hurts! Go away and let me die.'

Anna remembered something she'd heard when she was working in the forest. It appeared that some convicts, maddened by hunger, would resort to chewing and swallowing tree bark with horrible consequences. She thought quickly.

'You're not going to die,' she said sternly. 'I am going to cure you. Sit up and tell me what you have eaten beside your rations. Have you eaten tree bark?'

He nodded miserably and whispered,

'But what am I to do? I'm large and always starving hungry.'

He knelt there, on the ground, like a monstrous savage. Tears were streaming down his face and freezing in his beard. Anna had a sudden idea.

'I wonder if I can convince him I have magic powers,' she thought. She spoke slowly, almost intoning the words,

'Listen very carefully, Krivosheyev. I have the power to cure you but first you must swear, on your soul, never to eat tree bark again. If you break this promise, you will be lost for ever.'

'I can't swear on my soul, lady,' he sobbed. 'My soul is already lost because I'm a sinner and a murderer.' Anna heard the utter despair in his voice. She remembered something her mother had once said to her.

'Only God can decide whose soul is lost and He is all merciful. It is not your place to make His decisions,' she repeated. 'Promise me that you'll never eat tree bark again and, in return, I promise to make your pain go away.'

The old man nodded several times and mumbled,

'I promise.'

Anna had remembered her nanny's remedy for a sore stomach and decided to embellish it. She held up the loaf of new bread and made the sign of the cross over it.

'This is very special bread, Krivosheyev. It has healing powers. You must take it to your hut, cut it into thin slices and dry it on top of the stove. You must then eat one slice of dried bread every two hours, with a mug of hot water. Do this for two days. Don't eat anything else and don't smoke. On the third day, you may start eating small amounts of porridge again and drinking tchay. When you've eaten all of the bread, the pain will go.'

She put the loaf of bread into his hands, reverently and stood up to go. He stared after her, mouthing his thanks, his eyes wide with wonder. Then he struggled to his feet and shambled back to his hut.

'Meet me in the dining hut when you've collected your food,' whispered a voice behind Anna, as she stood in the queue for bread, three days later. Startled, she turned in time to see Avgust Gustavitch walking away. Intrigued, she joined him fifteen minutes later. She sat down opposite him.

'Don't make it obvious,' he said softly. 'In a moment, look over there. It's the group of Poles who arrived recently. I think your friend may be among them.'

Anna's heart lurched. She dropped her knife and turned round to pick it up. About a hundred people were milling around inside the dining hut but she saw Severyn immediately, thin, stooping and with a big grey beard, which obscured half his face.

Anna gasped as she turned round, her face burning.

'He's there, isn't he – your sweetheart? Which one is it? Tell me and I'll ask him to come over.'

'No, no. You don't understand,' Anna said quickly. 'He's not my sweetheart. It might be dangerous for us to be seen together. I don't want anyone to know...'

August Gustavitch suddenly understood.

'Please don't worry,' he said gravely. 'I won't tell anyone else. I could speak to him privately and tell him you're here. I'll be very careful'

'Yes, do that, please,' Anna whispered. 'He's the old, stooped one in the corner – the one with the long grey beard.'

Five minutes later, Severyn sauntered casually over to Anna's table and, barely looking at her, sat down next to her.

'At last, Annechka,' he breathed. 'At last I know you are safe. I've been worrying about you all these months. Thank God you're all right. It's not safe for me to stay and talk for long. They watch us nearly all the time. Three Polish colleagues and I have been transferred here from a hard labour camp because of our expertise in mechanics and all things electrical. The large generators here have deteriorated badly because of the ignorance of the Russians, in charge, who call themselves engineers. The remedy for any fault seems to have been a hearty kick! The four of us are already working very hard to make ourselves indispensable and to oust the Russians. This will put us in a powerful position.' Severyn looked around and then said quickly, 'I'd better go now. I'll try to meet you again soon.' and then, before Anna could reply, he was gone.

Preoccupied by thoughts of Severyn, Anna was unprepared for the tragedy which struck a couple of nights later. Mrs Piotrowska and Irka had been moved into her hut several months previously. The reunion had been joyful but she had noticed that Mrs Piotrowska seemed quieter and more tearful than usual and that her

115

daughter, Irka, sulked in a corner of the hut when she was not working. As Christmas was approaching and many people were sad and homesick Anna thought nothing of these things until she was woken one night, at midnight, by a piercing scream. It was absolutely dark. She leapt up and opened the boiler door so that the firelight gave a flickering orange light. There, on the floor, lay Irka, writhing in agony amidst a rapidly spreading pool of blood, which oozed from between her legs, from where a thick wire protruded. Her shrieks of pain and terror filled the hut. Her mother, screaming also, was attempting to staunch the flow of blood with a towel. There was a moment's stunned silence and then pandemonium. Anna and a couple of others tried to calm and comfort Irka and Mrs Piotrowska while the rest of the women screamed for the guards, hammering on the door and windows.

When the guards finally arrived, and saw what had happened, they sent two women to the hospital hut to fetch the lekpom and a stretcher.

'Please, please,' Anna pleaded with one of the guards, 'send for the Polish woman doctor in the next hut. She will know what to do for the best.' Reluctantly, he agreed and fifteen minutes later Irka was carried away, to the hospital, accompanied by the doctor, the lepkon and two guards. Her mother was not allowed to go with her and when the hut door was re-locked, she sat on a bench, immobile, in a state of shock. No-one had any more sleep that night and as soon as day began, the women attempted to scrub the blood from the floor with ash and melted snow.

Three days later, news came of Irka's death and that evening, Mrs Piotrowska was found, kneeling in a deep snowdrift at the edge of the camp, frozen to death. The two pathetic victims were buried together, in a shallow grave, in the corner of the convicts' cemetery, under the gaze of the guards. Anna, Ninka and Zosia, the three Polish inmates closest to the Piotrowskas were permitted to stand at the graveside for a few minutes. There, they prayed, silently for the two tortured souls.

Anna had learned from the other two the whole tragic story.

'It seems that Irka was seduced by one of the guards,' explained Ninka. 'He promised to marry her and get her and her mother out of the camp.'

'Then when she became pregnant,' Zosia continued, 'he threatened to report her for misconduct with a male prisoner. She was frightened and confided in her mother, begging her for help in terminating the pregnancy. But you know how religious Mrs Piotrowska was. She wouldn't hear of it and said that all they could do was report the matter to the authorities and trust in God. They both knew that once they'd made the report, they would be separated, probably for ever.'

Ninka finished the story.

'Obviously, driven wild with fear and anxiety, Irka took matters into her own hands. What a terrible, terrible thing!'

Life resumed its normal pattern and Lyuba, concerned at Anna's lack of appetite and general malaise after the death of her friends, announced that she was going to make a feast for her and the other Polish women. She had smuggled some frozen potatoes, an onion and a small bottle of caster oil from the kitchen. She was not discouraged when the potatoes melted to an unappetising pulp and Anna protested that the castor oil would upset their stomachs.

'Nonsense,' was the reply. 'It won't harm you once it is cooked. Just leave it to Lubya, she'll make your mouth water.' True to her word, the potato pancakes, flavoured with onion and cooked until crisp were delicious – and she was right about the caster oil. No-one suffered any ill effects at all.

CHAPTER 9

Siberian Christmas 1940

It was early morning just over a week before Christmas. Anna was woken by a commotion outside the hut. A man was shouting and another was swearing. Anna lay still and tried to catch the words the first man was repeating over and over again.

'These are for my barishnya/lady. Let me give them to her.'

All at once, Anna recognised the deep rough voice. It was Krivosheyev. She jumped out of her bunk and was over by the door as the guard unlocked and flung it open, letting in a draught of freezing air.

Krivosheyev stood there, his arms full of logs. The guard was swearing and trying to push him away but he was no match for the enormous, bear of a man, who stood firm and seemed to be growling under his breath. His eyes lit up when he saw Anna, who, clutching her blanket round herself, tried to bring calm to the situation.

'Now, now Krivosheyev,' she said lightly, with a smile, 'stop this clowning. You know you're not allowed into this compound without permission. We all have to obey the rules, you know.'

The huge man beamed at her, ignoring the guard.

'These are for you. Lady. You'll never lack firewood while Nikita is around, I promise. Where shall I put them?'

'Tchort!/The devil!' exclaimed the guard, spitting in the snow. Then, looking from Anna to Krivosheyev, he suddenly laughed and walked away.

The tension was broken. Anna and the crowd, which had gathered round the door, laughed too and so did Krivosheyev.

'Thank you very much,' Anna said. 'Leave them outside by the door, please. Are you quite well now?'

'Yes, thank you, my lady. You cured me.'

'I'm glad, Krivosheyev. I shall see you soon because my sign writing work has finished and I've been told I'll be working with you for a few days.'

If possible, his smile became broader. He turned, put the wood down and walked away.

'You're a deep one, Aniuta,' laughed Zosia. 'What kind of witchcraft did you use to tame that wild animal?' And for the rest of the day, Anna's friends teased her unmercifully.

Two days later, Anna and Krivosheyev were working together again. The latter talked non-stop, while managing to work hard at the same time. Anna found his dialect hard to understand but tried to make appropriate responses until he started to speak so fast that she had real difficulty keeping up and then she realised that he wasn't talking to her at all. It was as if some long suppressed emotion had been unstoppered and was pouring out, whether or not anyone was listening.

'I hate women, every one of them. I hate them all.' He shouted. 'All they do is nag, nag, nag. They get inside your head with their nagging – nag, nag, nag.' He was starting to shake and Anna wondered if she should call for help. But she knew this could lead to trouble for the disturbed man so she put a hand firmly on his arm.

'Krivosheyev,' she said gently, 'Look at me.' He fell silent and looked directly into Anna's eyes. She went on, 'I'm a woman. You bring me logs for the fire. We can talk together while we work. Do you hate me?'

The old man started to whimper.

'You're different, Lady. God has given you mighty powers to cure people and to save them from eternal damnation. Your blessed bread made me well.'

Anna became alarmed. She could not allow such stories to get back to the Commandant. This time she spoke sternly. 'Listen to me very carefully and remember what I say. You must never tell anyone at all about what happened the day I found you and you were so ill. That's a secret between us. I forbid you to mention it again, even to me. If you do, I shall never speak to you again. Do you understand?'

Krivosheyev nodded and placed his hand on his heart. Anna's solemn voice seemed to have calmed him. He turned quietly back to his work.

An hour later, the labour of the day was over. It was time to return to the huts. As they were parting, Anna smiled at her subdued companion.

'We've done a good job, Krivosheyev. You've worked very hard. Thank you. Goodnight, sleep well. I'll see you in the morning.'

He beamed at her and shambled away into the darkness.

It would soon be Christmas. In spite of a resolution not to mope, Anna could not help remembering the wonderful Christmases past, when she had been surrounded by family and friends. One night, she lay awake and pictured the table, at home, glowing in soft lamplight and laden with the Christmas Eve food. The huge, richly decorated tree stood in the corner of the room. The sound of laughter filled the air as presents were exchanged. And, after the feast, Anna saw herself, her parents and brother and sisters, decked in furs, tramping through the crisp snow to midnight mass.

'Stop this!' she said grimly to herself, as tears ran down her cheeks. 'No self-pity. It's the same for all of us here.'

It was Christmas Eve, a rest day, and Zosia ran into the bath hut, where Anna was dressing after taking her bath.

'Anna, Anna, be quick. There's a guard outside our hut and he says you're wanted in the Commandant's office immediately.'

Anna was apprehensive, though a little annoyed.

'My one chance of privacy and leisure ruined!' she complained but, nevertheless, she hurried into her clothes and followed the guard who was waiting for her outside. Although the sun was bright, the temperature was about -40 degrees centigrade and by the time she had reached the office, her lashes and eyebrows were white with frost.

Major Kondrashkin greeted her with a smile.

'How would you like a ride to Asino?' he enquired. Thinking she had misheard or that the question was some sort of trap, Anna simply stared at him. He laughed.

'I understand that there is a parcel for you at the post office in Asino,' he explained. 'It's been opened, cleared by security and awaits collection. I thought you might like to collect it yourself. A

120

lorry leaves for Asino in half an hour and you can ride down but you'll have to walk back. I'll provide an armed escort who'll help you carry the parcel if it's heavy. You should be able to make it back to camp by supper time. What do you say?'

Anna couldn't check the hot tears that streamed down her cheeks as a vision of her family gathering gifts together and carefully packing and mailing the package swam before her. She stammered her thanks. The Major laughed and handed her a permit to leave camp and collect the parcel and then she was outside, running to the hut with her news.

Twenty minutes later, wrapped in several layers of clothing, some borrowed, she reported to the lorry park. At the last moment, Lyuba had produced a small, roughly made sledge, usually used for transporting logs to the hut.

'Take this,' she'd said. 'It might be useful.'

Now, the driver placed the sledge in the back of the lorry and told Anna to climb into the cab, next to him. The guard sat on her other side and they were off.

As they drove through the prison gates, Anna took a deep breath.

'Free air,' she thought to herself and savoured the idea.

After fifteen minutes, they entered the town, picturesque under its layer of snow. The decorative gable-end of each house was hung with glistening icicles and although the windows of shops displayed few goods, there was a bustling market place where local wares could be bought and sold. It was here that the lorry dropped Anna and the guard, next to a booth where a woman was selling tea and Siberian pilmyeni/tiny, meat-filled ravioli.

'Come,' the guard said suddenly. 'Let's have some pilmyeni.'

'I haven't any money, I'm afraid,' Anna answered, her mouth watering.

'Nitchevo, I'll pay,' he said and ordered two plates full and two mugs of tea. The woman smiled at Anna as the guard placed the order and put a second spoonful on to her plate.

'Thank you very, very much,' Anna said to the guard and looked at him curiously. He flushed at her glance.

'We're not inhuman, you know,' he responded. 'Now eat.' Anna needed no second invitation. The pilmyeni was deliciously spicy and the tea sweetened with honey. They both ate with relish but when the guard offered payment to the woman, she shook her head, saying to Anna, 'May my pilmyeni give you health and strength. There's no need to pay. Goodbye dievochka/young girl. God be with you.'

'And with you. Thank you,' answered Anna gratefully.

Next, the parcel, which turned out to be a large wooden box, was retrieved from the post office. The guard helped to secure it to the sledge and Anna and he were ready to start their walk back to the camp.

'It's 2p.m. If we walk fast,' said the guard, 'we'll reach camp before dark.' He strode ahead, Anna lagging a little, dragging the sledge and negotiating the slippery road. Sometimes the guard walked beside her, regaling her with stories of travellers who had been savaged by wolves or murdered by bandits. Anna didn't reply. She needed all her breath for the brisk walk and longed to be alone.

'Anyway,' she told herself, 'He's probably making it all up just to make me hurry.' But she couldn't help glancing apprehensively into the deepening gloom of the taiga. The temperature was dropping sharply, Anna's feet ached and she felt tiredness creep over her but she knew she must keep going. Then, an hour or so later, when darkness was falling and she thought she must stop, she heard the jingling of bells and heavy hooves, pounding the icy road. The guard and she leapt to the road-side just in time to escape a heavy sleigh, on which three men sat, wrapped in furs.

'Damn sons of bitches,' muttered the guard, wiping down his snow-splattered coat. 'There they go. There's no ride for the likes of you and me.'

But he was wrong. The sleigh stopped about a hundred metres on and a voice called,

'Hey you two! Want a lift to the camp? Hurry up if you do. We can't wait all night.'

In moments, the two of them were in the sleigh, the parcel wedged one side of Anna. Regretfully, she had to leave her little sled by the side of the road. With a start, she realised that two of the men were NKVD officers. They were merry with drink and the one next to Anna, opened his great sheepskin jacket.

'Here, come inside, little one,' he said. Anna dared not refuse, though his vodka breath revolted her. He put his arm around her and she could feel his row of medals against her face. She snuggled inside the sheepskin and the sleigh started to move. She couldn't help smiling wryly to herself.

'What would my family and friends say if they could see me now?' she wondered. 'Under the arm of a NKVD officer, riding in a Russian 'troika' on this starry Christmas Eve?'

Everyone was at a compulsory meeting when Anna arrived back at the hut, earlier than expected. She placed her precious box on the table, removed her surplus clothing and, with trembling fingers, opened her present. At the top lay a letter from her sister.

September 1940
'My dearest little sister,
Your post card arrived last week and we are so happy to know that you are well. We, too, are well. The girls insist I enclose an apple from each of them. Clara made the handkerchiefs especially for you. I hope you will find some use for these few things and I'm sorry the parcel could not be larger. We miss you very much and send you all our love and best wishes, Justa.
P.S. Your mother, sister and brother are well but, unfortunately, we still have no news of Papa.'

Inside the box were unbelievable treasures. There were a pair of laced shoes, warm underwear, woollen stockings, a thick sweater, a warm pink nightdress, a two metre length of winceyette, sugar, a small piece of soap, a packet of tobacco, twelve pastel, lace-edged handkerchiefs and three dried and shrivelled apples.

Anna's tears flowed. She was moved to think of the sacrifice the little family must have made so that she could have such a parcel. She imagined them getting ready for their Christmas Eve feast and wondered just what they had found to put on their own table.

She carefully re-packed the box and when her friends returned, crowding around and asking how the day had gone, she said, 'I promise I'll tell you all about it after supper. I'm going for a walk now. I'll see you later.' And, refusing to say more, she went out into the cold, clear night.

Looking up into the sky, she found her special star and stood, for a moment, thinking of all her family.

'Happy Christmas,' she said, silently. 'I wish... I wish...' But she knew she mustn't wish.

After the evening meal, Anna collected her bread ration and, seeing Severyn with his friends, at the other side of the room, had a sudden idea. She walked over and Severyn greeted her with a smile, 'Do you want to join us?'

'Forgive me for coming uninvited,' she replied quietly, 'but it's Christmas Eve. Although we have no holy wafer, I wondered if we could share some bread together instead.'

And so it was that in the crowded, overheated, noisy canteen, a small group of Polish exiles, solemnly broke off crumbs of black and bitter convicts' bread and shared it in Christmas communion.

'I told you Anna was a witch!' cried Lyuba, half believing it. Anna was back in her hut and had just related her day's adventures to her incredulous friends. Anna gave Lyuba an affectionate hug but Lyuba looked serious.

'That NKVD officer could have done anything to you. They're all bad men. You're unharmed because you cast some sort of spell on him, I'm sure.'

Everyone laughed and Anna, retrieving the parcel from her bunk, said, 'Well, here's more magic.' She spread her treasures out on the table and her friends gasped in wonder. 'I shall share what I can among you,' she said. Everyone deserves gifts at Christmas.'

'No!' was the surprising response. Zosia and Lyuba spoke together and the rest of the group were agreeing.

'Anna, your family sent these things for you. You've shared so much with us already,' Zosia went on.

Then Lyuba spoke to the room at large, 'I'm warning you, if

even the smallest item is stolen from Anuita's parcel, I shall find out who took it and deal personally and very harshly with the thief.'

That night, Anna went to bed, wearing her new pink nightdress.

'Perhaps I'll be home in Warsaw to celebrate next Christmas,' she thought as she drifted off to sleep.

After Christmas, Anna's work with Krivosheyev came to an end and she was transferred back to the sawmill, where her sign writing skills were needed. So, once more, she joined the ragged line of convicts each morning and evening, for the gruelling three kilometre march across the snow-covered plain and through the forest.

Too often, with horror, she saw the frozen corpses of those who had died at work, being dragged on small sledges, back to the camp. Looking at the contrast between the exhausted, undernourished prisoners and the fat, warmly clad Russian guards, Anna felt her anger rise.

'I will survive. I will survive,' she'd mutter to herself, in time with the tramping of the marching feet.

Tovarishch Tabadze, a short, irascible Georgian, himself a convict, was her new boss. He owed his privileged position to his expertise in timber production. He was even allowed to sleep at the mill with a small unit of fire-watchers. On her first day, he regarded Anna with suspicion.

'A girl to paint signs! Whatever next? As if I haven't got enough to worry about. This man can help you.' He indicated a tall, emaciated Jew, who stepped forward with a smile.

'What a lovely pair,' sneered one of the Russian workers. 'A Polish lady and a dirty Jew!' Tobadze said nothing but slammed out of the room. Anna ignored the remark and put out her hand to the Jew and said, in Russian, 'My name is Anna Grzymala Siedlecka.' The man took her hand, with a smile.

'Mine is Marcus Shapiro. We were told you were coming and I've made space for you to work at the end of my table over here.'

Marcus helped Anna bring boards, a large tin of black paint and brushes from the carpenter's room and Anna set to work.

By the end of the week, Tobadze had stopped glaring at Anna and even grudgingly admired her neat work but as she painted the black letters, she longed to have the freedom to draw once more. As if in answer to this longing, two of the guards approached Anna timidly outside the canteen one day.

'We have heard that you drew a magnificent portrait for Politruk Byeriosov,' said one.

'And we wondered if you would draw our portraits too,' added the other. Then, quickly, 'We'll pay you.'

Anna was astonished but knew she couldn't miss this opportunity.

'I will draw the pictures for you but I don't want any money. A little extra food for me to share with my friends would be payment enough. Also, you must get written permission from the authorities. I don't want to be in trouble. Finally, you will have to supply your own paper and pencils for me to use.'

Her first sitter arrived two days later, by arrangement. He carried an official permission slip, a grubby grey piece of packing paper, a pencil stub and an army mess tin full of thick, meaty stew, which smelled delicious. Anna started to draw the young, blond soldier, who reminded her of Grisha. She used his pencil and a dark brown one from her precious store. She marked the highlights with a white crayon. She sketched quickly and was well rewarded by the man's delight. He blushed, as he looked at it, until his ears glowed like poppies.

'You must be a very famous artist to draw so beautifully,' he stammered. 'Would you please write at the bottom, "to Grisha from…" and then sign your name?' Anna did as he asked, thinking what a coincidence it was that he had the same name as her friend from her days on the train. That seemed so long ago. This Grisha, still perspiring and red with embarrassment, pulled something wrapped in greaseproof paper out of his greatcoat pocket.

'I know this is inadequate payment for such a work of art,' he said. 'It's all I could get in the time – and you said you wouldn't take money.'

'Thank you very much. This is quite sufficient,' Anna answered, although she had no idea what was in the parcel. 'You have already given me the stew.' Still stuttering his thanks, Grisha went and Anna unwrapped the package. She couldn't believe her eyes. Inside was a large piece of salted pork fat – enough for her and her close friends. She smiled as she thought, 'Fame at last. I'm a professional artist!'

The second portrait was equally well received and several other guards approached Lyuba, asking her to petition Anna to draw their portraits.

'They say they'll pay handsomely,' Lyuba reported.

'It's too difficult to do portraits from life, really,' Anna said. 'It would be better if I could borrow photographs and work from them during my midday break at the mill.'

'If the men who have asked me have photographs you can use, shall I tell them you'll do it?' asked Lyuba eagerly.

'You can tell them I'll probably be able to,' Anna answered, thinking hard, 'but I don't want money as payment – only stuff that we can all share. I need permission to draw, from the Commandant, otherwise Tabadze could well lodge a complaint. Leave me alone for a bit. There's something I must do.'

It was a rest day and there were three hours before the compulsory re-education meeting. Anna retrieved the last prized sheet of cartridge paper and her pencils from their hiding place and began to draw.

The meeting was as long and as tedious as usual. Anna slipped away quickly afterwards and was standing next to the door as the Commandant came out.

'Please, Major Kondrashkin, may I speak with you?' The Major turned in surprise. It was almost unheard of for a convict to approach him without being invited to do so.

'Oh it's you, Anna Grzymala Siedlecka. What do you want now?'

Undeterred, Anna asked, politely.

'Sir, I wish to obtain your permission to do some drawings during my free time at the sawmill. The drawings will have no religious content, I promise, nor will they interfere with my work in any way.'

'All right. You have my permission on those terms. I'll see that Tabadze is informed tomorrow. Is that all?'

'No sir.' Anna responded quickly and handed him the rolled sheet of cartridge paper. He opened it, stared for a moment and then laughed heartily.

'Why, you crafty young woman! Would you have given this to me if I'd refused you permission to draw?'

'I would, sir,' Anna was earnest. 'It's to say thank you for your great kindness in allowing me to go out of camp to collect my parcel. Thank you.'

The Commandant gave her an amused nod and turning, shouted across to the Politruk,

'Byeriosov, Look at this portrait of my dog. It's Mishka to the life!'

The next morning, Tabadze spoke to Anna.

'The Commandant has given permission for you to draw pictures during your mid-day break. I don't care what you do in your spare time, as long as your work doesn't suffer. If it does, I won't hesitate to report you. There'll be no favouritism in my office.'

CHAPTER 10

The Bouran

'Anna Grymala Siedlecka, come outside immediately. I have something to say to you.' Startled and apprehensive, Anna followed Tabadze out of the workroom. He had been standing behind her, watching her pencilling the outlines of letters on to boards.

'What can this be about?' she wondered, searching her mind for something she may have done wrong. Tabadze hurried over the sunlit yard, deceptive in its brightness, for the temperature was minus thirty degrees. He halted by an empty rest hut and motioned Anna inside. The old convict, who tended the stoves, had two cups of hot tchay ready on the table. He handed one to Anna, the other to Tabadze and then made himself scarce.

'Sit down,' ordered Tabadze. Anna obeyed, still puzzled. She took a sip of the hot liquid.

'I would like you to paint my picture,' said the manager, not looking at her. 'I hear your portraits are very successful and life-like. I want you to paint me wearing my national Georgian costume. Do you think you could do that, if I explain all the details of the dress to you?'

Astonished, Anna managed to reply, 'Well, yes I could. Actually, I know what the costume is like... My father... but is it allowed for a c...?' She tailed off, embarrassed.

'For a convict to have his portrait painted?' Tabadze laughed. 'Yes, don't worry, I've got permission and, what's more, I've got some watercolour paints and brushes for you to use. Now what were you going to say about your father?'

Pulling herself together, Anna explained.

'My father travelled all over Europe before the First World War. He used to say that one of his favourite places was Georgia. He had some pictures of your mountains and forests and also of some dancers, in national costume.'

Tabadze's smile was so wide that he was unrecognisable as the dour, strict master Anna had known.

The paints comprised a small palette on which twelve round cakes of watercolour were stuck and the brushes were thin and of poor quality. Nevertheless, this children's kit was riches to Anna and, for the next four midday breaks, she and Tabadze were closeted together in his office, while the painting progressed. The manager spoke with passion about his beloved Georgia and Anna reciprocated by telling him of the many Georgian friends her family had. These proud people had been exiled after the First World War and had settled in Warsaw.

'They wore their national costume on special occasions,' Anna told him. 'I think I can remember it but to make sure, I'll sketch it in pencil and you can correct anything that isn't quite right.'

When the portrait was finished, Tabadze gazed at it in delight.

'How can I ever thank you, Aniuta? This is my face looking back at me. You have the dress just right too. This tight black tunic, with its row of rifle bullets above the pockets. You have even decorated the kinjal/curved dagger and scabbard correctly... and as for the belt and papakha/sheepskin hat... well, words fail me. How can I ever repay you?'

Anna smiled at his pleasure.

'I'm just happy you like it,' she replied. 'And... well, if I *could* keep the paints and brushes, please... if you don't need them?'

'Take them, they're yours. I do have something else for you.'

From under his desk, Tabadze produced a two kilogram tin of condensed milk. Anna was stunned.

'Oh... I had no idea such a luxury was to be had in camp, or even in the whole of the USSR,' she gasped, 'and it's for me – all of it?'

Tabadze laughed at her incredulity.

'It's for you. Take it. I promise you I didn't steal it. You've earned every drop. You need to drink it to give you strength. Now get back to work and collect it at the end of the day.' He brushed aside her thanks and picked up the frame he'd prepared for his portrait.

After work, Anna borrowed a small sled from the office hut, secured the tin with rope under a bundle of firewood and joined the convicts on their return journey to the camp. How she wished she had enough milk to share with all of these emaciated, ragged men and women.

That night, everyone in the hut enjoyed a hot mug of tchay, richly laced with a spoonful of the delicious contents of the tin. Anna kept back one spoonful to give to Krivosheyev and then the tin was washed and dried to take its place among the hut's communal cooking pots.

The weather continued with bitterly cold temperatures falling to minus fifty degrees. The prisoners had to be constantly vigilant in spotting frostbite on themselves and others. A white patch would appear on the skin, which would have a waxy appearance. The only remedy was to grab a handful of snow, immediately, and vigorously massage the affected area until the circulation returned. Neglected, the skin would become inflamed and fester, leaving scars that disfigured for life. Makeshift masks, with narrow slits for eyes were fashioned from the silky bark of silver birch trees to offer some protection against inflammation of the eyelids and snow blindness, which affected Anna along with most other inmates.

One night, soon after Anna had completed the portrait for Tabadze, the Bouran struck. This hurricane, which blows through parts of Siberia once a year, wild, furious, flattens all but the sturdiest buildings, destroys fences, uproots trees and swirls the snow into deep, deep drifts. As Anna lay, curled in her bunk that first night, she was sure the hut roof would be blown away and she and her friends would be whipped into the air by the vicious wind and be lost forever.

However, the huts had been built to withstand the Siberian winter and, with all gaps between planks filled with moss and clay, they were warm and safe.

There could be no outside work while the hurricane raged. It was even difficult to get to the canteen for meals and, after it was reported that two people from another barrack had lost their way and perished in a snowdrift, dry rations were issued and food was cooked inside the hut.

'This would be quite cosy and restful,' Anna remarked to Zosia, 'if only we had proper latrines in easy reach.'

But there was no such luxury. The unpleasant fact was that the overflowing parashas, used by almost a hundred prisoners, had to be emptied just outside the hut door.

Thanks to the well organised collection of firewood, there were plenty of logs stacked under the bottom bunks but as the wells were frozen and out of reach; snow must be melted and used for cooking and washing.

In the dark of the nights, when the howling of the Bouran seemed most fiendish, Anna often thought of Tabadze, marooned at the mill. She had grown to like and respect the gruff Georgian and wondered how he fared.

The days were spent in resting and storytelling. There were impromptu concerts, the groups of Ukrainians, Russians and Poles vying, good naturedly, against each other to sing the most moving or the funniest songs. In spite of its hardships, Anna always looked back on this oasis of time with pleasure and nostalgia.

It came to an end as suddenly as it had begun. The Bouran exhausted itself one night and the relentless clearing up began. While many of the prisoners stayed to repair damage at the camp, the others, including Anna, set out for the mill. The devastated forest lay all around as they walked. On reaching the mill, Anna could hardly believe what she saw. Most of the huts had been destroyed and the large shed, housing the chainsaw and conveyor belts, had collapsed, damaging the machinery. The huge generator stood, stark and silent, covered only by strewn planks and snow. Shattered planks, pieces of equipment, sawn tree trunks lay as far as the eye could see, as if a fearsome giant had plucked up everything within sight and thrown it at random. Tabadze was almost incoherent with fury and anguish. He ran among the prisoners, swearing, shouting and waving his fists. His world had tumbled about him, quite literally. One wall of his office had caved in, the windows were broken, wood, plaster and documents lay heaped on the floor but, strangely, Anna's neatly stacked, finished notices still stood in one corner. Anna and the three other office workers spent the morning clearing the office as well as they could. They propped up the ceiling with planks, threw out the debris and retrieved what was useful. Suddenly Tabadze rushed in.

'What are you doing wasting time in here?' he screamed. 'Get outside and do some proper work!' Then, seeing that Anna's hands were cut and bleeding from the rough work, he shouted at her, 'You stay here.' Surprised, Anna stood still, while he ran out and returned, in a moment, with a clean rag, a pair of woollen gloves, a large tin kettle and two briquettes of pressed fruit cores.

'Light a fire,' he ordered, 'then heat some water and clean those hands, for pity's sake. Do you want to lose them? Blast all stupid women! Then put on the gloves and boil the kettle. Make as much tchay as you can.' He stamped out of the room before Anna could reply.

Somehow she managed to light the fire, fill the kettle with snow, clean her lacerated hands and bind them with rag. As the circulation returned to them, the pain became almost unbearable. Crying, she pulled on the gloves and set about preparing the tchay. While she waited for the kettle to boil, she wondered how Tabadze had managed to survive here in the hurricane. She looked through a half open door at the undamaged end of the hut. There she saw his room, small, tidy and Spartan. There was a roughly made chair and a small chest. Above a truckle bed hung the portrait she'd painted, lifelike, glaring. Anna withdrew hurriedly. Just then, Tabadze, the brigadiers, including August Gustavich and the office staff came in. They sipped the tchay gratefully.

By 3pm, the prisoners were lining up to return to camp, for dusk fell early. On a whim, Anna ran back to the office. It was dark and quiet, the only light given by the roaring fire. Tabadze was sitting at his desk, shoulders hunched, head in hands. Anna suddenly realised exactly what the disaster had meant to the manager. He had been alone, in danger and in the most frightening conditions. Helplessly, he'd watched his precious mill and his carefully constructed life disintegrate around him. Not wanting to disturb him, she tried to leave the room silently but he heard her. Lifting his head he asked, sharply, 'Who in God's name is it? Can't you leave me in peace in this cursed place?'

Distressed, Anna faltered, 'I didn't mean to disturb you, Tovarishch Tabadze but I came back to thank you for sparing a thought for my hands in the midst of all this upheaval.' There was no answer so she went on, 'I'm so sorry that this terrible disaster has struck your mill… and here are your gloves. I return them with deep gratitude.' The manager still didn't reply so Anna handed him back the woollen gloves and turned to leave.

There was a sudden snort from Tabadze, which became a deep sob. Then he spoke, his voice distorted with grief.

'I'm, grateful to you, too, Aniuta, for coming to see me before you go. You've been a good friend and I'll remember you until my dying day. Keep the gloves as a memento from an old Georgian. Run now, or you'll be in trouble. I'll see you tomorrow.'

But on the morrow, Major Kondrashkin sent for Anna.

'There's no point in your going to the mill to work for the next couple of weeks,' he told her. 'You can return when the clean-up and reconstruction is complete. Until then, you'll work in the camp office occupied by the draughtsmen. You can use your artistic skills helping to prepare the graphs illustrating how well we're doing in our timber production and other industries. There may be the odd sign writing job too.'

'We're producing brightly coloured graphs, based on reports given by tally men and brigadiers,' Anna told her friends, in the canteen, after her first day in the draughtsmen's office. 'They're very impressive and are sent to some higher authority.' Then, lowering her voice, 'Doubtless they join all the other fairy tale statistics beloved by our Soviet masters.'

As everyone laughed, Anna noticed August Gustavitch standing near the door, beckoning her. She went over to him, alarmed by his grim face.

'What's wrong?' she asked.

'Anuita, I've some bad news. Our friend Tabadze died last night. He set fire to his hut and his charred body was found, hanging from a rafter.'

Shock shot through Anna. She leant against the doorframe for support. August continued.

'He liked and respected you, Anuita. He often spoke of your kindness and artistic prowess. We've both lost a friend. If you still remember how to pray, say a prayer, tonight for Tabadz.' Before Anna could respond, he walked away, leaving her stricken and distressed. She pushed her way out into the Siberian night and, through her tears, gazed at the dark blue, star-filled sky. She hadn't the heart to look for her special star, but silently prayed that the gruff old Georgian had found peace at last.

CHAPTER 11

Spring

Anna woke with a start. It was an hour before the usual reveille time but someone was banging on the iron pipes, which hung outside the hut. People were banging on all of the iron pipes, which hung over all barrack porches. The clanging was deafening and it meant there was an emergency. Someone opened the door and a guard called,

'Everyone out! Get to the main square immediately.'

Alarmed, the prisoners quickly pulled on some clothes and made for the square.

Major Kondrashkin and Politruk Byeriosov arrived straight away. The faces of both were grave. The major addressed the expectant crowd.

'You will have noticed that the temperature has risen rapidly over the last three days,' he said. 'I have just received an urgent telephone message from the main saw mill to say that the melting snow and ice have caused the river to burst its banks. The mills are in danger of being flooded. All able bodied convicts must join their brigades and march to the site to repair the damage to the riverbanks and to make sure there is no loss of timber. Go, immediately to the canteen, where extra soup and bread will be issued then report to your brigadiers, here in the square. Anyone trying to avoid going to the mill will be treated as a saboteur and dealt with severely.'

Anna, Zosia, Ninka and Lyuba hurried to obey the orders. As they stood in the canteen queue, a series of revolver shots rang out from the direction of their hut. Shocked, they stared toward the women's compound and saw two Jewish girls they knew. They were flanked by armed guards and growling dogs and followed by Byeriosov, carrying a revolver. Crying and ashen-faced, they were marched past to face the Commandant, who stood nearby.

'Here are the two dirty Jews who tried to hide and avoid the work,' snarled Byeriosov.

'No time to deal with them now,' said the Major. He swore at the girls and ordered them to join their brigade. Terrified, and looking at no-one on the way, they did so as quickly as possible.

'Poor little things,' Anna whispered to Lyuba but her friend was stony faced. 'If we have to do it, so should they,' she answered.

As Anna's brigade marched toward the mills, she remembered the recent reports brought back by prisoners who worked there. They'd said the ice on the frozen river had begun to crack, which was a sign that spring was on the way – they had never imagined that the spring could bring disaster. In fact, spring had been what she longed for. After the suicide of Tabadz, Anna had felt very depressed.

'What's the point of going on?' she thought. 'Death is all around. It's such a struggle simply to stay alive. I'd like to give up and drift away.'

She hated drawing the garish, lying graphs. Her friends irritated her. She ate very little and avoided all company, even that of August Gustavich and Severyn. One evening, Severyn had joined Anna in the canteen queue.

'Meet me outside when you've collected your food,' he said.

Severyn's face had been stern as he looked at Anna fifteen minutes later.

'Listen carefully, Anna,' he said seriously. 'I am speaking not only as your friend but also as your superior officer. It seems you have forgotten a night at Kazio's house when you undertook certain obligations. It's your duty to behave with dignity and calmness during this harrowing time. I'm sure that the political situation will change quite soon. Germany and Russia have such different philosophies, they won't be able to remain allied for much longer. It will end in armed conflict between them and we can only benefit from that. Now think about what I've said, Anna, and remember that your anger, hatred and depression will prevent clear thinking.'

Anna had been unable to reply. She turned away and went back to her hut, feeling ashamed of her weakness. She spent much of the next night thinking about what Severyn had said. She realised the wisdom of his words and resolved to change. She forced herself to eat, converse with her friends and be cheerful at work and, gradually, it became easier.

Anna's train of thought was interrupted by the most beautiful sight. Just before the mills came into view, the first rays of the rising sun illuminated the bushes on each side of the path. Sometime, recently, the temperature had risen to just above freezing and started to thaw the snow. The temperature had then dropped again and every bush was covered in a glaze of millions of tiny icicles, glittering against the deep rose sky.

The magic was short lived for by the time the prisoners reached the main saw mill, the sun had melted some of the snow into ankle-deep slush. As they waded through the gates, they could see the full extent of the flood disaster. Planks and tree trunks were swirling drunkenly, coming to rest against huts or being carried away by the current. Trucks from the narrow gauge railway, which ran between mills and even small huts were afloat like little Noah's arks. Anna saw a night watchman, standing on a table inside one of these. With a terrified face, he was shouting down a telephone the broken flex of which trailed in the muddy water.

The larger huts were intact and the new manager, standing in the doorway of the main one, was shouting, 'Do something! Save the timber!'

Each brigade was assigned to a different hut. The prisoners collected planks and tree trunks and lashed them around the huts with strong ropes. This served the dual purpose of strengthening the huts and securing the timber. By early afternoon, each large hut had a makeshift platform around it. Everyone was exhausted, soaked through, cold and hungry. They clambered on to their platforms, unable to work any longer.

August Gustavich addressed his brigade.

'The manager says we must go back to camp. All the food here has been destroyed and there's not even hot water for tchay.'

'We'll drown on the way,' a man remarked. 'Look at the depth of the water now and it's getting deeper by the minute.'

'The manager has detailed two of the brigades to dismantle the railway line. We must summon our strength and help to lash the wooden sleepers together. In that way, we'll construct a floating bridge to take us from here to higher ground.'

Anna never knew how the exhausted, frozen convicts managed to build that life-saving 'bridge', but an hour before sunset it was done and the first workers were walking on it, heading back to camp.

When it was Anna's turn, she stepped carefully from sleeper to sleeper, each submerged under the weight of the prisoners, each slimy and hazardous. Several people slipped, fell in and were hauled up by their neighbours. Progress was deadly slow. Anna's boots finally disintegrated. As she flung them away, she was glad of the rags in which her feet were wrapped and relieved that the temperature was a few degrees above freezing. She found she was quite nimble without the heavy felt boots but as the column reached the final rise to the main road and prison gates, there was a sudden surge behind her and she slipped, falling into the mire.

Anna lay in the mud, unable and unwilling to move. Hundreds of feet rushed past her, churning the filth. It covered her face. It was in her mouth,

'Just let me die,' she thought.

Then Lyuba was there, shouting at her to get up.

'Leave me alone.' Anna begged. 'Just leave me.'

But Lyuba's strong arms were round her, dragging her, forcing her up the slope. Then Lyuba, too, tripped and fell at Anna's side. She cursed and gasped for air.

'Get up you two!' screamed a guard, then, seeing how exhausted they were, he levered Lyuba to her feet before shouting at someone else and moving ahead.

'Come, Aniuta, please try to get up,' pleaded Lyuba. 'If we don't get into the warm soon, we'll both die.' Anna knew this was true and she also knew that her faithful friend would not leave her. She forced herself to move and managed to get to her knees, shaking with effort. Then she saw the flowers.

A few inches from the muddy rutted path, under a spindly bush, were three large, pale violets. Amidst the chaos and despair, nature triumphed – spring was on its way.

Those violets gave Anna the will to get up. Slowly she joined the last stragglers and rear detachment of guards as they entered the camp.

A guard on the gate said, 'Go immediately to the canteen. You will be given a hot meal.'

The stoves had been lit and rich fish stew, potatoes and carrots were served, followed by thick millet porridge, sprinkled with sugar. Mugs of scalding tchay completed the meal. Then a full day's ration of bread was distributed and a fresh set of clothes for everyone who had been at the mill.

'They're scared we'll be ill after such a day,' Lyuba whispered. 'We're no good to them if we sicken and die.' Anna didn't care what the reason was for the unusually good food, the new clothes or for the day of rest they were told they could have on the morrow. Life was suddenly worth hanging on to.

Back in the hut, wet clothes were spread around the hot stoves and then the exhausted women crawled into their bunks and fell asleep immediately. Anna's final thought was one of gratitude to Lyuba, her faithful friend, who had certainly saved her life that day.

The long awaited spring arrived at last. By mid May, the midday temperature was 10 degrees. The taiga came to life. Bright orange flowers, poppy-like blazed against the deep brown of the forest floor. Tiny pale green tufts of new growth appeared at the tips of the conifers. These were nipped off and chewed by the convicts, to avert tzinga/scurvy.

With the rise in temperature, mosquitoes and dreaded moshka, the vicious, microscopic black midges, reappeared in their millions. Mosquito hoods were issued once more. The latrines and hillocks of excrement, outside the huts, frozen hard during the winter, thawed with a nauseating stench. Swarms of iridescent bluebottles hovered round the mess. Rivulets of yellowish effluent oozed out of it, covering the paths around the living quarters.

One of the Polish women doctors, with whom Anna had become friendly, spoke to her in the canteen queue.

'The Commandant has agreed to a meeting with two of my colleagues, the lekpom and myself this evening. We're going to ask him to order a cleansing of the camp area. Without it, an epidemic of typhoid fever is inevitable.'

'It is,' Anna agreed 'and you mustn't forget to mention that such an epidemic is certain to spread into the gorodok/camp personnel compound.'

Two days later, Anna, along with all prisoners who were employed within the camp, was issued with a wooden shovel and a rake. She couldn't help heaving as she helped to pile the offending filth into barrows and wheel it to a far distant part of the camp. There, it was buried in deep trenches, dug by another brigade. Then she was detailed to work with others to dig new latrine pits and construct huts over them. While this was in progress, a small detachment of women sprayed all the cleansed area with pungent disinfectant. The whole operation took a week. The camp had been saved from a typhoid epidemic and the doctors and lekpom were publicly congratulated by the Commandant.

Lulled by a return to normality and the spring weather, no-one was prepared for a new calamity. Meningitis spread rapidly through the camp, causing panic and claiming over a hundred lives.

Anna's brigade helped to convert two large store huts into a hospital. A team of doctors and nurses, from a large hospital in Novosibirsk, joined the Polish doctors to care for the sick. All huts were washed inside and out with Lysol and all floors were sprinkled with chlorine. Every morning and evening, each inmate was dosed with a vile medicine called 'Protargol'. No unnecessary gatherings or visits were permitted.

Anna's hut was spared, No-one there contracted the disease.

There were positive outcomes of the epidemic. Shocked by its severity, Major Kondrashkin allowed those who recovered to convalesce and then take on less strenuous work. This heralded a slightly more sympathetic approach to prisoners who became ill. The Polish doctors were highly praised by the visiting hospital team. In recognition of this, they were made permanent medical officers and were joined by four trained nurses. Thus, there was proper medical care for the convicts at last.

Anna availed herself of this facility, one day – not for herself but on Severyn's behalf. She had noticed how pale he was and that he was limping badly.

'What's wrong with your leg?' she asked.

'Nothing,' he replied sharply. 'Stop fussing, Anna. I'm all right.' He turned and started to limp away but Anna caught up with him and looking round to make sure they were not observed, she persisted.

'Severyn, that's not true. You're my superior officer. How will I and other Poles know what to do if you become too ill to command us – or if you die.'

Without a word, Severyn rolled up his trouser leg. Anna gasped at the sight of his emaciated leg, which was covered with suppurating ulcers.

'Severyn, you must see a doctor immediately. Whatever caused this to happen?'

'I have to carry buckets of fuel from a container outside the power hut to the engine inside,' he explained. 'It's not possible to do so without spilling a little on to my trousers. It soaks through and the ulcers are the result.'

'Can't other workers help you? Couldn't you take it in turns to carry the fuel so that your trousers aren't permanently wet?'

'I'm in charge of the generators and the only person allowed to go to the tank. There are armed guards there all the time.'

Anna said no more for the moment, but, at her next midday break, she sought out the doctor and told her what Severyn had said.

'Can you do something for him, please?' she asked.

'I could make up a salve to reduce the inflammation,' she answered 'but I need to see him at the clinic first. You must persuade him to come.'

Severyn was angry when Anna met him outside the canteen the next day and told him what the doctor had said.

'Who do you think you are, Anna Grzymala Siedlecka? I didn't ask you to worry the doctor on my account. I didn't have you down as a fussy woman but I see you're no different from all the rest.' Anna was mortified. Not daring to answer, she turned and walked away. Suddenly, Severyn was behind her, his hand on her shoulder.

'I'm sorry for being rude and bad tempered, Annechka. I know you sought help because you care about what happens to me and I'm grateful. I will go to the clinic and I'll do everything the doctor advises. I must be fit when it's time for me to take the lead. I think that will be quite soon now.' Anna looked at him enquiringly and he went on, 'I'm convinced something serious is happening outside. I don't know what yet but I'm sure it's time to start planning for the future.'

CHAPTER 12

Warmer, Warmer, War. 1941

Over the next couple of days the atmosphere in the camp changed. All rules were tightened. Punishments became harsher. The guards seemed more vigilant and unapproachable than ever.

On June 24th, Avgust Gustavich came to the door of the room where Anna was working alone. His face was grey and strained.

'What's wrong, Avgust? Are you ill?' Anna asked, alarmed.

'No, I'm not ill but I've come to say "Goodbye" to you, Annuita. I've been transferred to another camp. I leave tomorrow.' Anna was stunned by the news.

'Oh, but you've been such a good friend to me,' was all she could manage, afraid that she would give way to tears.

'I've something very important to tell you,' the brigadier went on. 'It's secret and I beg you, for both our sakes, not to tell anyone, except perhaps, your Polish officer at the power station. Doubtless he can be trusted.' Seeing Anna's look of surprise, he smiled and said, 'I've known for some time he's an officer. I've gathered that you were good friends before you came to the camp.' Anna nodded, still waiting for the important news. Avgust Gustavich continued gravely, 'Don't show any emotion now. Keep your face expressionless in case someone is watching us. Five days ago, Germany attacked the Soviet Union. Russia is now at war with Germany. Several of us have been offered pardons and discharge from this camp, if we join the Soviet army as volunteers. I'm a soldier and I love my adopted country so I've accepted the offer.' Then Avgust bent down and, kissing Anna's cheek, whispered, 'Farewell, my little friend. I sincerely hope that you will be able to return to your own country soon. Wish me luck and spare a thought, sometimes, for a convict who loved you dearly.' Striving to keep her face passive, Anna reached up and returned the kiss.

'May God bless you, Avgust Gustavich. I love you too and I'll never ever forget you.' She turned to hide her tears and when she looked back, Avgust had slipped silently away.

Anna had little sleep for the next few nights. She tossed and turned, thinking of Avgust and the new situation. She worried about whether she should tell Severyn. She was afraid that he would feel it necessary to take some action or to share the information with other Poles, which in turn, might endanger the chance of Avgust reaching his destination safely.

On 27th July, the radio amplifiers, which ever since Anna had been at the camp had blared out patriotic Russian songs through all daylight hours, crackled and fell silent.

Prisoners exchanged frightened glances. What could it mean? The silence was uncanny, unsettling.

Anna was on her way to her hut, alone, when Nikita Krivosheyev appeared unexpectedly from behind a store hut. He stood, huge and ragged in front of her, kneading his cap in his enormous hands.

'Please Lady, I must talk to you,' he said in a low voice. 'Strange things are happening in this camp and I don't understand them. I feel that something dreadful is going to befall us all and I'm terrified. You're the only one who talks to me. Everyone else calls me "mad old Nikita," You helped me before. Will you help me now?'

The words had tumbled from his mouth. His agitation was obvious. Anna tried to soothe him with calm words.

'I will always try to help you, Krivosheyev. You know that. Just tell me quietly what is frightening you so much.'

'It's the Devil, Lady,' he answered shrilly. 'He's waiting for me. Everyone tells me to go to Hell. "That's where you belong," they say. Please help me to pray. I want to ask God to take me to Heaven but I don't know how – I don't know the words.'

Anna looked around. There was no-one about. It was strictly forbidden to participate in any religious activity, yet here was a poor, unbalanced creature, suffering and bewildered. She decided she had no alternative but to take the risk.

'We'll go over there,' she said, indicating deep shadow between

145

the hut and a stack of firewood. 'Now, kneel beside me, close your eyes and put your hands together.' The man obeyed.

'Now, say this after me, Krivosheyev.' Anna took a deep breath and conjured a prayer.

'Heavenly Father, please forgive me for all my sins and make a place for me in your Heavenly home. Amen.' Krivosheyev repeated the words slowly and solemnly. When he'd finished, they both stood up, Krivosheyev grinning broadly.

'Thank you Lady. Thank you. You have made me safe.' And patting her gently on the shoulder, the old convict shambled away.

Waking early the next morning, Anna determined to tell Severyn what Avgust had told her. Relieved by her decision, she lay for a moment and then was roused by shrieks outside the hut. The door burst open and Zosia and Ninka rushed in, crying, laughing and shouting,

'We're free! We're free! All Poles are free!' They rushed over to Anna and seized her by the arms.

'Get up Anna. Get up. Hurry! We are free, free, free! There's to be a meeting of all Poles in the main square. Do hurry up.'

Bemused, Anna pulled on her rubber boots. The non-Poles in the hut could only stare in puzzlement while all the Polish women dressed and hurried out of the hut. Anna joined the excited crowd in the square. There was a sudden silence as a slim, clean-shaven man, ramrod straight, addressed them.

'Friends,' he said in a clear, strong voice, which, with a jolt, Anna recognised as Severyn's. 'Two hours ago, while repairing the Commandant's radio, I heard the following news. On the 21st June 1941 – that is over one month ago, war was declared between the Soviet Union and Germany. An amnesty was announced for all Polish citizens being detained in Soviet prisoner of war and labour camps as well as for those who were forcibly deported from their homes in Poland. The leaders of this camp chose not to tell us this. Nor did they tell us that all imprisoned Poles must be released immediately and treated as free men and women. Apparently, at this very moment, the Polish army, under the command of General Wladyslaw Anders is gathering in the mid Asian region of the USSR.

All able-bodied men and women are requested to join the Polish army. The Soviet Government has promised to supply the necessary transport and aid. Long live Poland!'

'Long live Poland! Long live Poland!' The cry was taken up by the men and women in the square. Then someone started singing the National Anthem of Poland.

'Poland will not perish
as long as we're alive...'

Anna joined in, her voice breaking with emotion, tears streaming down her face.

At that moment, the door of the Commandanture opened and the Commandant came out, followed by Politruk Byeriosov. Anna saw him hesitate when he realised what the Poles were singing. Then he slowly raised his right hand to his hat in a salute. Byeriosov, face thunderous, followed suit. Silence fell again at the end of the anthem. Severyn turned to face the Commandant, addressing him as an equal.

'Commandant,' I am Captain Severyn S... a serving officer of the Polish forces, representing all Polish citizens in this camp. I wish to discuss two things with you. First, the immediate release of all my compatriots, secondly, a means of contacting the Polish Embassy in Moscow or the Polish Government representative in Kuybyshe without delay.'

The Commandant stared at Severyn for a moment and then, with a wry smile, exclaimed, 'Tchort!/The Devil! I always had my doubts about you but your grey beard fooled me. Please ask your people to return to their quarters quietly. Then come with me to my office where we will discuss all necessary arrangements.'

Seeing the Commandant smiling at Severyn, the Politruk stepped forward to speak to him.

'Tovarishch/Comrade Kapitan...' he began but Severyn broke in sharply, 'I'm not your tovarishch, Lieutenant Byeriosov. Please stand to attention when you address a superior officer.' He turned to the waiting crowd and spoke to them in Polish.

'Friends, return to your huts peacefully and with dignity. At the moment we are still under the jurisdiction of the camp authorities and must obey the rules. Meet me in the largest dining hut this evening and I'll tell you what has been arranged with Major Kondrashkin.'

Back in the hut, Anna and her friends, watched enviously by the Russian women, chattered excitedly about the change in their circumstances. Lyuba sobbed all the afternoon at the thought of losing Anna and there was nothing Anna could do to comfort her.

At 6pm, the Polish men and women gathered in the large dining hut. Anna was pleased to see Marcus Shapiro, whom she hadn't seen for some time.

The expectant Poles cheered as Severyn and Major Kondrashkin entered the room. Anna, stomach churning with excitement, stood on tiptoe to see them. Severyn spoke first, shouting to be heard above the hubbub.

'Dear friends, I understand your joy and exuberance and share it, wholeheartedly. There are, however, many important issues to be clarified with the Soviet Authorities. I've been chosen as liaison officer and I've had preliminary discussions with Major Kondrashkin. He assures me that immediate steps will be taken to notify the Polish Authorities about us. He will ask them to send a special official envoy, who will bring instructions about our future. As this may take up to three weeks, the Commandant has suggested that we remain here until the arrival of the Polish delegate. We'll be employed as free citizens, paid properly and receive better food and accommodation. My advice is to accept this temporary arrangement. Anyone who wishes to leave earlier should apply to the Commandant, in person.'

'Oh no,' Anna whispered to Zosia, 'I really thought we'd get out of here straight away. Who knows how long we'll have to hang around.' Before Zosia could answer, the Commandant stepped forward with a smile.

'I promise I'll do all in my power to expedite your departure from here. I'll interview all Polish citizens tomorrow so that release documents can be issued immediately. I sincerely hope that Polish and Russian soldiers will soon be fighting side by side to vanquish the treacherous Hitlerites. One last thing – I must ask you not to talk about any of these matters with Soviet convicts.'

As soon as Major Kondrashkin left the hut, there was uproar. Everyone started to discuss what had been said, arguing, shouting and pushing. Anna looked to see what Severyn's reaction was. He was standing on a table, arms raised. He called, loudly, for silence.

'Please, please be patient and behave as decent Polish citizens should. I understand your disappointment at the delay but remember that each of us is a representative of our beloved country. I think the camp authorities have promised a lot to keep us quiet. I don't trust them and it maybe that, after consulting their superiors tomorrow, their attitude to us will change. Remember, the Soviet Union is at war and it would be easy for the Soviets to accuse any of us of sabotage, which carries a death penalty. We're in their power so all we can do is abide by their rules and be patient. I'll make sure you are moved to better accommodation tomorrow. I'll keep you informed of developments. Whenever you have any interviews, my advice is not to sign anything at all. I'm sure you will be asked to sign various documents or contracts. Don't! I can't stress that strongly enough. We must all be careful and patient and, most of all, we mustn't antagonise the Russians but don't commit yourselves to anything without discussing it with me. Now, please return to your huts in an orderly fashion.' Chastened, the Poles left the room.

Back in the hut, the Russian and Ukrainian women were subdued. They had been called to a meeting of their own. Clearly they had been warned not to ask questions. Anna smiled across at Lyuba, who tried to smile back as the tears coursed down her cheeks.

'I'm not leaving this hut without saying a proper "Goodbye" to Lyuba,' Anna said to her friends. 'She's saved my life on more that one occasion. I'll go over and speak to her after lights out.'

But before she could put this plan into action Lubya, herself, was at Anna's side as soon as the lights were extinguished.

'We've been told that this is the last night we'll spend together, my dearest friend,' she whispered. 'We were warned not to speak to any Poles but I couldn't bear to see you leave without saying "Farewell" and wishing you all the happiness in the world.' Then she embraced Anna and her friends in turn, wishing each well, returning, at last, to Anna.

'Will you remember old Lyuba who loved you as a daughter, Anuitka? I shall miss you every day. May God and his angels take care of you.' She clung to Anna for a moment and amidst tears, Anna stammered, 'Lyuba, I shall never forget you. Not only have you saved my life several times, you have also shown me great kindness and love. Thank you and may God bless you.'

The next morning, after the Russian and Ukrainian women had left for work, a guard came into the hut and spoke to the Poles.

'Collect your belongings and assemble in the dining hut in an hour's time. From there you will go to new barracks.'

Anna looked through her few belongings. She pulled out the headscarf and the dozen handkerchiefs along with a piece of dark red winceyette, which had been in the parcel from her sister. She wrapped the material and handkerchiefs in the scarf and left them under Lyuba's pillow with a note, scrawled with a stump of indelible pencil on one of the handkerchiefs.

'To my dearest friend Lyuba, with love from Anuita. 29 July 1941'

Anna still had the dainty shoes, sent to her by her sister. Although they were completely unsuitable for the Siberian climate, she thought she might be able to sell them or exchange them for food some time. She rolled her nightdress round them and put them, a tin can, mug, wooden spoon, bowl, spare underclothes, foot wrappings and mittens and, most precious of all, a few crayon stumps, paint brushes and watercolours, given to her by Tabadze, inside her blanket. Then she tied the bundle neatly with a strip of material. She was ready to leave the hut, which held so many memories.

As she stood looking round, two young men arrived and stood in the doorway talking to a guard who had been posted there.

'Captain Severyn S... has sent us to escort these ladies to the dining hut.. He is on duty at the powerhouse. You do realise that these people have had no breakfast, don't you?' The guard mumbled something and the two men walked past him into the hut.

'Ladies,' said the taller of the two, 'I am Yurek and this is Zenek.

Please bring your belongings and follow us.'

With a last look round, Anna and her friends obeyed. In the dining hut, they joined the rest of the Polish inmates and were served with porridge and tchay by four Russian convicts.

Then began a long day of waiting for Anna. First, a Soviet official listed the names of everyone in the hut and then, two hours later, the first Pole was called to see the Commandant. A guard had been left on the door and when Yurek asked him if he could go out for some fresh air, the request was refused.

'Isn't it odd,' Anna remarked to Yurek and Zenek, after a while, 'people are being called out of the room, one after the other but they never come back.'

'Yes, that worries me a bit,' Yurek replied. 'I'll ask the guard what's happening.'

Anna saw the man shake his head and turn away at Yurek's question.

'I've had enough of this. We're supposed to be on the same side now. I'm going to find out what's going on,' exclaimed Zenek. He doubled up and gave a loud groan. Clutching his stomach, he staggered across to the guard.

'I need to go to the latrine,' he gasped. 'Quickly, or I'll have a very nasty accident.' The guard looked round hopelessly but there was no-one to ask so he opened the door and pushed Zenek out. From the window, Anna saw Zenek swerve away from the latrines and dash towards the powerhouse.

By midday, the Polish group had dwindled to about eighty, each remaining person anxious to be called for the interview. A meal break was announced and the food arrived. Suddenly Severyn strode in, followed by a Soviet lieutenant and a grinning Zenek.

Severyn turned to the lieutenant.

'What's the meaning of this?' he shouted. 'These people have been released from captivity. They are free. The Commandant said they would be treated with consideration and dignity. Why is there a guard on the door, preventing them from moving about freely?'

The lieutenant, in his turn, shouted at the hapless guard.

'These people are not convicts. You were left here to offer

assistance, not to be obstructive!'

Anna, and everyone else in the room knew that, in the eyes of the lieutenant, the only mistake the guard had made, was to let Zenek out.

After the meal, Severyn addressed his waiting compatriots.

'The people who have seen the Commandant have been conducted to new living quarters, where their food is being served. I have told the Commandant that I want to make sure that all of you are given discharge papers as soon as possible. I have said that I won't go back to work at the powerhouse until that has been done. As he is anxious for me to carry out some urgent repair work, I think he will do as I ask. Think very carefully before you decide whether to leave immediately or stay until the Polish Legation arrives and, remember, don't sign anything.'

At that moment, Anna's name was called and as she got up to walk to the door, Severyn came to her side.

'At least I don't need to worry about your saying or doing the wrong thing,' he smiled. 'Just be calm and firm and, for heaven's sake, don't argue.'

Major Kondrashkin looked up and smiled as Anna entered the room. The Politruk stood behind him.

'Ah, here is our young artist,' the Major said amiably. 'The time has finally come for us to talk about your future. Please be seated.' Anna sat down. The Major continued.

'Have you decided what you want to do, Anna Grzymala Siedlecka?'

'I'd like to leave the camp as soon as possible.'

The Commandant, smiling almost indulgently, said, 'Anna, I want you to know that we, in the Soviet Union, encourage and take great care of intelligent, talented and hardworking young people such as you. If you agree to accept our offer of Soviet citizenship and study art in the USSR, a brilliant future awaits you.' He stopped, awaiting a reply.

Anna thought for a moment and then spoke slowly, 'There is a war on, Major. Surely you expect all your young people to do their duty, join the army and defeat the enemy.'

A flicker of annoyance passed across the Commandant's face but it didn't show in his voice.

'Our army is invincible. We'll crush the German aggressor in no time and utterly destroy him.' Anna didn't answer.

'I must be careful,' she thought. 'Severyn warned me not to argue. I've said enough.'

The Major resorted to sarcasm.

'We all know what a little fire-eater you are. I shall waste no more of my valuable time trying to convince you that a decision to leave the camp and undertake a difficult and dangerous journey on your own is irresponsible and foolish. I wanted to spare you the hardships of travelling thousands of miles in war time, searching for your army – but you are free to decide for yourself. My advice to you is to wait patiently until the official representative of the Polish Government arrives. Then transport and other facilities will be properly organised. If you leave then, the journey will be much less strenuous. However, as I said, you are free to decide what to do.'

Anna saw the sense in his argument. His advice was the same as Severyn's.

'This is all too easy and comfortable,' she thought. 'Politruk Byeriosov has been watching my face all the time. There's a catch somewhere.'

The Major's next remark confirmed her suspicions. He took a piece of paper from a folder and pushed it towards her.

'To legalise your position as a free person, employed temporarily in this establishment, here is a six month contract, entitling you to an appropriate wage, living quarters and food. You will be employed as a draughtsman, with a bonus if you work overtime. Of course, you'll be free to leave the camp and visit the local town when you're not working and you'll be able to use the special camp shop. Should the Polish Envoy arrive here before the six months is up, this contract will be automatically cancelled.' He held out a pen to Anna.

Severyn's words rang in Anna's head, 'Don't sign anything.' She didn't take the pen.

'Please Aniuta,' his voice was almost wheedling, 'Be sensible. Sign the contract. You know I have always tried to be fair to you.'

Anna took a deep breath and looked directly into the Major's eyes.

'Thank you, Major Kondraskin, for your consideration and advice. I'm willing to stay here and work until the Polish Envoy arrives without signing a contract. However, my resolve to join the Polish Army as soon as possible is unshakeable. Please will you issue my discharge papers and my travel document, allowing me to travel to Uzbekistan, as you have promised.'

The Commandant's face became red with anger but, to Anna's surprise, he handed her both documents, already signed and stamped.

'Follow the guard outside the door. He'll take you to your new quarters.' Was all he said. The interview was over.

A large store hut, divided by a wooden screen into male and female quarters, was Anna's new home. Twenty men and thirty women, all of whom had refused to sign contracts, comprised the Polish group housed there. Some Poles had elected to leave immediately, others had signed and were accommodated separately.

The hut was empty except for two iron stoves.

'New bunks will be built in here for you, tomorrow,' promised a Russian lieutenant. So the first night was spent on the floor. As Anna tossed on the thin mattress, trying to get comfortable, she heard mysterious noises from outside – crashes, thumps and shouts. In the morning, the mystery was solved.

A tall wire fence had been erected, separating the Polish living quarters, kitchen and dining hut from those used by the Soviet inmates. A large notice suspended above the gate, set in the fence, read,

'ZAPRYSHCHENAYA ZONA'/ 'FORBIDDEN ZONE'

'Except when we go to work, we'll be isolated,' Severyn explained. 'The Soviets don't want us to contaminate their citizens. Be very careful what you say and do in your workplace. We have been warned against fraternisation. Remember what I said about sabotage. Our rations are being increased to top grade although wages will still be paid according to quotas. None of you will be sent to work away from camp and working hours are to be shortened.'

'What sort of work will we do?' asked Ninka.

'You'll each be told later today,' Severyn replied. 'I shall continue in the powerhouse with the team of electricians and four extra Polish workers. Some of you will clean and fumigate our living quarters daily. Some will work in the clothing repair shop or laundry and men are needed to mend the board walks around camp and carry out general repairs.'

After breakfast a Soviet official arrived in the dining hut to give the promised work instructions. Anna was delighted to return to her sign writing, though she'd been moved to a small room on her own. Gavsiuk met her with her instructions.

'I'll come each morning and tell you what you have to do,' he said in a subdued tone. 'Apart from that I have orders not to speak to you.' And he hurried away.

It was a strange new life. Anna missed Lyuba and some of her friends from whom she was now separated. Two weeks passed and there was no news of the Polish Envoy and no reply to the Commandant's letter. The first rest day of the new regime arrived but Anna decided against going into Asino with Ninka and Zosia.

'No thank you,' she said. 'I want to spend a long time in the banya and then see if I can have a proper talk with Severyn. He's always so busy or working. There are some things I want to find out.'

Refreshed after her visit to the banya, Anna made her way to the powerhouse, which was outside the Forbidden Zone. The armed guard outside took no notice of her so she stepped inside the hot noisy room. Severyn saw her immediately and hurried over.

'Are you all right, Anuita? How can I help you?'

The clanging of the huge diesel generators made conversation impossible. Severyn took Anna's arm, led her into a small office and closed the door.'

'I'm sorry to bother you, Severyn,' she said, 'but I wondered if there were any news from Kybyshev.'

'No, there isn't, I'm afraid,' replied Severyn 'The Commandant blames war-related communication problems. I expect the Polish Legation is short staffed and inundated with requests similar to ours from many parts of the USSR.'

'Wouldn't it be possible for you to get a permit to travel to Kuybyshev to speak to the Polish Authorities, in person?' Anna asked. Severyn shook his head and said, wryly,

'I thought of that but the Commandant wouldn't give me a pass. He was very polite but, nevertheless, he refused. I have some news, though. When a group of us went into Asino a couple of days ago, we met a large group of Polish women and children and a few elderly men. They, along with some Ukrainian and Jewish families were deported from Poland, last year, and forcibly re-settled in a place called Sosnovka. It's about seven kilometres from Asino, on the other side of the railway line. They've survived by selling belongings they managed to bring with them and by working in and around Asino. They were notified of the amnesty earlier than we were – on the day it was announced. At the same time, they were advised to stay put until the Polish Envoy arrives. The group we met were astonished to discover there are Polish inmates in this camp and very willing to do anything they could to help us.'

'Couldn't we leave here and join them in their settlement?' asked Anna, thinking longingly of getting out of the camp to freedom.

'They've so little, Anna. We couldn't expect them to support us and it's not easy to find work. I think it's best to stay. It can't be for much longer.'

Just then, someone called for Severyn. Anna left the powerhouse and saw her friends returning to the hut after their trip to Asino.

That evening, there was a long discussion about the best way forward. Those who had been to the town that day were of the opinion that leaving the camp to stay with the Poles in Sosnovka would be the best course.

'If we unite and demand that we are given transport away from here, they may agree. We'd be quite a large group. They might listen to us,' someone said.

'And they might accuse us of causing unrest and send us back here,' retorted Anna.

'Sosnovka is nearer the railway station than we are. It will be much easier for the Polish Envoy to reach us there,' suggested Ninka.

'Severyn strongly advised that we should stay for the moment,' Anna reminded everyone. 'At least we have food and shelter and are sure of earning some money, however little. I respect Severyn as our leader. I shall be guided by him.'

In the end some went and some stayed. By the end of August, the only Poles left in their section of camp were Anna, Ninka, Zosia, three other Polish women and nineteen men, including Severyn and his powerhouse team. On 1st September 1941, the second anniversary of the German attack on Poland, Severyn called a meeting in the dining hut.

'You've all been very patient,' he began, 'but I don't think we can wait any longer for the Polish Envoy. I've been to the Commandant and he has agreed to help us in our endeavour to reach the Polish Army. His only stipulation is that the generators should be in tip-top condition before we go. We'll work hard over the next two days to leave everything in order. You go to work, as usual. If you want to leave when I do, get your belongings together so that you'll be ready to leave on 4th September. Which of you wishes to join me?'

Anna's heart seemed to miss a beat as she put up her hand. She looked round. Everyone in the room had raised a hand.

'We'll all soon be free,' she thought, 'at last.'

That night, in spite of the armed Soviet guards, one of the three generators was almost completely destroyed. Byeriosov burst into the dining hut as breakfast was being served.

'Treason! Sabotage! He shouted. Which miserable son of a bitch sabotaged the generator last night?' When he was met with astonished silence, he went on. 'Don't think for one moment that any of you will be leaving this camp until the culprit is found and punished or until the generator is back in working order.' He crashed out of the room and, almost immediately, Severyn came in, looking upset.'

'I gather you've had Byeriosov shouting at you.' he said. 'It's obvious to me that this whole incident has been cleverly staged by the authorities because they don't have their own skilled technicians to work in the powerhouse. They simply can't spare us. Our only hope is to repair the generator over the next weeks and never to leave it unattended. We must place our own guards there. If the Polish Envoy comes to the area, meanwhile, the Poles who have already left will tell him we're still here. I'm so sorry this has happened but my team will do its best to repair the wretched generator as soon as possible.'

Anna couldn't help feeling despondent.

'So near and yet so far,' she thought as she lay on her bunk. 'How many more nights must we endure? It's not being here that's keeping me awake. It's the hope that's been dashed. In a way, the hope's the hardest thing…'

Over the next week, Severyn and his team dismantled the ruined generator and tried to re-assemble it. They worked well into each night and returned filthy and exhausted but with small tools, nails, screws and bits of metal, secreted in their clothing.

'You never know when you might need stuff like this,' grinned Yurek and he handed Anna a small soldering iron and some strips of solder, which she slipped inside her bundle. 'I almost got caught by Byeriosov, as I was tucking this into my boot,' he added. 'He's in and out all day, chivvying and bullying us. It's hard not to lose your temper with him but Severyn keeps reminding us that lashing out will only make a bad situation worse. He's a wise one!'

At the end of the week, Severyn reported,

'All our attempts to repair the damage have failed because we can't reproduce some of the parts which were broken and we haven't got all the necessary tools. I've been to see the Commandant and he's given permission for Yurek, Zenek and I to go to the Tomsk scrap yard, where broken machines of all types are taken. There's no chance of getting new parts at the moment. I also reminded the Major that sooner or later, the Polish Authorities will hear about our plight and will be sure to notify the Soviet Government that the powerhouse workers are being detained unlawfully. He re-iterated his pledge that we'll be free to leave as soon as the generator is repaired. We are to leave tomorrow morning and travel by lorry. We'll be away for two days. Two of our team will maintain constant watch at the powerhouse, while we're away.'

After two days, the heavily loaded lorry returned to camp. Bits of broken machinery and scrap metal were carried into the powerhouse and further gruelling work for the team followed. A few evenings later, Severyn spoke to the residents of the Polish hut.

'I'm afraid there's no chance that the new parts we're making out of scrap, for the generator, will keep the thing running for more than a couple of days. When we do actually get it working, those who wish to leave must be ready to go immediately. I'll quite understand if anyone chooses to stay safely here and wait for the Envoy.'

Anna spoke first.

'I'm coming with you, Severyn, whatever the hazards.'

'So am I.'

'Me too.'

There was no-one in the room who wished to stay behind. Severyn smiled and outlined his plan.

'When the reconstructed generator is ready, we'll let you know so that you can be prepared to leave. Then I'll notify the Commandant and invite him to be present when the motor is restarted. When he's seen proof of the repair, I'll ask him to make good his promise of allowing all remaining Poles to leave. Zenek will bring you word straight away and you must all leave the camp, with your belongings, immediately. You must walk towards Asino and find shelter at the edge of the taiga to wait for the remaining electricians and myself.

When we meet up, we'll take refuge at Sosnovka until the Envoy finally arrives.'

Work continued as usual for Anna. She saw Lyuba, once or twice, at a distance. They exchanged furtive smiles but dared not speak. To her regret she never saw Nikita Krivosheyev again and could get no news of him. In after years, she often thought about the strange old man and wondered what had become of him.

On the morning of 14th September 1941, Severyn announced that the generator would be re-started on the morrow.

'Be ready to leave as soon as Zenek gives the word,' he said. 'It's a rest day so you won't be noticed if you saunter out in groups of two or three. Wear your spare clothes under your everyday ones and carry your belongings in pockets, up sleeves, tucked away so that you have only inconspicuous bundles. Take any small tools you have. Those will be useful. You won't have time to collect your wages, I'm afraid. Save any food you can from meals today and, above all, make sure you have your documents and travel permits. Put them somewhere absolutely secure. One last thing, if something goes wrong here and the team and I can't get away, don't on any account, come back. Wait about two hours and then make your way to Sosnovka. Now we're going back to do all we can to make sure the generator comes up trumps tomorrow. We'll be there all day and all night. This nightmare is nearly over. Good luck!' With that, Severyn and his team departed.

Anna and her friends looked at each other.

'I can't believe it's really going to happen,' whispered Zosia.

'Nor can I.' Anna paused and then admitted, 'You know, suddenly the camp seems secure, safe. I feel quite scared of "out there." It's so... so... unknown.'

'Would you rather stay here, then,' joked Ninka.

Anna knew she wouldn't, but nevertheless, she lay awake for a long time, filled with anxiety and foreboding.

The next morning, after breakfast, everyone in the hut stood ready. They took it in turns to watch through the door. About an hour elapsed and Anna was watching when she saw Severyn, the Commandant and the Politruk enter the powerhouse. People gathered round the hut door. There was a sudden silence. The two working generators had been switched off. The waiting group hardly dared breath. There was a spluttering sound from the powerhouse, a pause and then the sound of one generator.

'It's working!' The words were hardly out of Ninka's mouth when the generator stopped. No-one said anything. Anna felt sick, almost faint.

She squeezed her eyes shut and prayed

'Please, please let it start.' Then, sweeter than any music, the air was filled once more, with the sound of the generator.

It wasn't until an hour later, when the generator was still working, that Zenek and a lieutenant came out of the powerhouse. As they came across to the hut the crowd at the door dispersed. Everyone became occupied with his or her own affairs, looking up only when the lieutenant addressed them. Zenek stood behind him, grinning.

'Those of you who wish to go to Asino may leave now,' said the officer. 'Please return before nightfall as the Commandant wants to talk to you about your final release.' He beamed at them, Zenek mouthed.

'Good luck' and then both men went back to the powerhouse.

Not much was said as everyone stood up, ready to leave. They went out, in small groups. Anna, Ninka and Zosia were the last to go. Anna passed through the gates without looking back. Winter had arrived. The day was frosty and bright and the snow crunched, crisply under their feet.

PART TWO

CHAPTER 13

From Tomsk to Tashkent

Four hours later, the elation had disappeared as Anna and the other women huddled together, in the bushes, trying, in vain to keep warm as they waited for the powerhouse crew.

'Let's light a fire,' someone suggested.

'Too risky,' said Ninka. We mustn't draw attention to ourselves.

'We can't wait much longer for Severyn,' Anna said at last. 'We'll have to move soon if we're going to get to Sosnovka before nightfall.'

'I think we should move now,' this from Zosia. 'We'll freeze to death if we sit around any longer. Severyn told us what to do if he didn't come. Let's obey orders.'

With heavy hearts, they crawled out of the bushes. As they stood at the edge of the road, Anna saw Severyn and the others. She felt almost weak with relief.

As the group grew closer, Severyn shouted to them.

'Don't stop! Hurry up. Keep moving. We'll catch you up.' When he drew abreast, he explained.

'Can't talk now. We must get further from the camp. The generator is likely to stop at any moment. If that happens, Byeriosov is bound to come looking for us.'

Everyone began to run, terrified of re-capture. Anna thought her lungs would burst but she kept repeating, as she ran, 'Freedom, freedom, freedom.'

At last, on the outskirts of Asino, Severyn called a halt and everyone collapsed, gasping, into a snow-filled ditch at the side of the road.

'Let's stop for a few minutes to recover and talk,' he said. 'So far, we are not being followed. As the generator is bound to fail, the powerhouse team is in real danger of being arrested and charged with sabotage. We must leave the district. We're going to try to board a train and make our way to Tashkent. I advise the older men, all of the women and anyone who is too exhausted, to continue to Sosnovka. I promise that I will inform the Polish legation of your whereabouts at the first opportunity. You must decide now what you want to do.'

Anna knew, at once, that she wanted to go with Severyn. Having come this far, she couldn't bear the prospect of more waiting. She looked at Ninka and Zosia.

'I'm going with Severyn,' she said quietly. 'What about you?'

'I can't go on,' answered Ninka. 'I might just make it to Sosnovka but I simply can't keep running and hiding. I'm sorry, Anuita.'

'I feel the same,' said Zosia. 'I'd love to get right away but I just haven't the energy. Come with us, Anuita. Come and rest for a bit. The Envoy is sure to be here soon.'

Anna bit her lip. She hated the idea of parting from her good friends but she felt an iron resolution within herself. She shook her head and turned to Severyn.

'I'm coming with you.'

'Are you sure, Anuita? I don't think you should. The journey will be extremely dangerous.'

'I'm coming with you.' Anna repeated. Severyn looked annoyed.

'Take my advice, Anna. Go with your friends.'

'I want to come with you.'

'Then expect no favours or special treatment.' Severyn snapped. Anna reddened, looked away and kept silent.

'I'll show you,' she thought. 'I'll prove I'm as good as any man.'

Finally, ten people, including Severyn, opted to go on, Anna being the only woman. She didn't trust herself to speak as she gave each of her friends a farewell embrace. She was determined to display no sign of weakness in front of Severyn. Then the two groups separated. The women and older men followed the Sosnovka road while Anna's group, walking in twos and threes to avoid unwanted attention, made for the railway station.

Darkness was falling. They found a sheltered, deserted spot in a siding. A long freight train stood on the single track in the station and they could hear a babble of voices from the platform. Severyn, Yurek and Zenek crept cautiously towards the noise to investigate what was happening. They soon returned with excellent news.

'The train in the station was full of Germans,' explained Severyn. 'They come from the Volga German Republic. The Russians have decided to deport them to Siberia, fearing a subversive element amongst them. The empty train will return to Tomsk as soon as everyone is out and it is made ready and – we'll be on it!'

'There's only one drawback,' added Yurek. 'There are a lot of armed guards and NKVD officers around. Some of them are bound to go back on the train. We'll just have to be very careful.'

An hour elapsed before the train was cleared. Anna shivered with cold, excitement and fear. What if they were caught now? All this effort would come to nothing. They'd be sent straight back to camp, punished severely and… She gave herself a shake.

'I said I wanted to come. I'm glad I'm here with a chance of escape. I *will* be positive.' She thought.

Severyn whispered that they should all move silently until they were abreast of the train, on the side further from the brightly lit platform. Once there, Yurek and Zenek moved slowly along the line, searching for an empty, unlocked truck. They found one, at last, and beckoned to the others.

'We'll hide in the shadow of the embankment just there,' said Severyn softly, pointing to a dark patch close by. 'We won't get in until just before the train leaves. The guards are bound to check the trucks to make sure they're empty.'

Twenty minutes later, the searchlights on the platform were suddenly extinguished. The station was now lit by a few dim bulbs. Steam hissed from the engine and a large group of guards and NKVD officers boarded the front of the train.

'It appears there won't be a search. Get in quickly everybody,' ordered Severyn.

Stiff with cold, Anna climbed into the truck. She could make out the familiar tiers of wooden shelves and the hole in the centre of the floor. The door on the station side was still open.

'We'll squeeze under the bottom shelf,' whispered Severyn, 'And pray that whoever shuts the door doesn't look inside. You first, Anuita.'

They crushed themselves into the dark, dusty space and for ten excruciating minutes, no-one dared speak or stir. Then there was a voice outside their truck, the door slammed and, almost immediately, the train jerked. They were off. For a moment, nobody spoke or moved. Then, stiffly, cautiously, they crawled out and stood upright.

'Now we must try to sleep,' Severyn said. 'We don't know what lies ahead. We'd better save our food for later.'

Anna curled up with her bundle, on the middle shelf. The temperature in the truck was below freezing. Her hands and feet were numb, every bone ached, she was shivering uncontrollably and she was very hungry. However, remembering Severyn's words to her, she said nothing and eventually fell asleep.

'Time to wake up, Anna.' Yurek was grinning down at her and, to her surprise, she realised her head was on his knee.

'Hope you don't mind. Thought you'd be more comfortable,' he said. 'You've been sleeping like a baby. It's morning and we'll be in Tomsk Station in a few minutes.'

Anna stood up. Grey morning light was seeping through the slats of the windows.

She felt warmer and rested.

'Thank you so much, Yurek. I slept so well because you made sure I was comfortable.' Yurek laughed.

'We're all soldiers,' he said. 'We must help each other to defeat every one of our enemies, whether it's the cold, hunger or the NKVD.'

Zenek climbed on to the top shelf to peer through the slats.

'We're just coming into a large station,' he reported. 'The lines crisscross and there are sidings and loading areas, sheds and stationary trains. We're drawing into a siding.' The train stopped, doors banged and Zenek continued his commentary. 'I can see the crew and officers leaving. They're going towards the main station.' He clambered down.

'What next?' he asked Severyn.

'As you and I speak the best Russian, Zenek, we'll go to the station to see if there's any chance of getting some food. We'll also find out when the next onward train leaves. The rest of you stay quietly here for the moment. One of us will be back soon.' They pushed the sliding door slowly aside and jumped on to the deserted embankment. Yurek pulled the door almost closed after them. Anna stood by the narrow gap looking out at a spectacular sunrise. The sun was just above the horizon and because of a hard frost, the very air glittered. To the east, the sky was bright orange-pink while on each side of the flaming orb, two columns of fire glowed and shimmered. Anna gasped and called Yurek to look.

'Words can't describe it,' he said softly. 'I think it's a good omen.'

Fifteen minutes later, Zenek returned.

'There's a train due to leave for Novosibirsk in two hours,' he reported. 'There's no food on the station but there is hot water. Severyn is talking to the Station Master. He thinks he'll be able to get us some travel documents. Come on, follow me.'

The station was crowded but they spotted Severyn outside the Station Master's office.

'I explained to the Station Master that I'm a Polish officer, in charge of a group of volunteers en route to join the Polish army. I've got travel documents as far as Novosibirsk, where, he says we should report to the Voyenkommat/Military Office. He couldn't give us any food but says we can wait in the waiting room if we like.'

'Do you trust him?' Yurek asked. 'If we sit in the waiting room and members of the NKVD ask who we are...'

'Exactly what I think,' broke in Severyn. 'Let's mingle with the crowd, get some hot water, have something to eat and get on the train as soon as it arrives.'

They found a sheltered place at the end of the wooden platform then Anna, Zenek and another of their group went off to find the hot water boiler.

'If there's nothing else I like about the Soviet system, I do love the inevitable hot water boiler on every station,' remarked Anna. Then she smiled sweetly at the old man in charge of the boiler and begged for the loan of a large kettle.

Soon everyone's mugs and cans were full of hot water, into which they crumbled the dried prison bread. It was their first meal for twenty four hours.

'Wonderful,' Anna murmured. 'The best meal I've ever had.'

Afterwards the men sat around, smoking, talking and dozing but Anna had other ideas. She filled a large can with hot water, held it and picked the kettle up with the other.

'Just going to return the kettle,' she said.

This she did then she pushed her way through the crowd, stepping over sleeping forms, bundles and battered suitcases towards the ladies' lavatories. The huddled figures had been waiting for hours, shabby, cold, apathetic. They didn't even glance at the small grubby young woman as she passed by.

The toilets were even worse than those in the camp, reeking and filthy. There were no cubicles, just a series of holes in the ground, open to view. Nor were there any washbasins. Anna found a corner to put down her can of water and then washed as well as she could, watched by several surprised and amused women.

In spite of the limitation on her ablutions, she returned to her friends refreshed. No-one smiled as she came up and she saw that there were militiamen nearby and that they were examining people's documents. Severyn turned a furious face to her.

'We've all been very worried about you, Anna. We didn't know where you were. You said you were just going to take the kettle back.'

'I'm sorry, I only went for a wash,' Anna replied.

'Don't leave the group again, without permission,' he snapped. 'This is no joy-ride. Understand this, if there's an emergency and we have to disappear fast and you've wandered off, nobody will wait for you. You'll be on your own.'

Anna could hardly believe her ears. She was angry and hurt and spoke icily.

'I would like to remind you, Captain, that I have never asked to be treated differently from the others. I don't want – or expect any favours from you. If you think I'm a burden, please tell me now and I'll leave the group immediately. We're only at the start of our journey and I would hate to think I'm jeopardising your plans.' She picked up her bundle and was about to walk away when a militiaman approached.

'Show me your documents' he said. Anna froze, everyone stood up and Severyn hissed at her.

'Go back and stand with the others. That's an order.' He turned to the man, with a smile.

'Certainly Officer. Here is the travel pass for all ten of us and we've each got our own personal papers. Here are mine.' As the man scrutinised first Severyn's papers and then those of the rest of the group, Anna could only pray that he had not been notified of their exodus from camp and told to detain them. The soldier came to her last and seemed to stare at her papers for a long time. Then he smiled and handed them back.

'They all seem in order,' he said to Severyn. 'I hope you'll get on to the train. There are a lot of people travelling.' He moved off to the next group.

Anna's legs felt so weak that she sat down abruptly. Severyn came across and, crouching beside her, put his arm round her shoulder. His voice was conciliatory.

'Come on, Annechka. Don't behave like a child. I apologise for losing my temper. It's only because I was so worried about you. It's imperative we all stay together. You do see that, don't you?'

Anna looked at his face, lined with worry and felt remorseful.

'I do understand,' she replied. 'I'm sorry I was so thoughtless.'

The friendly atmosphere was restored.

The hours passed slowly. In spite of more hot water and bread, Anna was once more very cold. At 7pm, someone shouted, 'Here's the train!' Anna rushed to the edge of the platform and peered into the darkness. Through the thick curtain of falling snow, she could just make out two flickering yellow dots in the distance, growing larger all the time. Then she heard the muffled rumble of wheels and a shrill whistle. Next moment, the huge locomotive, belching smoke, sparks and steam hissed past them, cattle trucks in its wake. It stopped at the end of the platform.

The impassive crowd transformed into a heaving mass, which pushed towards the train. There was shouting, cursing, fighting. Anna was lifted off her feet and propelled forward. Severyn grabbed her arm, pulled her back for a moment and lifting her up high, carried her to one of the wagons, screaming at the rest of the group to follow. He threw Anna forward into the truck and scrambled in after her, followed by the others. Anna had landed on top of other passengers who pummelled her, swore at her and pushed her roughly away. Novak, one of their number, came to her aid and, apologising on her behalf, helped her over to where the others stood.

After a few minutes, the hubbub subsided and someone lit a tallow candle. Then everyone tried to find a space on the floor on which to sit and, at least it was warm. Instead of the usual hole in the middle of the floor, there was an iron stove and a good supply of logs. Anna turned to Severyn.

'Thank you for saving me out there,' she smiled. 'I would have been trampled underfoot by the frenzied mob if you hadn't come to my rescue.' He smiled in return.

'Let's spread out coats and blankets and try to sleep,' he said. Anna counted thirty people in the truck as she curled up to sleep. Then, huddled close to Yurek and Severyn, head on her bundle, she was asleep before the train left the station.

They arrived at Novosibirsk at 9am. It was a modern, clean station with a friendly, helpful Station Master.

'Don't walk the four kilometres into Novosibirsk town,' he advised. 'A train going to Semipalatinsk, which is in the direction you want, leaves in five hours. If you miss that, you'll have to wait four days and travelling's getting more difficult all the time.'

'What about travel documents and food?' asked Severyn.

'As you are soldiers, you can eat in the station canteen free and I'll give you the appropriate documents.'

It all seemed too good to be true but they tidied themselves as well as they could and washed hands and faces. Then they walked into the warmth of the spotless dining hall. Behind a long counter, stood four women in white aprons, presiding over an array of steaming cauldrons. Severyn gave the first woman the note from the Station Master and she gave him a menu. Years later, Anna could repeat that menu. It seemed to glitter in Severyn's hand, the black print dancing before her eyes.

'Rice with milk
Noodles with milk
Fish soup
Sauerkraut soup with meat
Sour cucumber soup with meat
Buckwheat kasha with dripping'

They stared at the list for a long time, marvelling at such wonders.

'Lady and gentlemen,' Yurek said, at last, 'Please make up your minds what to order before I die of starvation. Anna?'

'I just can't choose,' she answered. 'What about everyone else?'

'Why choose, then?' said Novak. 'Let's have everything!'

So they approached the counter and each of them ordered every item on the menu. The food had to be spread over two large tables and, using their wooden prison spoons, they consumed every morsel of the magnificent feast. It took them three hours.

Anna could hardly move when she had finished.

'It'll be worth the indigestion,' she laughed as she picked up her bundle.

Sated, warm and sleepy they thanked the women behind the counter.

'Congratulations,' said Anna. 'Every dish on the menu was delicious.' Surprised and pleased by the praise, the manageress pointed to a store behind the dining room.

'If you knock on the door, the storeman will issue you with dry rations for the journey,' she said.

Anna, Novak, Yurek and Zenek volunteered to go. The elderly storeman handed them portions of millet, flour, oatmeal, sugar, haricot beans, pork fat and tchay briquettes. He gave Novak a sack of potatoes and Anna two large round loaves to be shared.

'You've been prisoners of war, eh?' he asked. When Anna nodded, he added an extra packet of sugar to the groceries. 'Wish I could give you more,' he said softly 'but everything has to be accounted for.'

They thanked him warmly and he laid a hand on Anna's shoulder.

'I envy you, lad,' he said. 'How I'd love to be young enough to fight the filthy Germantzy. I'd willingly give my life for my country.'

'I'm not a boy,' Anna replied, 'but I feel exactly as you do, dyadya/uncle.'

'That's the spirit,' he laughed and, taking a tin box from a shelf, stuffed a dozen small, hard honey biscuits into her pockets. Then the old man shook hands with them and wished them a safe journey.

Later they repacked their bundles and sat in the waiting room to await the train. Once their documents had been examined, they were told they would share a truck with some young Soviet army recruits travelling to Semipalatinsk. The men were young, eager and merry with beer.

'Annechka, I think it best if you masquerade as a boy in this company,' whispered Severyn. 'Tuck your hair away. Try not to speak. We'll pretend you've got earache.' Anna obeyed as the train arrived. This time, they had a truck specially reserved for them so there was no scramble. The soldiers brewed some tea on the central stove. They shared it with the Polish group. It was sweet, delicious and liberally laced with vodka.

Once more, Anna fell asleep before the train left the station.

When she woke in the morning, the train was stationary. Anna sat up.

'Where are we?' She asked blearily.

'Toilet stop,' answered Severyn. 'As there aren't any on the train, we'll be stopping regularly and making do with bushes by the track. Off you go. I'll screen you with my coat.'

As day followed day, the atmosphere in the truck became more and more genial. Discovering the Poles were also on their way to join an army, the Soviet recruits insisted on sharing their ample rations with them, saying,

'Save yours for later.' One of them had a battered accordion and there was much noisy singing of Russian and Polish songs. To her disappointment, Anna could take no part in the jollities as she kept up her pretence of being a boy with severe earache and had to stay quietly in a corner.

On 27th September, they arrived at the heaving, noisy station of Semipalatinsk and said 'goodbye' to the soldiers. Anna looked round at a different sort of crowd. Here were Tartars and Kazakha, with flat Mongolian features, colourful, quilted kaftans and tiny embroidered skullcaps. The language spoken was strange to her.

'It's Turkic,' explained Severyn.

The Station Master refused to help them.

'I can't give you travel permits. You must report to the Voyenkommat' he grumbled.

Shouldering their bundles the group walked into town. The icy wind blew dust and dirty leaves into their faces.

'Wait here,' instructed Severyn, indicating a small patch of sooty lawn outside the Voyenkommat. 'Zenek and I will go in and we'll be as quick as we can.'

Three hours later, they returned to the group, each one of which was shivering and numb. Severyn was angry and frustrated.

'We'll have to go back to the station to sleep tonight,' he reported. 'At first, the officials in there denied all knowledge of a Polish army. Then we were sent from one office to another and, finally, were promised travel permits for everyone tomorrow. No-one was concerned that we have nowhere to sleep tonight.'

Dispirited, they returned to the large hall in the station. Cold and hungry as she was, Anna dropped off to sleep, to be awakened at midnight by a militiaman, demanding to see her documents. When he had looked at everyone's papers, he shook his head.

'These permits, issued by a Major Kondrashkin aren't valid. You haven't got train tickets so get out of the station now, all of you. Don't come back without the correct documentation.'

There was nothing for it. They had to walk the streets of Semipalatinsk all night.

At 8am they reported to the Voyenkommat. Different officials were on duty and no-one knew anything about the promised passes. Once more, they were sent from office to office, kept waiting in draughty corridors and ignored for hours. Finally, at 4pm the passes were produced and, weak with cold and hunger, they returned to the station.

The train to Tashkent wouldn't leave until 3pm the next day but this time they had a pass for the canteen and for dry rations for the journey – and they could stay in the relative warmth of the station hall.

The next morning, after a breakfast of porridge and tchay, all the men except Severyn decided to visit the town.

'I don't advise it,' Severyn said. 'Let's wait here, safely, together and get on the train as soon as we can.'

'Severyn, we've done nothing but wait and sit around for days,' objected Novak. 'Surely it'll be OK to walk about the town for a bit this morning. We'll be back by midday.'

Severyn looked unhappy but nodded and the men disappeared.

'Are you bearing up, Annechka?' he asked kindly, when they were alone in the station hall. 'You're certainly not one to complain.'

'I wouldn't dare!' she laughed. 'I'm fine but sometimes do get very homesick. I've no idea, of course, what is happening to my mother, father, brother and sisters. But that's the same for all of us.'

'It is,' Severyn sighed, 'I'm desperately anxious about my wife and Konrad, my little son. Also my elderly mother – they all live together in Warsaw.' His voice shook as he spoke. Then, as he and Anna spoke quietly about their experiences and about the friends they had lost, she began to understand him better. In her heart, she forgave him for his occasional brusqueness. He had willingly taken on the responsibility for the safety of many people, never letting his personal fear and despair interfere with his duty.

At midday, Yurek, Zenek and two others of the group arrived back.

'The others probably went straight to the canteen,' Yurek said. 'Come on, I'm starving.'

They found Novak already eating.

'The other three wanted an extra hour in town,' he explained. 'I'm sure they won't be long'.

By 2pm, it was time to get on to the train and everyone was worried.

'I'll stay in the hall and rush them on to the platform as soon as they get here,' said Yurek.

'Don't wait for more than half an hour,' ordered Severyn angrily. Then, as they went towards the train, 'I should never have let them go, From now on if any of you go off on your own, we won't search or wait for you if we have to make a hasty exit. You'll be on your own.'

They managed to secure a corner in the wagon directly behind the engine and waited anxiously. Just before 3 o'clock, Anna who was looking out, shouted,

'Here's Yurek!' They dragged him into the truck just before the guard slammed shut the door.

'No sign of them, I'm afraid,' he panted. Severyn looked grim but said nothing.

Once more, monotonous day followed monotonous day as they journeyed south. They stopped regularly and replenished their supplies whenever they could. The weather became warmer and Anna felt her spirits lifting.

On 3rd October, after the train had been travelling over a dry, treeless steppe for hours it ran alongside a huge lake. To the east they saw the Torbagatey Mountains. Two hours later, they stopped in a siding at a place called Aktogay.

A guard opened the door and called, 'We're stopping here for the night for some urgent repairs to be carried out on the engine.'

'Who wants to explore the town?' asked Severyn.

They passed women and children selling sunflower seeds, pungent home-grown tobacco, hard dry goat's cheese and fermented milk. Anna's fingers itched to draw the stall-holders, in their rainbow clothes. In the main street, they found a tchaikhana/tea shop, serving real tea.

'Can we treat ourselves, do you think?' begged Anna and everyone nodded. They sat under a striped awning and were served with tea, poured from a china teapot into small porcelain bowls. All around was the soft murmur, not of Russian but of a strange tongue, Anna had never heard before. She leaned back, letting the comfort and warmth flow through her.

'How wonderful to feel like an ordinary person,' she sighed, contentedly. They spent a relaxed hour sipping tea and eating raisins and dried apricots and returned to the station, much refreshed, at about 4pm.

Severyn went to see the Station Master about breakfast for the next morning and Anna said to the others, 'You go on to the train. I'll have a wash and then join you. I haven't had a proper wash for almost a week. I'm filthy and feel disgusting.'

'That's all you ladies think about – keeping clean,' Yurek laughed. 'I'll come with you and wait outside the ladies toilets for you.'

'I wouldn't hear of it, Yurek,' Anna protested. 'I'll be fine. I won't be more than half an hour.'

'Are you sure?' he persisted. 'Severyn would want me to stay with you.'

'He wouldn't mind my going for a little wash on my own, I'm sure,' and before he could argue further, she had slipped away into the crowd on the platform.

She filled her largest can with hot water and took her place in the queue outside the toilet.

It took her longer than she had anticipated to reach her goal of a dirty, cracked wash basin. She took about fifteen minutes to wash. Darkness had fallen by the time she was making her way back to the train.

'Severyn will be annoyed with me,' she thought as she crossed the main line, in front of the northbound locomotive, to the siding. Then she froze, unable to believe her eyes. The siding was empty.

Sick with fright, she rushed back across the line and along the platform, searching, in vain, for a familiar face.

'How could you leave me behind, Severyn?' she cried aloud. 'How could you?' At last she stopped, convinced now, that the train, carrying her friends, had left without her. Sobbing, she realised, with mounting terror what had happened. Severyn must have been told of the change of plan and hurried back to the truck. By then it would have been dark and the others were probably already asleep, huddled together as usual. Severyn would have no idea that one of their number had ignored his warning and was missing. He wouldn't find out until the next morning.

Anna was on the verge of panic when there was a hiss of steam from an engine, a shrill whistle and the sound of wheels on the track. The northbound train was moving off. The platform was deserted, except for three railway workers and half a dozen militiamen. She stepped back into the recess of a building, realising that if she were caught without documents, she would be handed over, immediately, to the Authorities. She stood still, shivering until the voices on the platform subsided. Then cautiously, she felt her way along two walls of the building until she was at the back of it, in a narrow space between it and the fence. There, she ate a little bread, wrapped herself in her thin blanket and lay down.

The night seemed endless. At first, she allowed herself to cry and to wallow in despair. Gradually, though, she began to think rationally.

'I won't give up,' she told herself sternly. 'I've come this far and I *will* join up with the army. It's my fault I'm in this position but there's no point in weeping and wailing. I have some bread, tchay and millet. I can easily survive for a couple of days. The most important thing is *not* to get caught. I have to stay out of sight until another southbound train arrives – and – I must change my appearance. I still look like a convict.' She dozed fitfully and woke when she heard voices on the platform. She was stiff with cold and desperate for food and a hot drink but before she allowed herself to mingle with the crowd, she set about making herself look as different as her limited resources allowed.

She hid her cap in her bundle, plaited her hair and took a reasonably clean piece of linen out, which she tied, as a kerchief, round her head. She tied a spare foot-wrapping round her neck as a scarf and tucked it into her quilted jacket. The only give away now were the rubber tyre moccasins, almost always worn by convicts. Anna remembered, wryly, the elegant shoes she still had in her bundle. She'd try to sell them as soon as possible and use the money to buy felt boots.

Anna emerged on to the platform, which was even more crowded than on the previous day. She sat down on the edge of one of the Russian-speaking groups of women and children, trying to be as inconspicuous as possible while finding out whether a southbound train was due that day. She gathered that no such train was due for two days and that these people had already been travelling for many weeks away from the horrors of war.

Painfully hungry and longing for a hot drink, she joined the queue for hot water and fifteen minutes later was sitting amongst the Russian refugees, dipping some of her remaining dried bread into tchay.

The day dragged by. Anna took shelter in the hall but, as night fell, she crept back to her refuge of the previous night. Once more she curled up in the darkest corner and eventually fell asleep.

It was still night when she was awakened by an uproar from the station. For a moment, she couldn't remember why she was lying on rough ground in the open. Then she heard the unmistakeable rumble of wheels on railway track and, a few seconds later pandemonium. Without wasting a moment, she wrapped her blanket round her bundle and rushed on to the platform, just in time to see a freight train grind to a halt, amidst steam, smoke and sparks. Anna joined the screaming mob, pushing towards the trucks. She saw that they were, in fact, already full and that the current passengers were trying to pull the doors shut against the invading hoards. This was to no avail and they gave up, after a short struggle. They were pushed inwards by the surging tide of newcomers as they scrambled on to the train.

Struck with terror lest she would be left behind, Anna dived into the crowd, frantically clutching her bundle in on hand and trying, in vain, to grab the doorjamb with the other. Again and again she lunged for and missed the jamb, trying desperately to stay on her feet. She knew that if she fell, she would be trampled underfoot or shoved under the wheels of the train. In her despair, she heard herself crying, as if from a long way off,

'Mama! Mama, save me!'

Two strong hands lifted her off the ground and she found herself inside the truck, sprawled on top of a squirming mass of humanity. She never discovered who had saved her but she knew that, without his help, she would have perished that night.

When Anna finally managed to stand, still clutching her bundle, she found herself looking into the kind face of an elderly Russian woman.

'Try to follow me to the corner of the truck,' the woman said. My friend and I have secured a small space. You are welcome to share it with us.'

Gratefully, Anna pushed her way in the direction indicated and sank down between the two friends. Suddenly she felt hot and feverish. There was a loud rushing in her ears. She tried to thank the women but found no words. Then she lost consciousness.

Anna was to remember little of the four day journey to Alma Ata, the capital of Kazakhstan. She developed a high temperature, slipping in and out of consciousness.

She was aware of the overheated, overcrowded truck, of the women offering her water and placing her bundle close to her when she cried out that someone had stolen it. On the fourth day she felt better and was able to sit up, drink some tchay, eat a small piece of bread and thank her two kindly companions.

'Whenever I am on the point of death, someone is sent to save me,' she said. Looking round to make sure no-one was listening. One of the women whispered.

'It is God who is keeping you. May you continue to be blessed by him.' Furtively, she crossed herself and her friend and Anna followed suit.

The next morning, the train stopped at Alma Ata.

'Everyone out!' came the order. 'Train goes no further.'

In the scramble for the platform, Anna lost her two friends and never saw them again. Once more, she was alone. She was still weak and dizzy but determined to continue her journey south to join the army. There was no sign of a southbound train and she noticed militiamen, on the crowded platforms, examining people's travel passes.

'I'll just have to manage without a hot drink,' she thought. 'I can't risk going on the platform.'

She found a sheltered spot but the temperature was dropping and a cold wind penetrated her clothes. She noticed, on one of the lines, a row of strange trucks. A large box took up most of the flat surface of each but attached to the side of the box was a small sentry box. The boxes, which had grills, were covered in a thin layer of ice. Anna thought they must contain a chemical substance. She realised that an engine was slowly backing towards this odd train.

'It's going to travel south east,' she whispered to herself. 'The way I want to go! Once it's moving, I'll jump on.'

She waited for the coupling of the engine, stood up and slowly, with a nonchalance she didn't feel, wandered towards the train. She saw the crew get in and heard the steam blast that brought the engine to life. Enveloped in a cloud of smoke as the train lumbered past, she was invisible to the crew. She waited for the last truck, sprinted forwards and managed to hook her hands round the ladder, which was attached to its side. Gripping it desperately, she found a foothold on the bottom rung and started to climb. Her bundle, which was tied to her arm, hampered her but she went doggedly on towards her goal, the sentry box. With horror, she realised the rungs were covered in ice. Her clumsy boots slipped and the palms of her hands stuck to the metal. When she reached the top, her hands were raw and she was trembling from the exertion. The train was gathering speed. She stopped to rest for a few moments and then looked up, ready to climb on to the platform in front of the sentry box. She almost fell off when she saw a man, in a sheepskin coat and hat glaring down at her. She couldn't hear what he was shouting but his face and attitude were hostile. Frantic with terror, she clung on and shouted, 'Help me, please help me!'

He took a step forward and slowly, with deliberation, he stamped on her fingers, leant over and pushed her off the ladder.

With a scream, she catapulted through the air.

'This is it, then,' is all she had time to think before she hit the ground with a sickening thud.

She lay there, not trying to move at first. It was getting dark and she could see the station lights. She could feel pain in every part of her.

'What's broken?' she wondered. 'Back, leg, arm?' She felt the cold seeping through her clothes and knew she must try to move. Slowly, she rolled on to her side and sat up. She moved her arms and then her legs – no bones broken there. She forced herself to stand. She was sore all over and every breath she took caused pain so bad it made her dizzy.

'I must get to the platform for help or die,' she told herself. Miraculously, her bundle, was still attached to her arm. Staggering, falling over railway lines, she half shambled, half crawled to the platform. She could see families dozing by their luggage. She reached the first group and collapsed.

Helping hands lifted her and placed her carefully on to a sheepskin. Someone covered her with a woven blanket. Someone else poured some vodka into her mouth, which almost choked her. A third person washed her face with warm water and dried it gently. All the time, Anna could hear anxious whispering but she couldn't make out any of the words. Slowly, she drifted into oblivion.

When she opened her eyes, dawn was breaking. She was still on the sheepskin. She tried flexing each part of her body. She was sore but less so than last evening and felt much refreshed from a warm night's sleep.

Anna sat up. She was surrounded by a small group of friendly, smiling people. There were men and women, in colourful quilted khalats/robes. They had flat, Oriental faces and slanting, black eyes and spoke in a language she didn't know. A young woman crouched down and offered her a bowl of delicious hot broth, which Anna drank, to the accompaniment of encouraging nods and smiles from all around. When she had finished it, a warmth and feeling of well-being filled her. She said, in Polish,

'I thank you all, from the bottom of my heart for what you have done for me. I have no way of repaying your kindness but please take my last few roubles in return.' She stood up carefully, fished the money from her pocket and held it out to the young woman who smiled more broadly but shook her head.

Suddenly Anna spotted a militiaman close by. She froze as he pointed at her and said, irritably, 'Are you from the Polish transport to Tashkent? I can't understand you people. You were warned not to stray far from the train but you never listen. Get a move on. Your train leaves in fifteen minutes.' He strode away without another word.

Anna was stunned by this sudden change in her luck. Turning, she saw the train, ready to leave. She bade a hasty and grateful farewell to her bewildered rescuers and limped as fast as she could across the line to the waiting train. Many people were already sitting inside the cattle trucks but there were still a few on the platform – and everyone was speaking Polish. An elderly, energetic looking man was talking to a railway official and directing people on to the trucks. He seemed to be in charge. Anna waited for him to finish his conversation with the official. Then she approached him.

'I'm sorry to bother you,' she began 'but I am stranded here on my own.' Briefly she told him her story, finishing with, 'I'll show you my release documents if you like. Please, please let me come to Tashkent with you. If you leave me here, I'm likely to be re-arrested for travelling on my own without a pass. I could well be accused of carrying false papers and of being a fifth columnist. Please help me.'

'Get into the truck at once,' he replied sharply. 'Militiamen are watching and it would look suspicious if I examined your papers.' He helped her up into the nearest truck and she found herself, once more, amongst her own people.

CHAPTER 14

Between the Devil and the Aral Sea

As the passengers disembarked, wearily, from the trucks at Tashkent, their spirits were lifted by the unexpected sound of a Russian military band, playing a medley of Polish tunes. They were further cheered by freshly baked white bread and rich stew, served in the canteen. Anna saw Captain May, the officer she had spoken to in Alma Ata. She decided now was the time to secure her future travel arrangements.

'Excuse me Sir,' she said. 'I wish to join this military transport officially now. Is it possible, please, for you to issue the necessary permit so that I am no longer an illegal traveller?' The captain smiled as he recognised her.

'Actually, I have the pass here for you, right now. I don't like being responsible for "illegals." I was on the lookout for you. Please fill in your personal details on both of these forms. I'll keep one, you keep the other.'

Elated, Anna complied.

'Thank you very much indeed,' she said. 'May I ask you a couple of questions, please?'

'If you're quick, young lady. I've some other people to see before we leave.'

'Are you able to tell me our final destination?' Anna asked.

'We've just received a telegram from the Polish Embassy, delivered by an NKVD officer,' he replied. 'We're directed to make for Chardzhouy, on the Amu Dar'ya River, in the Turkmen Republic. That's the area to which all Polish army personnel will be sent, in due course. What else do you want to know?'

'I wondered if there were any way I could find out what has happened to Captain Severyn S... He's the officer I was travelling with originally. He's in the Polish Air Force.'

'I can't help you there, I'm afraid,' answered Captain May. 'All I can tell you is that if he reached one of the recruiting centres in time, he will have been sent to Great Britain for further training and will operate as an Air Force officer from there.'

'Thank you so much for helping me and for the information,' Anna said. She returned to the truck encouraged by the conversation.

On 8th October, the train arrived at Farab, a river port on Amu Dar'ya, on the bank opposite Charzhouy. Everyone squeezed into the main port building, waiting for further instructions. Some NKVD officers appeared and spoke to the Polish officers. Standing on tiptoe, Anna could see that there was some sort of argument between the two groups of men. Finally the NKVD members withdrew and Captain May addressed his people.

'Bad news, I'm afraid. The Soviets say there is neither food nor adequate accommodation for us in Chardzhouy or here. They have ordered us to travel, by barge, five hundred kilometres downriver to a place called Nukus, which is the capital of the Kara-Kalpak Republic. We have refused to move until we get orders from our own Command. Therefore we'll be staying here until telegrams can be exchanged. There should be room for women and children to sleep in here. Men will camp outside.'

As he finished speaking, an NKVD officer appeared and spoke briskly to him. The other Polish commandant came over and an argument ensued. Anna couldn't hear what was being said but two more NKVD officers arrived and the discussion became more heated. Finally, Captain May turned to the crowded room and spoke.

'The Soviet Authorities, in their wisdom, have cancelled distribution of all food rations until we agree to move to Nukus. We've sent word to our high command and await instructions from them. We can't change our plans without their permission. I'm sorry about this. There are some dry rations left over from what we were allowed on the train. These will be distributed. Please let me know if your position becomes desperate. I'll inform you as soon as we have news.'

Eight days later, on 16th October, word came from the Polish

Authorities, that Anna's group should comply with the Soviet order immediately.

'Just as well,' Anna commented to Marta, who had been occupying the neighbouring space on the floor. 'The food's run out. At least, we'll get rations for the journey.'

These consisted of 800 grams of bread, a few spoons full of sugar, one salted herring, a small piece of pork fat and 500 grams of uncooked millet.

'Make this last,' they were told. 'No more food will be issued during the voyage.'

More and more groups of Polish people had been arriving, over the last few days. A harassed Captain May told Anna that he was now in charge of about four thousand people.

During that day, five biskirs/small river tugs arrived, each towing three large, open, iron barges. Anna and Marta, clutching their bundles, lined up to get on one of these.

Conditions on board were appalling even before the journey started. No benches had been provided. The rusty sides of the barge were running with water and pools of stagnant water had gathered on its floor so that within half an hour, Anna's clothes were damp and slimy.

'We can't sit or lie down in this rust bucket,' complained Marta. 'If we do either we'll be soaked through in a moment.'

The barge began to move and Anna said, as cheerfully as she could, 'Off we go. One more journey started. At least we're one step nearer the end of our seemingly endless search for the elusive Polish Army.'

Anna spent most of the journey standing. She felt most sorry for mothers of small children who, weak, hungry and suffering from diarrhoea, whimpered continually. She felt pity, too, for the elderly, many of whom looked more dead than alive. Because of the uneven nature of the river bed, with its unexpected sandbanks, the barges could travel only during the day.

After sunset, the passengers left the boat and made camps by the river's edge. There, they lit fires, dried clothes, cooked the millet and made hot tchay. Thick dry rushes, which were used on the fires, lined the riverbank. Beyond these lay the desert sands.

'Don't wander far from your fire,' they were warned. 'Wild boar and tigers roam close by.' As the rushes burned quickly, everyone took turns to 'firewatch' throughout the nights, which were very cold.

On the third day, they stopped at the ancient city of Turktul. A woman had set up a tea stall nearby. Anna and Marta each bought a bowl of the fragrant, hot liquid and, noticing thick slices of sweetmeat for sale, asked what they were. They gathered they were long strips of melon, dried and plaited. Unable to resist such luxury, they spent some of their remaining money on a strip each.

'Delicious,' murmured Anna as she chewed hers on the way back to the boat. 'It's sweet and chewy and like honey.'

That night, she developed excruciating toothache. The next morning, one side of her face was balloon-like, on fire and throbbing.

'I'll never eat anything sweet again,' she moaned.

On the fifth day, they reached the Port of Nukus. Although her toothache had abated, Anna felt sick with cold as the icy wind penetrated her clothes. Somehow, she and Marta became separated as the hundred and fifty passengers streamed on to land. It was late afternoon. Some people started walking towards a nearby fishing village, which they were told was a kilometre away. Others stood around, waiting for orders from someone. Anna couldn't see Marta. When she heard a man say that the Polish Commandant and lorries were in the village, she decided to walk there, rather than freeze on the riverbank.

The temperature had dropped to about zero. A gale was raising clouds of dust and pieces of dried desert bushes around Anna's head. She became even colder as she laboured in the direction of the village. Two figures appeared from behind her – two men, dressed in prison clothes. Anna forced her numb lips to form the desperate words, 'Can you help me, please? Do you know where the Polish

Commandants are? I'm at the end of my tether. I must find help soon or I think I'll simply drop down and die.'

'Good Heavens, it's a girl!' exclaimed one of the men, as he took her arm. 'We've been trying to find someone in authority without success so, for the moment, we're just going to look for a teashop in the village. We're cold and hungry and will be no good to anyone until we've had food and drink.'

'Come with us,' insisted the other. 'You look as if you need food even more than we do.'

Unable to resist, Anna walked with them to the edge of the village, where they found an eating-house in a little clay hut. An elderly crone, wrapped in layers of quilted clothing, sat grimly behind a counter. She spoke in broken Russian.

'The only food I can offer you is tzingotnoye/raw shredded cabbage.'

'Could we have some hot tchay, please,' begged Anna.

'No tea, only vodka,' was the reply. Anna turned to the men.

'There must be somewhere else we could go. I can't face tzingotnoye and I never drink vodka.'

'Come on, just take a couple of sips,' urged one of the men. 'It'll give you the strength to go on.'

Anna complied. Afterwards, she remembered drinking one mouthful from a not too clean glass and then... nothing.

When Anna opened her eyes, she was lying on a quilt on the floor of a tiny room. Three women stood round her and one was kneeling on the floor at her side, massaging her left hand.

'She's waking up. Thank God,' she said, in Polish. 'Bring her a cup of soup. Are you feeling better my dear?' Anna nodded and sat up, her head thumping. A cup of thin broth was handed to her.

'Thank you very much,' she managed.

'My name's Wanda Puchalska,' the woman said. 'You poor thing – the men who brought you here found you unconscious in the street.' Anna smiled, inwardly, at the story the Polish men had told. She decided not to contradict it.

'Now try to rest, my dear. Later we can swap our stories of how we've ended up in this God-forsaken place.' Anna finished the broth and then she lay back on the quilt and fell asleep.

The next day, Anna learned that a considerable number of Polish people were billeted around the village. The little room in which Mrs Pulchalska and her three friends lived, was in fact, the projector room in the local cinema. Many Polish families lived in the main hall, itself. Mrs Pulchalska was an opera singer, married to a Polish army officer. She had no idea where he was or even if he were still alive. A year ago she had been exiled to her current abode.

In spite of the kindness she was shown over the next couple of days, Anna felt awkward and painfully aware that her presence made the small room even more overcrowded. Also, although she made efforts to rid herself of lice, there was no soap or disinfectant to be had and her appearance was ragged and dirty.

She tried, in vain, to contact Captain May or the other commandant, Captain Nieczuya. She discovered that they had both been sent back to Farab to deal with recruitment for the Polish army and with the welfare of the many Poles there. As soon as the two officers left, the Soviet Authorities had issued orders that all resident Poles should find employment.

In despair and feeling she must try to pay her way, Anna laid out her few belongings. She thought she'd try to sell her sister's shoes and nightdress and then she came across the soldering iron. She remembered the strips of solder she'd sewn into the lining of her trousers.

'My salvation!' she exclaimed aloud. 'You can't buy pots and pans anywhere at the moment, can you?' she said to Mrs Puchalska. 'Lots of people will want theirs repaired.'

This proved to be the case.

She knocked timidly at a back door.

'Go away!' shouted an irate woman. 'No beggars.'

'I'm not begging,' responded Anna. 'I mend pots and pans. Have you any which need mending?' The woman's attitude changed.

'Come in, come in. I'm sorry I misjudged you.' Anna mended a large enamel kettle and a selection of leaking pans. The woman gave her some tchay and a bowl of tasty stew.

'Try next door,' she suggested. 'I'm sure my neighbour will have work for you.'

By the end of the day, Anna had earned enough to invite her friends to supper.

During the next week, she soldered scores of kitchen utensils and was paid well in cash and in goods. Mrs Puchalska patched her clothes with scraps of cloth she was given and Anna shared all food with the little household. One evening, Mrs Puchalska spoke seriously to her.

'Annechka, we've found employment in Nukus, at the cotton processing factory. There's hostel accommodation and a canteen. We'll be warm and secure for the winter and should be able to save some money. We'd like you come with us.'

Anna was silent for a moment. Her heart sank at the idea of even more time lost. She made a sudden decision.

'Thank you very much for your offer. I wish you well but I can't come with you. I want to go back to Farab now the army is assembling there. I should be able to get transport from there to join our troops. I've almost enough money for the boat trip and for food to eat on the journey. I'm so grateful to you for letting me stay here. I'll never forget you.'

'But you haven't got travel documents,' Mrs Puchalska protested. 'Please don't risk it. Wait until the Polish Envoy comes. Come with us and stay safe.'

But Anna would not be persuaded and two days later, she bade her friends a tearful farewell as they left.

Once more, she spread all her worldly possessions in front of her. She had one small kerchief, a strip of solder, the soldering iron, a few rusty nails, a short length of thin wire, some string, a little dry bread, her precious crayon stumps, two cans with wire handles, a wooden spoon, fifty nine roubles and a Polish coin of silver, a two zloty piece, given by Mrs Puchalska, as a memento.

'It's not much but it'll have to do,' she told herself. 'At least my clothes are fairly clean and the holes have been patched and I have good boots. I'll be fine.' This she repeated to herself again and again as she prepared to spend her last night in the little projector room, alone.

A tumultuous noise hit Anna as she approached the booking hall at the port. Inside, it was heaving with would-be passengers, most of them locals, though she noticed a few Russians among them. Stacks of crates and baskets littered the floor. An unruly queue had formed outside the closed ticket office. Men pushed, swore and shouted while the women and children looked after the luggage. Anna took her place at the end of the queue noting, with relief that there were no militiamen in evidence.

Suddenly the booking hatch was thrown open and the angry face of an Uzbec woman appeared. The queue swayed then erupted forward. Anna knew she must take drastic action or lose all chance of gaining a ticket.

Clutching her fare in her hand, she dived into the thickest part of the crowd. She was so desperate that she hardly noticed the kicking and pummelling. Several times she was lifted off her feet and carried forwards. Twice she grabbed and held on to the person next to her to prevent herself from being trampled underfoot.

Miraculously, she found herself in front of the ticket office. From behind and beside her, she was aware of large hands, waving bank notes but the woman was looking at her.

'What do you want?' she shouted angrily.

'One deck ticket to Farab, please,' Anna shouted back as she threw the fifty seven roubles on to the sill.

The woman handed Anna the ticket and shouted something else which Anna couldn't hear for she was pushed from her place, by a large man and then borne away by the mass.

'Just as well,' she thought, jubilant as her hold tightened on her ticket. 'She was probably asking for my travel permit.'

On board, Anna found a space near the wall of the engine room and, hoping it would afford shelter, settled down to await departure, worried that militiamen might appear.

At noon, the gangplank was removed and her journey began. With the relief of being on the way, came exhaustion. She slept until late afternoon. When she awoke, she was hungry and thirsty. The crew was tying up the boat and everyone disembarked to cook supper and camp for the night.

Anna collected a few rushes and, borrowing some embers from her neighbour's fire, lit her own and supped on warm river water, into which she crumbled some dry bread. She hadn't the energy to collect enough fuel to keep a fire burning all night so she returned to her place in the boat to sleep.

By the end of the fourth day, Anna had eaten all her bread. She didn't bother to leave the boat that evening. Strangely, she didn't feel hungry or thirsty – just tired beyond belief. Her body was numb with cold and her brain was numb too. She simply felt that death was near and that she didn't mind.

On the fifth morning, she was awakened by a tapping on her shoulder. With an enormous effort, she opened her eyes to see a very young Uzbec woman crouching at her side.

'Apa, apa,/Sister, sister,' she was calling in a high child-like voice. Anna saw she was holding a painted bowl and spoon out to her. Anna forced herself to sit up. Laughing delightedly, the girl handed her the bowl, which was full of rich onion soup. Embarrassment and gratitude, in equal measure, swept over Anna. Blinded by tears, she clutched the bowl. The girl spoke softly in her native tongue, caressing Anna's cheek with a small hand. Then she lifted a spoonful of soup to Anna's lips and smiled broadly when she drank it.

'Thank you,' Anna said, in Polish, and took the spoon. After such a long fast, she couldn't manage to take much soup. The girl seemed to understand and left the bowl with her, walking towards the skipper's cabin and looking back at Anna several times.

She returned that afternoon, carrying a bowl of rice and meat pilau. She sat next to Anna, urging her to eat and giggling when Anna tried to thank her and apologise for not being able to speak Uzbec. For the first time, Anna was able to look at the young woman properly. She had beautiful Oriental features with a tiny filigree ornament fixed in one nostril. She wore colourful quilted clothing and a little embroidered skull cap. Her black, lustrous hair was plaited into a dozen braids. Golden bracelets jangled on her wrists and necklaces of coins swung at her neck.

'Just like an illustration from 'The Arabian Nights,'' Anna thought.

When the boat stopped for the night, the Uzbec girl reappeared. She took Anna by the hand and pulled her towards the skipper's quarters. Inside the cabin, an elderly Uzbec was sitting on a bunk, which was piled high with quilts and cushions. He didn't look too pleased to see Anna, who hesitated in the doorway.

The girl ran to him, pigtails flying. She flung her arms round his neck and started to talk to him, with animation. The old skipper listened for a moment then, as if under a spell, smiled over the girl's shoulder and motioned Anna into the cabin. He spoke in heavily accented Russian.

'Please come in and drink tea with us. My wife and I are pleased to welcome you.'

'His wife?' Anna was incredulous. 'There must be at least forty years difference in their ages.' She smiled back at the skipper and thanked him warmly.

The real tea was delicious. As they sipped, Anna learned that the couple were returning to their winter quarters in Farab. The girl seemed very happy and fond of her elderly husband and he was obviously bewitched by his vivacious bride. They wanted to hear her story and were amazed to hear of her adventures and could not understand her wish to join the army.

'Come and spend the winter with us,' they urged.

When it was time to retire for the night, Anna rose to go, thanking the couple, warmly, for their hospitality.

'No, no,' protested the skipper. 'We want you to stay here, with us, in the warm.'

The girl handed her two warm quilts and lay some cushions beside the double bunk.

They would brook no argument, so Anna snuggled gratefully under the quilts although she was a little embarrassed at her proximity to the married couple.

For Anna, the rest of the voyage passed as if in a wonderful dream. During the day, while the skipper was in the wheelhouse, she and the Uzbec girl sat in the cabin. Anna tried to teach the young wife to speak Russian but her attempts usually ended in fits of laughter. The girl played hostess, producing bowls of delicious food with a graceful flourish. Several times, Anna saw the skipper watching them through the window. He seemed delighted that his wife was enjoying herself so much. Each night, Anna slept in the cabin. Each day she grew stronger.

She desperately wanted to show her appreciation to the kind pair. She suddenly remembered the Polish coin, given to her by Mrs Puchalska. Loathe as she was to part with it, she had nothing else to give. Waiting until the girl was busy cooking, she slipped into the engine room and begged the mechanic to pierce a small hole near the rim of the coin. She made a hook out of a piece of wire and at the final meal together, she presented her hostess with the gift. The girl squeaked and clapped with delight and, flinging her arms round Anna's neck, cried, 'Apa, apa.'

Once more, the skipper tried to persuade Anna of the recklessness of her plan and his little wife wept at the prospect of losing her friend.

The boat reached Farab late that afternoon and Anna took her leave of the Uzbec couple, who had saved her life.

Anxious to find the Polish representative as soon as possible, Anna hurried through the crowded streets around the docks. Refugees, most of them Polish, huddled round little camp fires at the side of the road or in doorways of shops. All looked starving, ragged and cold. No-one Anna asked knew where she could find the Polish representative. Then, by chance, she stumbled upon a cold drinks kiosk. In the doorway, she saw the familiar figure of Captain Nieczuya. He had just locked the kiosk door and was turning to leave.

'Please, Captain Nieczuya, may I speak to you?' Anna spoke timidly. The Officer looked at her and answered in a flat, tired voice.

'Not now. Please come back tomorrow. My office is closed.'

'Sir.' Anna persisted, 'I have just arrived from Nukus. I'm alone and have no money or friends. I'm cold and nervous about being out in the open all night. I apologise for bothering you but I'm in desperate need of help.'

Captain Nieczuya stood silently for a few minutes, staring at Anna, but not seeming to see her. She felt something inside her snap.

'I'm not standing here to be stared at and ignored,' she thought and started walking away, head held high.

'Where do you think you're going?' he called after her sharply. She turned back, but said nothing.

'How do you come to be here?' he asked.

'After I was with your group in Tashkent, I sailed with the other Poles to Nukus. There seemed no chance of joining the Polish forces there so I decided to return, on my own, to Farab.

'I see,' he unlocked the kiosk door. 'I'm afraid this is all I have,' he said and handed Anna a thick slice of stale bread and a tin mug of lukewarm water. 'Now sit there,' indicating the doorstep, 'eat and drink that and then I'll tell you where you can stay. Come back here tomorrow and we'll see what to do with you.'

Anna obeyed, feeling like a beggar, but too hungry and thirsty to object.

She spent the night curled up in the waiting hall of the port building, surrounded by other refugees. In the morning, she had a hot drink, washed and put on clean foot wrappings and scarf and made her way to Captain Nieczuya's office. He and some other officers were talking to groups of Poles outside the kiosk. Anna joined the queue of people waiting for information. When it was her turn, she smiled up at the Captain.

'Thank you very much for the food and for finding me somewhere to sleep last night. While I am waiting for my orders, would it be possible to find temporary work in Farab, do you think? I'll do anything at all. I'm not fussy. I just need to earn enough to buy myself food and, perhaps a cheap lodging.'

The officer looked her over and said, impatiently, 'Can you speak Russian?'

'Yes sir, I can,' she responded, needled by his manner, 'and French and English. I can also write and count.'

His tone softened a little.

'You do realise that this is only a transit point don't you? Polish citizens, arriving from all over the USSR are registered in this office and then transported to whichever destination seems appropriate. At present, all recruitment to the Polish Army has been stopped by the Russians. Until that situation changes, all Poles are being sent to a variety of communal farms and factories, where food and accommodation are provided for them. As a representative of the Polish government, I'm entitled to retain a small group of office personnel. It has to be small and the NKVD are always counting!'

Black disappointment swept over Anna. She felt a sense of hopelessness. At every attempt to join the army, she was thwarted. For a moment, she couldn't speak. Then she took a deep, calming breath and tried to hide her disappointment.

'Thank you, Captain, for explaining things to me. I won't bother you any more. Please tell me which transport I should join and I'll leave immediately.' She turned away abruptly and started to walk away without waiting for an answer. She was afraid she might break down and cry. She was walking disconsolately back towards the port building when a young officer caught up with her.

'Please stop,' he said. 'Captain Nieczuya wishes to speak to you.'

Reluctantly, Anna returned to the kiosk.

'What a hothead you are,' exclaimed the Captain, when he saw her. 'Do you always leave in the middle of a conversation?' Then before Anna could reply, 'I can't promise you a permanent job here but I'd like you to stay and help in the office for the time being. I'll try to persuade the NKVD that you should be a member of my staff.' He turned to the young officer, 'Bring the young lady some food.'

Half an hour later, a space had been cleared at the table of the tiny office and Anna was given a box full of scraps of paper, on which were the names and particulars of refugees recently interviewed by the Captain and his staff. Her task was to compile a list from this information. Then she issued coupons for everyone on the list, entitling each to three meals a day.

Over the next four days, Anna came to realise what an exceptional manager Captain Nieczuya was. He had an uncanny ability for getting what he wanted from the local NKVD officers. He dealt quickly and efficiently with emergencies as they arose. She later discovered his was the only transit point at which refugees were sure of getting three meals a day and dry rations for journeys. Above all, he worked tirelessly for his people and Anna quickly learned to respect him but could not warm to him.

'Are you afraid of corpses?' It was Anna's fifth day in the office and the question came from the Captain.

'No Sir.'

'Then go to the railway embankment with the Lieutenant. That's where the bodies of refugees who have died on the journey here are laid. It will be your job to try to identify them, list their names and organise, with the NKVD, their burial in a communal grave.'

It was heartbreaking work. She and the Lieutenant wept unashamedly at the sight of the many emaciated, half clad bodies. Most pitiful were those of the children, skeletal, shrunken. Anna wanted to scream aloud at the wanton brutality of war. Instead she said a silent prayer over each one.

In that arid, treeless land, there could be no coffins. Instead, the tragic remains were placed side by side in long trenches, dug in the desert sand. The trenches were then covered with quick lime and stones.

It was a sombre Anna who returned to the office a few days later.

It was then that she met Ela Majewska, a young mother of three daughters, who had been granted a temporary permit to stay in Farab because her youngest was ill. Anna and Ela had an immediate rapport. The latter rented a small room in the house of an Uzbec widow and she invited Anna to visit her.

She found the three little girls, Marzenka, Yola and Helenka sitting in a large bed, wrapped in blankets.

'They have to stay there almost all day. I can't get any fuel to heat the room so it's the only way to keep them warm,' explained Ela. Anna spent much of her free time helping Ela with the chores, playing with the children and telling them stories. They reminded her of her nieces.

In the middle of December, Captain Nieczuya was summoned away and the senior Lieutenant was left in charge. Arriving at the office the next day, Anna was surprised to see another woman in her place at the table. The Lieutenant called Anna outside.

'The Captain has given orders that you should be dismissed. You're to join the next transport to a kolkhoz/collective farm.'

Anna, reeling from the shock, found her voice.

'Why? What reason did he give?'

'That's not for me to say. Now please will you go?'

'I can't believe the Captain would ask someone else to give me such a message. I'm certainly not going to leave Farab until I hear from Captain Nieczuya himself, that I'm dismissed.'

With that, she turned abruptly and with angry tears running down her cheeks, she walked away.

She forgot her problem when she arrived at Ela's. Marenka and Helenka were obviously extremely ill. Both were unconscious, burning hot and struggling to breathe.

'Quickly, go for the Polish doctor,' said Anna. 'I'll stay here with the children.'

Ela ran out and Anna made up a separate bed on the floor, in the corner of the room, for Yola, who, although frightened, seemed not to be running a temperature. Anna sang softly to her and she fell asleep.

All she could do for the other two was sponge their faces with cold water and wait.

It was an hour before Ela and the doctor arrived. The doctor examined the children, gave them injections of camphor and promised to return on the morrow. As Anna saw her out of the room, the doctor beckoned her into the yard.

'I don't want to distress the already distraught mother tonight but the girls have both got pneumonia. I'm afraid there's no hope of recovery without proper care and medicine, which just isn't available. I honestly don't think they can last more than one or two days. I'm so very sorry.' With that, she hurried off to visit her next patient.

For the next two days, Anna stayed with Ela. They took turns to sit by the bedside of the sick children. The doctor visited several times, bringing what scanty medication she could lay her hands on.

On the third day, both Marzenka and Helenka regained consciousness and seemed slightly better. Ela was overjoyed and full of hope. Yola sat on her bed, happily playing with an old rag doll. Reassured by all of this, Anna decided to see if Captain Nieczuya had returned.

She met him in the street leading to his office.

'Excuse me, Sir,' Anna said to him. 'I expect you know that while you were away I was dismissed from the office, with absolutely no explanation offered by your Lieutenant. I'm not asking for my job back but I'd be grateful if you could tell me why this happened. I've no money so I must work and don't mind working on a kolkhoz, if necessary. It's just that I can't understand why I was so rudely dismissed.'

Anna paused for breath, her heart beating hard in her chest.

Captain Nieczuya gave her a long look.

'My dear girl,' he answered coldly, 'maybe we'll all be sent to a kolkhoz soon. Who knows? However, my officer was entitled to dismiss you if he deemed it necessary. I certainly don't have to explain his decision to you.'

Then taking a twenty-five rouble banknote from his pocket, he held it out to Anna.'

'I'm afraid this is all I have. Please report to the train early tomorrow morning.'

Anna reddened. She seethed with anger at his reply and his tone but she managed to answer calmly.

'Captain Nieczuya, I'm not a beggar and I don't want your money. I'll leave Farab in my own time, when I'm ready. I hope that one day we'll meet in different circumstances and that by then, you'll have realised that I've been very unfairly treated and will apologise to me.'

Turning her back on the officer, she marched stiffly away, head held high. Part of her felt sorry she'd refused the money.

'But at least he's found out he can't browbeat me,' she thought, with a little spurt of triumph.

When she reached the house where Ela lived, she was met, in the yard, by the Uzbec widow, who was crying and agitated. Anna couldn't understand what the woman was saying and with dreadful foreboding hurried to Ela's room.

On a little bunk, near the window, lay Marzenka, dressed all in white and obviously dying. Her mother knelt on the floor, her arms encircling the child's wasted body.

'Please Marzenka,' she sobbed, 'don't leave us. Don't you want to see your Daddy? He'll come soon. Please stay with us. We all love you so much. Don't close your eyes.'

Anna heard Marzenka's weak whisper, 'Mummy, I'm so tired. I want to sleep…'

Anna rushed to the larger bed, where Helenka lay, flushed and breathing with great difficulty. Her huge black, shiny eyes stared at Anna, unseeingly. A thin rivulet of blood ran from one nostril, staining her ashen cheek. Anna took the little body in her arms and held her close, trying to frame some words of prayer. A few moments later, the laboured breathing ceased, the eyes lost their lustre and the small heart stopped beating.

Ela was still talking to Marzenka but there was no reply.

Suddenly Anna heard a sound from a dark corner of the room. Yola was sitting on a pile of blankets, eyes wide, lips quivering. She stared at Anna, uncomprehendingly, knowing something dreadful had happened. Anna gently closed Marzenka's eyes, lay her in the still warm bed and went across to the frightened child. She sat next to her and put her arm around her.

'Am I going to die?' Yola whispered.

'No, no, you're not going to die, darling,' Anna replied softly. Yola snuggled against her and Anna could feel her little heart beating strongly against her own chest.

CHAPTER 15

Kolkhoz Voroshilov

Ela and Yola left Farab two days later, under the protection of Captain Nieczuya's young Lieutenant. Feeling desolate, Anna decided the time had come for her to leave too. She discovered that a train transporting Polish refugees to various kolkhozes around Bukhara, was due to leave that very afternoon. She would be on it.

As she queued for hot water, at the station, she noticed a group of eight Poles, chatting and laughing. With a start, she recognised the tallest of them, a young man with a bushy black moustache and eyebrows and very white teeth. He was one of a large family who had lived close to Anna's home in Warsaw. She and her brother had been friendly with his two younger brothers, their contemporaries, and had often visited his widowed mother's house. She was thrilled to see him but tentative about approaching him.

'Excuse me, Roman. Do you remember me?'

'Little Annechka!' exclaimed the big man and he lifted her off the ground and planted two smacking kisses on each of her cheeks.

'This is my cousin,' he lied to his friends. For the first time in a long while, Anna felt a delicious sense of security. She briefly explained her position and was delighted when Roman insisted, 'You must travel with us,' and turning to his companions, 'That's right boys, isn't it? We can't let a lady travel on her own can we?'

'Of course not.'

'Absolutely not.'

'Wouldn't dream of it,' were the replies and Anna offered up a silent prayer of thanks that she had found this band of protectors.

Roman introduced the young men as George, Piotr, Tadek, Marek, Henryk, Jerzy and Olek. He was clearly the leader and, at midday, sent Henryk and Olek off to forage for food. They returned with millet porridge and bread from the Polish kitchen. Anna thoroughly enjoyed the simple meal for, not only was she very hungry, she was with her own people and with people who laughed and chatted just as if they were out for the day and eating an ordinary picnic.

The train arrived soon after lunch, they scrambled for a comfortable corner in one of the cattle trucks and at 5pm, Anna left Farab for ever.

'How different this journey is, from some of those I've been on in the past,' mused Anna, as she swapped stories and jokes with her companions. By the end of the twenty four hour journey, she felt as if she'd known them all her life.

At their destination, they joined the other refugees to wait for allocation to a collective farm. Most of the groups were taken by lorries but theirs was greeted by something more exotic.

'These are our arba/carts,' explained a young Uzbek, in heavily accented Russian. 'My name is Istam and I'm your interpreter. Climb in please. We have a long journey ahead.'

The four camel-drawn carts were made of thick planks and each had two spokeless wheels. They were piled high with rugs and sheepskins. The 'drivers', clad in quilted kaftans and fur caps, walked slowly and silently beside the camels. The strange caravan, escorted by two horsemen, set off slowly through the frosty, starlit night.

Too tired to talk, Anna huddled next to Roman, dozing. She woke with a start, about three hours later, to see they had arrived at a compound. The drivers shouted something loudly. A door in the wall was unlocked and the arbas rolled in, stopping outside a large building.

'Please come inside,' said Istam. 'The stove has been lit for you and quilts will be sent soon for your beds. This is temporary accommodation for one night only, as it is too late to take you to your allotted hut.' The room was bare but warm. Kerosene lamps gave a cosy glow. As they stood inside the door, an elderly man entered, greeted them politely and said something to Istam.

'This is the predsedatiel khokhoza/chairman of the collective farm. He wants me to welcome you officially, to the Kholkhoz

Voroshilov,' he said. 'He apologises that no cooked food is available. Hot tchay will be brought and some dried fruit.'

'Please thank him for his welcome,' replied Roman. 'Tell him that we'll work hard while we are here and,' he pointed to Anna, 'we have one woman in our group – my sister, Anna.'

Istam related this to the chairman and then five small boys arrived, bearing quilts and sheepskin rugs. Three more came soon afterwards, with a cauldron of tchay and two large copper bowls, filled with raisins and dried apricots. Then the Uzbeks withdrew, leaving the friends to eat their strange but welcome meal.

An hour later, when they were all settled under quilts, Anna had the most excruciating stomach cramps. She heard Roman give a moan, then Olek. Soon it was obvious that the dried fruit had upset the stomachs of all in the room. Everyone felt bloated and to add to the dreadful discomfort, they discovered they were locked in. It was a memorable night. Morning found them bleary eyed and depressed.

They felt better after a breakfast of porridge and lyepioshki/small round unleavened loaves.

Istam arrived to take them and the other new arrivals to the chairman's office.

'You must divide into two teams,' he translated. 'Our crop is cotton. I need one team to work in the cotton fields and one in the cotton sheds.'

Roman was pleased that his group was chosen to work in the fields.

'The sheds will be very dusty,' he said to Anna. 'Also I don't think supervision will be quite as strict out in the open.'

Roman went on to discuss the conditions of work with the chairman. He was disappointed to learn how small the food ration would be.

'There's a general food shortage,' he was told. 'All we can give each of you, daily, 200 grams of flour, 200 grams of millet, one sugar beet, one onion and one carrot. 250 grams of sunflower oil will be allowed to your group each week.

'What about wages?' Roman asked.

The chairman shook his head and Istam translated, 'He's afraid that after the food is paid for, there will only be a few roubles each for you.'

Despite the heated discussion that followed, Roman couldn't persuade the chairman that his team would need fat and meat in order to have the strength to work long days in the field. The only concession he won was that Anna should be allowed to stay at the kibitka/hut during the day, to do the cooking, washing and other household tasks. She would receive the food ration but no money.

'I'll do my very best to be an excellent housewife,' she thought wryly. 'Still, it's a far cry from being a soldier.'

Their small kibitka was separated from the rest of the village by a seven foot aryk/irrigation canal. The only road was on the opposite bank and could be reached by a rickety wooden bridge. The flat roofed, clay bricked house had one door and two narrow unglazed windows. In one corner of the single room there was a big, shallow cast-iron cauldron embedded into a clay stove. The furniture consisted of three large wooden bedsteads with criss-crossed webbing forming the springs. Each of these was designed to sleep four people.

The room was dark and chilly but a stack of cotton twigs stood near the stove and bolsters and a dozen or so thickly padded, colourful quilts were folded on the beds.

'I can make this homely and comfortable,' said Anna, smiling at her housewifely thought.

They had received their first week's rations so they cooked a meal and spent the day settling in, discussing their position and planning for the future.

'We need to make sure we strike up a good relationship with the people of the village,' said Roman.

'We'll work really conscientiously, for a start,' commented George.

'And behave in an exemplary fashion,' added Tadek, with a laugh.

'I've been thinking how much these Muslim Uzbeks must hate the godless Russians,' Anna said quietly. 'Uzbeks are devout Muslims.

They aren't allowed to practice their faith properly. That must make them angry. We are all Roman Catholics and, although our faith is different from theirs, we should demonstrate that we are religious people.' There was a moment's silence, then Poitr said, 'I know, let's start and end each day by singing a hymn outside the hut. I love a good singsong and it'll demonstrate we take our religion seriously.'

'Good idea,' said Roman, 'and I think we should refuse to work on Sundays. We'll explain it's our holy day.'

After the meal, they arranged the beds along one wall so that they formed a sort of platform. Anna was allocated a space at one end, in a corner of the room. She rolled up a spare quilt to form a barrier between her and Marek's space, which was next to hers. It gave her the illusion of privacy.

Then they went outside into the clear cold evening and sang a well-loved Polish hymn.

'Accept our daily toils with compassion, merciful Lord
And let us praise you even in our dreams...'

They sang the familiar words, in harmony, deeply moved by the feeling of comradeship and renewed hope.

The villagers, curious at this strange happening, came out of their houses and stood on the opposite bank of the aryk, silent and mystified.

Back in the hut, they grouped themselves round the fire and watched the dying embers, chatting over all that had happened.

Then Roman beckoned to his friends, 'Come on boys, let's go for a little walk and leave Annechka on her own for a bit.'

Anna was grateful to have the chance to wash herself in a drop of warm water which was left from the tchay-making. She was already in bed, wrapped snugly on her two quilts, when the men returned. She turned her back on them, called 'Goodnight,' and tried to sleep.

Anna's ability to sleep anywhere at any time, deserted her that first night in the hut. The men snored; all was quiet outside but warm and comfortable as she was, her mind raced and sleep eluded her. The events of the last few months flashed before her. She must have dozed off just before daybreak but was wakened by voices outside. She put on her coat and, taking a tin, went out of the door to fetch water from the aryk. Several women and children were filling ewers from the other bank. They smiled and waved at Anna who returned their greetings.

The water was clear and ice cold. When she returned to the hut, the men were up, tidying their beds. Tadek and Jerzy were trying, unsuccessfully, to light the fire but the chimney wouldn't draw and the room was full of acrid smoke. Spluttering, Anna pushed past them and putting into practice techniques she had learned, long ago, with her father, she managed to get the fire going. It took some time to cook the millet porridge, which was grey, tasteless and lumpy.

'I'm sorry it's such a failure,' she said soberly. 'From now on, I'll get up earlier and light the fire before I do anything else. I won't keep you waiting for food again and I'll improve my porridge-making ability.'

They laughed and teased her good-naturedly but she knew it was important to produce the best meals possible, for the men would be working very hard. After breakfast, they sang the morning hymn outside the hut and then the men left for work.

It was a fraught morning. The cotton twigs were fast-burning so the fire needed almost constant stoking. In between, Anna ran to and from the aryk for water, chopped vegetables with a small, blunt knife belonging to Marek and tried to make the hut as comfortable as possible. She hadn't even time for a wash before the men arrived, cold and tired, at noon for a dinner of vegetable and millet broth.

'Delicious,' pronounced Roman. 'Our thanks to our talented cook.' Everyone murmured agreement though Anna knew that the best that could be said for her concoction was that it was hot and thick.

As the men were so tired, she didn't bother them with questions about their work, but she gathered that it was backbreaking. They had been digging irrigation ditches in the deeply frozen fields outside the village, using ancient, inadequate tools.

Anna spent the whole afternoon baking biscuits on top of the stove, using flour, water and a drop of oil. She served these to the exhausted workers with the re-heated remains of broth for supper. Then the friends dragged themselves outside to sing the night hymn, washed their hands and faces and fell into bed.

Left to herself the next morning, Anna decided to seek help from the chairman. She needed kitchen utensils, a bucket and more matches. She met Istam outside the office and explained her errand to him. He looked embarrassed.

'I'm sorry to tell you that the chairman will not see you or talk to you. You see, you're a woman and in our country, women cannot be involved in business in any way, nor can they approach a superior. Your brother will have to seek an appointment with the chairman and speak to him on your behalf.'

Anna reddened. She was outraged but felt impotent. She managed to keep her voice level. 'My brother and the other men work all day. The office is closed by the time they get back from the fields. How can any of them make such an appointment?'

Istam, seeming to know his words had given offence replied, 'I am very sorry but that is the custom. I shall speak to the chairman and tell him of your requirements. I'm sure he will want to help you.'

'Thank you,' was all Anna could say.

Then they both noticed that a crowd of curious women and children were watching them silently. Istam blushed and hurried into the office. Anna smiled at the onlookers and then retraced her footsteps to the hut. The children followed and formed a group round the door, watching her every move.

At dinner time she related her tale to the workers.

'Annechka, you know what you are, don't you?' laughed Tadek. 'It's now official. You're our slave.'

'Don't trust women with power!' chortled George. 'The Uzbeks have the right idea.'

'I bet there aren't any henpecked husbands here,' added Olek, amidst general hilarity.

Anna took it in good part. She threw her quilt over Tadek's

head and then threatened no supper if they didn't take her seriously.

'I'll pop into the office on the way back to the fields,' said Roman. 'I'll make an appointment to see the chairman and, Annechka, you'll be pleased to hear, we do take you seriously – very seriously indeed. On the way back to lunch, we decided that we'll take it in turns to stay with you each morning. We can do some of the heavy chores and liaise with the authorities. As soon as we're not needed here any more, we'll report for duty in the fields. Also, I thought I might ask for permission for you to visit some of the Uzbek women, if you'd like me to. You wouldn't feel so isolated if you had a few friends apart from us. Now, have I said enough to ensure you'll cook us supper tonight?'

In response to Istam's message and Roman's request, the chairman, his secretary and Istam arrived at the hut after supper, bringing a small bag of dried fruit and a packet of real tea as gifts. Roman greeted the guests and invited them to sit down. Anna served them with tea and then sat quietly in her corner, taking no part in the conversation.

After a little general small talk, Roman asked the chairman to supply them with two buckets, a small kerosene lamp, some spoons, forks and knives and a weekly supply of kerosene and matches. Each item was haggled over but finally agreed. The chairman was adamant that the food ration could not be increased except for the additions of 100 grams of oil, extracted from cotton seeds.

Once the official business was out of the way, Anna served more tea and the Uzbeks asked about Poland, its history and the personal journeys which had brought the men to their village. In turn, they said that all their young men had been conscripted into the Red Army, leaving the farm bereft of labour. Istam explained that he had been injured in the Russo-Finnish war in 1940. He had learned Russian while in hospital and convalescing from several operations. Finally, he had been invalided home with a small piece of shrapnel still embedded in his lung.

As the guests rose to go, Roman called Anna over and, placing his arm round her shoulder, said to the chairman, 'Sir, I would be greatly obliged if you would allow my young sister to meet some of the village womenfolk. She is lonely in the day when we are away and she would be very interested to learn your language and your customs. She is far from her mother and would benefit from the advice and companionship of other women. We have heard how industrious and friendly the Uzbek women are. It would be such a privilege if my sister were accepted into their company.'

The chairman, who had ignored Anna throughout the evening, now smiled in her direction, clearly gratified by Roman's diplomatic speech.

'I will speak to my wife and ask her to visit your sister soon,' he promised.

Over the next few days, Anna established a domestic routine, helped greatly by the presence of one of the men for a while each morning. On the first Sunday, Anna insisted that the men slept longer than usual, while she prepared the inevitable vegetable stew, this time flavoured with onion, fried in the thick cotton seed oil.

After an early meal, the household gathered outside for hymns and prayers. Then the men pooled their weekly earnings and delegated Roman to try to buy some black market meat for the Sunday roast dinner. When he had gone, the cauldron was filled, the fire stoked and the men prepared to wash themselves thoroughly. Anna left them to it and, crossing the rickety bridge, she walked through the village. As ever, she was followed by a group of small children, this time accompanied by two mottled bull mastiffs, who seemed friendly in spite of their fierce appearance.

Anna was fascinated by the ingenuity of the irrigation system, which she'd learned had been in existence here since ancient times. It was fed by the glaciers of the Alay Mountains and transformed great swathes of the desert into productive farmland.

When she arrived back at the hut, Anna found Roman and George, hacking at the carcass of a very skinny small goat, which had cost Roman every rouble of the hard earned wages.

'Curse these greedy Uzbeks!' he shouted. 'They wring every rouble they can out of you.'

'Let's cook half now and keep half for tomorrow,' Anna suggested. 'I can't roast it. It would be too tough. I'll make a stew.' She helped to chop the stringy meat into small pieces and added half to the vegetables and rice in the cauldron. Roman stayed with her while the others went out for a walk.

'Annechka,' he said soberly, 'I'm seriously worried about the physical condition of all of us who work in the fields. We're far too thin but Marek and Olek, in particular, are skeletal and some of the boys have festering sores all over their bodies. That's an early symptom of pellagra and scurvy, brought on by a lack of vitamins. I asked the chairman, this morning, for medical help. He said that the nearest doctor and pharmacy are in Ghizhduvan, fifteen kilometres away. He did say he'd notify the doctor of the men's condition, as soon as possible but I think that's just wishful thinking.'

'What about the communal first aid box? asked Anna, very concerned. 'Istam told us there's one in the office.'

Roman pulled two small bottles out of his pocket.

'I was allowed some iodine and potassium permanganate crystals,' he said. 'In real life, George is a chemist. I'll ask him if either of these will be any use.'

The others returned and dinner was served. Although the goat meat had been cooking for several hours, it was still somewhat tough.

'It probably died of old age,' commented Tadek, chewing vigorously. 'Still, it makes a wonderful change. Congratulations to the chef.'

George advised that the sores should be treated morning and night with a strong solution of potassium permanganate.

'It's a strong germicide and antiseptic so it'll keep the wounds clean even if it can't cure them.' He said.

A couple of days later, Istam brought Roman a message for Anna.

'Your sister is invited to a girls' party at my house. I'll escort her there now.'

211

Anna was thrilled to receive the invitation but knew she couldn't attend a party in her ragged state.

'Will you thank the girls very much indeed, please but I have to refuse their kind invitation, I'm afraid. You see, these are the only clothes I have and it would be an insult to them if I turned up at a party looking like this.'

An hour later, Istam returned, carrying a striped yellow and green quilted kaftan, a pair of white, hand-knitted stockings and embroidered black felt slippers, with toes which turned upwards.

'These are gifts from my sisters,' he announced. 'They are delighted to offer them to you and say that they will be offended if you don't come to their party.'

Moved and embarrassed, Anna changed into her new attire, while Istam waited outside. Then they walked into the village. Istam stopped outside one of the houses.

'It would be improper for me to enter now, while the house is full of women,' he explained. He opened the door for her. 'Please go inside. You are expected. I'll return for you in three hours' time.' And he walked away.

Hesitantly, Anna stepped through the doorway and went in. She was in a large room, full of laughing, chattering women. The floor was covered in thick white felt and bright cushions and folded quilts lined the walls, which were hung with rich Oriental rugs. A row of slippers stood by the door. Anna removed hers and placed them alongside.

A young girl, in an embroidered skull-cap approached her, smiling. She carried an empty, engraved copper bowl, a slender matching ewer and a towel. She indicated that Anna should hold her hands over the bowl, poured water over them then handed her the towel. A second girl then took her arm and led her into the centre of the room. The chattering stopped for a moment and then all the young women crowded round Anna, smiling and talking. She was certainly the main attraction of the evening. Next she was shown where to sit. Trays of dainty sweet cakes, dried fruit and jasmine tea were handed round.

Anna kept smiling and nodding. Her two regrets were, that she couldn't understand anything that was said to her and she couldn't see a way of smuggling any of the sweetmeats back to the hut to share with the others.

Later, there was singing and dancing to the tambourine and doutar – a lute like instrument. The girls danced gracefully, in a circle, beckoning Anna to join them. After a few false moves, she caught the rhythm and followed the dance with gusto, to everyone's delight.

During a break for more refreshment the girl in the skull-cap handed the doutar to Anna. She could play the guitar and zither and, calling on this expertise, tried out a few chords. Then she sang for the women, by way of repayment for all their kindness. She sang the Polish songs her mother had taught her and the women laughed and clapped and, in a mixture of Uzbek and Russian, begged for more.

'Apa, davai muzika! Davai concyert!' / 'Sister, give us music! Give us a concert!'

Too soon it was time to go back to the hut with Istam. Anna thanked her hostesses again and again.

'This evening has been a jewel in the drabness of my life,' she thought as she went into her hut. The men were still awake and avid to hear what had happened. She told them every detail, then, folding her precious new clothes carefully, she climbed into bed, fell asleep immediately and had the best night since arriving at the kolkhoz.

Another week passed and with it, the health of the workers deteriorated further.

'However well you do in disguising the starchy food, Annechka,' Roman said to her, 'it's still just starch and without the necessary vitamins. Most of us have got diarrhoea and Marek, Henryk and Olek are developing night blindness.' Anna looked at Roman.

His worried face was gaunt and grey and the skin round his eyes was puffy. Yet he never complained and encouraged the others with unfailing energy. 'I've had so many abortive meetings with the chairman and his committee,' Roman continued. 'They absolutely refuse to enrich our diet and the time has come for a council of war. We'll hold it when we've cleared up from supper tonight.'

'I know it's a nasty thought, but the village is absolutely crawling with huge, well-fed cats, many of them half wild. I propose we kill one and eat it, as an experiment,' George said as soon as the meeting began.

'Ugh!' Anna shuddered. 'I can't bear the thought. I like cats and the Uzbeks love them and think they bring good luck. We'd be in dreadful trouble if we were caught.'

'We'll just have to make sure they don't catch us then,' Tadek responded. 'Sorry Anna, desperate times call for desperate measures. I'm with George.'

'If we get one, I'll skin it,' offered Piotr. 'I think George and Tadek are right.'

In the end, Anna was the only one who voted against. That night she dreamt of giant cats invading the hut.

However, when the first cat was brought to her, skinned and quartered, it looked much like rabbit and tasted similar too. The pelt and inedible pieces had to be secreted out of the village and buried in the desert. Because of the ever-watchful Uzbek children the cat-meat meals had to be eaten at night. After two weeks, there was a small but noticeable improvement in the health of the men.

One night, just after everyone had settled in bed, George suddenly sat up.

'Soap!' he shouted.

There was a stunned silence so George continued. 'If we could get hold of some caustic soda or potash and some animal fat, I could show you how to make soap. There's a chronic shortage of the stuff as you know. The kolkhoz would get good money for it, the committee could pay us for producing it and then we could buy decent meat and forget the cats.'

'It sounds a brilliant idea,' Roman said, excitedly, 'but where are we going to find caustic soda?'

'We'll substitute it for potash,' answered George. 'We can make that quite easily from wood ash.'

'Fantastic! Let's approach the chairman, with the plan, tomorrow and...' he paused for breath as he had an inspiration, 'let's offer to build a bath-house, a real, Russian-type banya. We could do that instead of building irrigation canals. Between us, we'll offer to keep the village clean!'

The next morning, Poitr, a lawyer, rehearsed with Roman exactly what the proposition to the chairman and committee would be. Then the two of them and George made an appointment to speak to the officials later in the day. They arrived back at the hut triumphant, followed by a smiling Istam.

'They love the idea,' Roman reported. 'We can set up and start both projects as soon as we like.'

'They saw, immediately, that the manufacture of soap will make a lot of money,' grinned Poitr. 'They want to cash in on it. They've offered to help in any way they can but we'll have to keep the recipe a close secret or they'll start making soap themselves. This enterprise gives us some power.'

'They've offered to increase our rations,' added Tadek, jubilantly. And look, the chairman even gave us a piece of meat as a sign of the committee's good will.'

From that day, the position of those in Roman's group changed. The quality and quantity of their food increased miraculously. Small gifts of cheese, meat and goat or camel milk appeared, apparently as advance payments for the soap they were going to produce.

Preparations for the new ventures started without delay. The group was divided into two teams. George, Poitr and Tadek undertook the soap manufacture. At the back of the hut, behind a clay wall, they built a long brick stove, in which two shallow cauldrons were embedded. Clay troughs, to serve as moulds were made near the stove. In two days, they were ready to start production.

The rest of the group plus five Uzbek labourers, selected by the committee, commenced the construction of the banya in a small, disused house on the outskirts of the village.

Roman would help wherever he was needed but would be free to liaise with the committee when necessary. Anna was to remain cook, housekeeper and general factotum. She could call for help when she needed it and whenever she had spare time, she would be able to assist with the soap-making and learn its secrets.

The committee kept it's promise to help. First, they organised a regular supply of sheep's tails to provide the fat needed for soap. Then they sent bundles of gnarled saxaul wood to add to the cotton bush twigs. The saxaul is a stunted, desert tree, its wood hard, slow burning and was ideal for the production of potash.

Three days later, after a couple of failed experiments, the correct ratio of fat to potash was found and the first bars of light brown, slightly gritty soap were lifted triumphantly from the moulds. Everyone gathered round to admire them and to congratulate the soap team.

'I think we should cut them up into little squares and present a piece to every member of the committee,' suggested Anna. This was agreed, Anna cut the soap with care and Roman made the presentation, with appropriate ceremony.

It was three days before Christmas 1941, Anna's second Christmas in exile.

Anna and Tadek were tasked with preparing the Christmas feast. On the starlit Christmas Eve, the friends gathered in the hut to celebrate the birth of Jesus. Roman, as head of the 'family', solemnly broke a piece from a wafer-thin biscuit Anna had baked, and shared it with each of the group. Too moved to speak, they embraced, in silence. Anna's heart was full as she looked at the men who were sharing her life and then thought of her loved ones, so far away.

Then the mood lightened as they sat down to eat. Thanks to their new found opulence, Anna and Tadek had been able to concoct several tasty dishes of rice, herbs, nuts and vegetables, followed by a compote of dried fruit. Then there was real tea and some dainty sweetmeats, presents from Istam's sisters.

To end the evening, the friends sat round the stove and sang Christmas carols until midnight.

They had invited the chairman and Istam for a meal on Christmas day. Roman explained to them the Christian significance of Christmas. Then the Poles entertained the two Uzbeks with a concert of national songs and carols.

Despite much better conditions and the improved health of the team, they were growing increasingly impatient to hear about the promised recruitment to the Polish army.

When Roman attempted to discover the political situation from the chairman, the answer was, 'Why are you worrying about such things? Let the politicians worry about war. Stay with us.'

On New Year's Eve, Roman returned from his meeting with the chairman.

'The annual fair is being held in Ghizhduvan tomorrow and we're invited to join some of the Uzbeks in their arbas to spend the day there. It should be fun and we might be able to glean some information about what is happening in the rest of the world.'

Thrilled by the invitation, Anna and her comrades climbed into one of the camel-drawn carts early on New Years Day. The day was crisp and sunny and the mood cheerful as they arrived in Ghizhduvan town square.

'How will we know when to come and meet here again for the lift back?' asked Anna. As none of the Uzbeks spoke Russian and none of Anna's group spoke Uzbek, this presented a problem.

'One or other of us will have to come back regularly to check,' Roman answered. 'Say about every hour or so.'

The narrow winding streets of the town were flanked by open-fronted shops, full of local produce and artefacts. Peering into dark interiors, Anna could see hand-beaten copper bowls, trays and ewers, intricately engraved. Tall Russian samovars reflected lights from numerous oil lamps. Oriental rugs, silk scarves, jewelled skullcaps, slippers and saddlebags glowed richly.

The smells of spices, badly cured leather and grilled kebabs mingled with that of the camels and donkeys.

The noise of the streets was in stark contrast to the quiet kolkhoz. Shrill street vendors advertised their wares, camels grunted, donkeys brayed, dancers banged tambourines and the multicoloured crowd jostled and laughed. Anna, shouting to make herself heard, begged for a cup of tea at one of the numerous tchaikhanas. They joined the dignified, bearded customers who sat cross-legged on carpeted platforms, sipping tea, under striped awnings.

Roman ordered shashliks/ skewered diced lamb and onion, charcoal grilled and served with small pancakes.

'This is wonderfully like real life,' sighed Anna. 'I feel almost like an ordinary person.'

Having checked the town square regularly, they found the arbas and camels still there at 3pm.

'Let's go to the railway station,' suggested Tadek. 'We might find some Russian speakers who can tell us what's happening in the war.'

'Good idea,' said Olek. 'There might even be some Polish refugees there who can enlighten us.'

They were disappointed to find the station empty except for an Uzbek railway worker who spoke a little Russian. But he shrugged his shoulders at their enquiries.

'I don't know anything about politics or the war,' he grumbled. Then he brightened. 'But as it's New Year's Day, you can buy one kilogram each of Russian bread from the bakery round the corner. It's unrationed today.'

Disheartened at their failure to gather information, they walked away. The smell of freshly baked bread drifted towards them. Mouths watered.

'Let's treat ourselves,' said Roman. 'We can take the loaves back and enjoy them over the next few days.'

They joined the queue then, clutching their still warm loaves, they hurried back to the square. The arbas and camels had gone.

They were fifteen kilometres away from Voroshilov Kolkhoz and the light was failing. Roman returned from enquiring at a tchaikhana, about the best way to get back to the kolkhoz. He pointed along the main road.

'The owner spoke a little Russian and said we should follow the main road out of town for about seven kilometres. We'll reach a small bridge over the irrigation ditch. We cross that, turn left and follow the ditch which finally runs through Voroshilov.'

The night was cold but windless. Once through the town, the endless desert seemed empty. After walking for an hour and a half, they came to the bridge, crossed it and turned left, as instructed.

'This doesn't look right,' commented George. 'It's certainly not the way we came this morning. I remember noticing that the land was absolutely flat. There are hills over there, look.'

'Perhaps this road is a different route back,' answered Roman. 'We can't do anything but carry on by this ditch. It must take us somewhere.'

Two hours later, Anna, putting one foot in front of the other in a mechanical fashion thought, 'I really can't go on much longer.' But she said nothing. They rounded a hillock and there, perched on the side, was a small clay hut.

'Saved!' cried Tadek while Roman strode ahead to hammer on the thick wooden door. The windows were firmly shuttered but a ribbon of smoke from the chimney spelt hope to them all.

There was no reply to the knocking so Roman shouted, first in Russian and then the few words he knew in Uzbek. Still no answer.

'Roman,' Anna said, 'You're probably terrifying whoever is inside. How would you feel if a strange man thundered at your door and shouted at you in the middle of the night?' Roman laughed.

'What womanly common sense,' he said. 'You call out. Shout for help in your most helpless manner.' Anna called loudly several times, to no avail. Suddenly she was overcome with cold, exhaustion and hopelessness and she collapsed on the doorstep, sobbing. None of her companions took her seriously.

'Wail louder!' they urged. In spite of herself, Anna suddenly saw the incongruity of the situation. Her desperate sobs changed to hysterical laughter. At that moment, the door was flung open and a tiny, shrivelled and stark naked old Uzbek stood in the doorway, holding high a small oil lamp. His head was covered in an enormous shaggy fur hat, his feet encased in slippers and he was shivering with cold or fear.

He glared angrily at the shabby group and screeched shrilly, waving his arms. Shocked into silence, Anna stared up at the apparition while Roman tried to explain their problem. The man nodded when he heard the word 'Voroshilov' and, leaving the door ajar, he withdrew.

A couple of minutes later, he returned, clad in a long sheepskin coat and carrying a staff. He beckoned for them to follow him and trotted along without looking back.

'He's like a desert sprite,' whispered Anna to Tadek, as the old man leapt over ditches and climbed hillocks, disappearing into the shadows and then reappearing in the moonlight.

'Yes, and he's a sprite pursued by nine desperate human beings,' Tadek replied.

At last the old Uzbek stopped. He came close to Roman and pointed dramatically into the distance several times, nodding his head.

'Voroshilov, Voroshilov, Voroshilov,' he said loudly. Before Roman could thank him, he turned round and trotted away at a brisk pace, soon vanishing into the shadow.

Although Anna was weary and very cold, the thought that they were nearing the kolkhoz gave her strength to continue. The moon was high and Anna shivered, as much at the eerie stillness of the desert as with cold.

They trudged on for another hour, in the general direction in which the old man had pointed. Then Roman stopped.

'I'm sure we've passed that hill before. I think we're going in circles now. What does everyone else think?'

'It's so hard to tell,' responded Poitr. 'It all looks the same.'

They stood hopelessly and Anna shut her eyes, unable to bear the thought of being lost in the desert. When she opened her eyes, she gave a shout.

'Look, that's not a hill, Roman. It's a wall. I'm sure it is.' She ran forward, put her hands out and felt the rough clay of a boundary wall. She followed it for a few metres and found a wooden door, firmly locked at this time of night, of course. Anna hammered on it, shouting and crying. The others joined her but didn't shout for fear of alarming the inhabitants. Then they heard bolts withdrawn and, slowly, one half of the gate was opened. A sheepskin-clad man stepped forward and, in silence, beckoned them to enter. Once they were inside, he re-locked the door and led them across a yard, stopping outside a hut. In broken Russian he welcomed them and asked what they needed. He listened courteously to Roman's explanation.

'You must stay in my house for the night,' he said. 'In the morning, a guide will show you the way to the kolkhoz. Please come in.'

The hut seemed empty except for a fire of glowing charcoal embers set into the centre of the clay floor. Their host produced folded quilts from the corner and demonstrated how they should be arranged all round the fire, in the shape of a many-pointed star.

'You will sleep with your feet pointing at the coals,' he explained. 'With warm feet you sleep well. Here are more quilts to cover you. Lie down now and warm yourselves and I will arrange for some food to be brought to you.'

It seemed too good to be true. As the delicious warmth permeated Anna's body, she said a prayer of thanks and fell asleep. She was woken by the sound of children's voices. Two young boys had arrived with bowls of warm water and towels. Refreshed by a quick nap, Anna sat on her quilt and marvelled at the dishes of rice, vegetables and spicy meat two more lads brought in. The Poles were joined by their host for the feast, which was followed by bowls of real tea.

'How do you come to be at Voroshilov?' the man asked. Roman told him their story.

'You have had hard times,' he commented. 'I am pleased you have honoured us with a visit. My wife and daughters are anxious to meet your sister. Please may I take her to their hut for a few minutes?'

In spite of her exhaustion, Anna didn't want to miss this opportunity and it would have been rude to refuse. Roman nodded his head.

'Very well, but please don't take too long. We've walked many miles today and have further to go tomorrow.'

Anna followed their new friend outside. They had walked a few steps when he turned back, stepped past her, slammed the hut door and locked it.

'Forgive me!' he shouted.

Anna felt sick with fear. Expecting the worst, she looked round for some sort of weapon with which to defend herself but could find nothing. The men were banging on the door and shouting. She backed away as the man came towards her. He was agitated.

'Forgive me,' he said again. 'Forgive me for frightening you. Don't be afraid, please. I won't hurt you and I will take you to my wife and daughters but first I'll explain why I've done this. By custom, we are forbidden to refuse food and shelter to those who seek it but we're living in very dangerous times. Some of the strangers who knock on doors at night are dishonest and violent. In the past months, several of our communities have been robbed and there has even been a murder. I'm the only man in this household and I must protect my family and our livestock.' He looked so troubled that Anna felt reassured but she could still hear her friends shouting and banging inside the hut.

'I understand,' she said 'but please will you explain to the men. They'll be so worried about me.'

'I will speak to them once you have met my wife,' he answered. 'You must sleep with my daughters as it is unseemly for a young woman to sleep in the same room as men.'

Anna smiled to herself.

'If only he knew,' she thought.

Anna entered a large pleasant room, where an elderly woman, a younger one and two girls were sitting on quilts near the central fire.

'This is my mother and my wife,' he said. 'And these are my daughters. They do not speak Russian but they are very pleased to see you.'

The women smiled and indicated that Anna should sit. They pressed small sweetmeats on her and handed her a bowl of tea. The wife said something to her husband who turned to Anna.

'I'm going to explain to your friends now. Soon you can sleep. My wife thinks you are very tired.' He went out and Anna looked round the room. It had the same white felt carpet, rug hangings and bright, folded quilts as the house of Istam's sisters. A wide bed stood in the corner and the boys, who had served the Polish group earlier, were fast asleep on it. A tiny baby lay asleep in a wicker basket. A large loom dominated one wall of the room. On it was an unfinished rug of an intricate Uzbek design. Anna looked at it, smiled, nodded and clapped her hands to show how much she liked it. Then she admired the baby. Both women were obviously delighted with their guest. The wife brought a bowl of warm water so that Anna could wash her hands and face and then the husband returned.

'Your friends are happy to know you are safe,' he said. 'They have settled for the night now.' His mother showed Anna a quilt, she had put down and indicated this was where she should sleep.

'I hope you sleep well,' said the man. He and his wife withdrew through a door to their room, taking the baby. The mother retired to a small truckle bed in the corner and Anna snuggled gratefully under the quilt and fell asleep immediately.

The next morning, she was woken by sounds of the grandmother trying to hush the boys, who had gathered excitedly round Anna and were staring down at her. Refreshed, she sat up and smiled. They scampered off. Anna rose and folded the quilts, while the wife fetched hot water and towels for her and the grandmother served warm camel's milk and fresh lepyoshka. Anna could hear the host and her friends talking and laughing in the yard. Reassured, she enjoyed her breakfast.

'Apa, apa, thank you very much,' she said to the two women. They understood the first part of the sentence and obviously guessed the rest, for they each reached out and patted Anna's arm and smiled and nodded. Then she left her place of refuge and went out to join the men.

Their host was holding the reins of one of the finest horses Anna had ever seen. It was a white Arab stallion with a long silky mane and tail, dainty feet and flashing expressive eyes.

'I love to ride him,' he said. 'I shall lead him now and guide you back to the kolkhoz and then gallop home in a trice.'

The group was astonished and slightly embarrassed to find how near to the kolkhoz they had been. It was less then two kilometres. After thanking the Uzbek again and again for his wonderful hospitality, the man galloped off and they reported to the chairman. Istam was with him.

'Thank goodness you are back,' the interpreter cried. 'We thought some dire calamity had overtaken you. We were just about to gather a search party and scour the countryside for you.'

The unexpectedly warm reception was a pleasant surprise.

'Although I think the chairman is more concerned about the soap than about us,' Roman commented wryly as they went back to their hut.

The two teams worked hard for the rest of the week. The bathhouse was almost finished and the soap factory doubled its output. Anna was invited to two more parties and was beginning to feel one of the 'sisterhood'.

'Still,' she said one evening when she and the men were sitting round the fire, 'I don't want to get too settled. This isn't where I want to be for the rest of the war.'

'I've been pondering that,' replied Roman. 'I think that if we haven't heard any definite news once spring arrives, we should leave the kolkhoz and make for a larger town where we can find out what's going on. If we can contact the Polish representative, we may be able to join a transport to a Polish army camp.'

'Good idea,' Tadek was enthusiastic.

'But let's keep it to ourselves,' warned George. 'The Uzbeks won't want to lose us and our soap making expertise.'

'We've got to be extra careful,' added Marek. 'Istam told me that a group of Poles absconded from the cotton mill last week, stealing clothes and bedding which had been lent to them. We mustn't allow ourselves to be identified with criminals.'

'We won't take anything which doesn't belong to us,' said Roman. 'We won't need to as we're earning decent money now.'

One morning, after the men had gone to work, Anna sat on the doorstep, mending a hole in Roman's jacket. As usual, a group of children surrounded her, watching, smiling and chattering. Suddenly there was silence. Anna looked up to see a very old man, carrying a shepherd's crook and followed by a small flock of sheep. He was lean and bent and had a long, wispy, silver beard. He wore a blue and white striped khalat/robe and a white turban.

For a moment, Anna stared. He could have walked right out of an illustration from one of her childhood books of Old Testament stories. He smiled at her, she responded and then he passed on.

Enchanted by this patriarchal figure, Anna asked Istam about him.

'He's our mullah,' he replied. 'He's a religious teacher, very old and beloved by us all. Because of his great age, the Russians have allowed him to stay in the village, as long as he doesn't teach Islam to our young children.' He gave a big wink and added, 'Officially.'

Anna looked out for the mullah over the next couple of days. They always exchanged smiles and bows but Anna was very surprised when an excited Istam arrived with an invitation.

'The mullah and his wife wish you to go to their house this evening,' he announced. 'This is a great honour. They have been away for some time. That is why you haven't met them before. They have been asking about you and how you come to be here amongst all these men. Shall I say that you accept the invitation?'

Anna looked at Roman who nodded his head.

'Yes go, Anna, but I can't understand why it is you who gets all the invitations. The boys and I have never even been inside a proper Uzbek home.'

Anna washed and changed into her blue and white kaftan and felt slippers and followed Istam into the village.

'Istam,' she said, 'please tell me how to behave in the mullah's house. I don't want to give offence.'

'The only rules are, don't use your left hand when you're eating, only speak when you are spoken to and behave in a modest manner, as befits your lowly station,' he replied. Anna allowed this last the remark to go unchallenged.

'After all,' she thought, 'I just have to accept that I am the lowest of the low in this Muslim village. But when I get out, how I'll enjoy asserting myself!'

'And watch carefully what everyone else is doing and copy them. If you do that, you won't go far wrong,' Istam added.

Anna was greeted by a smiling elderly lady, the mullah's wife and two younger women, who brought warm water and towels. Anna thanked them and then, copying Istam, bowed towards the mullah and the group of elders around him. They sat at a low table in the centre of the room, their feet tucked under quilts. The women retired to sit on folded rugs at the side of the room. Anna hesitated. She was about to follow them when the mullah beckoned her, patting a spare cushion beside him. Istam sat down on her other side.

'Welcome to our home,' the mullah said in heavily accented Russian. The other men were pretending not to notice Anna, perhaps embarrassed by the unorthodox presence of a woman at the men's table. After a few minutes, however, they took their cue from the host and welcomed Anna, asking after her health, through the services of the interpreter.

An enormous dish of rice and lamb ragout was placed on the table. The mullah picked up a small piece of meat in his fingers, moulded some of the rice round it and put it in his mouth. The men did the same and Anna followed suit, eating the delicious food slowly and carefully. As they ate, the mullah plied her with questions.

'How do you come to be here?'

'Where are you hoping to go to?'

Then, 'You must long to be among your own people again and you must worry about your family.' Anna was grateful for the wise man's understanding and astonished at his grasp of history and world politics. She felt young and inexperienced and offered no comment on what he said, even when his pro-German sentiments became obvious.

'He hasn't suffered under the Germans,' she thought. 'He only knows the yoke of the Russians.'

The next few moments made an indelible impression on Anna. The mullah leaned forward and picking something out of the ragout, rolled it in rice.

'Before we go on with our conversation,' he smiled, 'I want to offer you one of our favourite delicacies. It is the eye of a sheep.' Before Anna could respond, he bent towards her and popped the hideous globule into her mouth. It was too large to swallow whole. Clenching her hands, she bit through the repulsive jelly and swallowed, praying it would stay down.

'I'm truly honoured,' she managed to say.

The almost empty dish was replaced by another, of millet milk pudding, flavoured with spices, which Anna ate gratefully. Then came dried fruit and bowls of tea. Finally, warm, moist towels were passed round as the conversation continued.

'Our prophet venerated the prophets of your Old Testament, Moses and Elijah, for instance,' the mullah commented. 'We Muslims, admire the life and teachings of Jesus and respect his mother, Miriam.'

By now Anna was very tired and weary of being on her guard against giving offence. Her bladder was also full. She leaned towards Istam.

'Could I make my excuses and withdraw now, do you think?' He shook his head. 'You'll be expected to spend the night here,' he whispered and Anna's heart sank but she kept an alert smile on her face.

The women appeared and placed quilts behind each guest. As the mullah's wife bent down to arrange one for Anna, Anna looked at her beseechingly, touching her hand. The woman understood and beckoned Anna to follow her to the yard, where they were immediately surrounded by snarling mastiffs. Chasing them away, the wife pointed to a corner of the yard. Embarrassed, Anna used the only facility the house offered and returned to the house. On the way back Anna tried, unsuccessfully, to indicate to the woman that she wanted to sleep in the women's quarters.

The men were still talking and drinking tea and were now surrounded by a number of cats. A large ginger one, on the mullah's lap, gave Anna a baleful glare.

'He knows we ate some of his kith and kin,' she thought and looked away.

Now there was ritual hand washing and then the mullah knelt and touched the floor with his forehead, chanting a prayer. The men followed and, unsure what to do, Anna knelt, folded her hand, closed her eyes and waited.

The prayers ended, the mullah turned to Anna.

'I've been told that you and your brothers are believers and are not afraid to praise God. I would dearly like to hear you pray.'

Still kneeling, Anna crossed herself and recited the Lord's Prayer in Polish. As she finished and sat back on the quilt, the mullah said, 'Please translate it into Russian for me.' When Anna had done this, he asked her to repeat it slowly. Then, line by line. He translated it into Uzbek for the elders.

'It is a beautiful prayer, truly beautiful,' he said. 'Now we shall sleep.'

Anna lay between the mullah and Istam and marvelled at the bizarre situation.

'This is stranger than any story I've read,' she thought. She knew Roman would wonder if something had happened to her and if it hadn't been for the mastiffs outside, she might have risked slipping out and finding her way back to her hut. At last, she fell asleep but was awake when dawn broke. She rose silently and went to help the women prepare breakfast. When the men finally arose, Anna went to the mullah.

'Thank you very much for your kindness and hospitality,' she said. 'I shall never forget the time I spent with you, your family and your friends.' With the good wishes of him and his wife ringing in her ears, she hurried back to Roman.

'Where on earth have you been?' he demanded angrily. 'We were just about to come to look for you. We've been very worried.'

Anna sat down.

'I'm so sorry, but there was absolutely nothing I could do.' She apologised. Then she told them of her extraordinary experience and by the time she got to the 'sheep's eye', they were roaring with laughter, quite forgetting their anxiety.

'You'll have to write it down, Anna,' cried Tadek. 'The only problem is, no-one will ever believe you!'

CHAPTER 16

The Ancient Walls of Bukhara

'We have been appointed by the family of Istam, to say that he seeks your sister's hand in marriage,' the Uzbek elder said solemnly. He and his fellow elders looked from Roman to Anna and then back again to Roman.

There was a stunned silence, then, before Roman could speak, the elder continued.

'Soon you and the other Polish men will be called to join your army. You will no longer be in a position to care for your sister. She will be safe and well cared for here. Also, we have noticed her modest behaviour and her keen interest in all our traditions. At a meeting, last night, the Mullah and all of the villagers agreed that this marriage will be a very good thing. Will you give your permission?'

The group of four elders, accompanied as usual by Istam, had been sipping tea in the Polish hut and amicably chatting for half an hour although Anna had felt that they had come with some sort of purpose in mind. Now she knew what it was.

Misinterpreting Roman's shocked silence for consideration of their offer, the elder added,

'The family of Istam is willing to offer you a small flock of sheep in exchange for your sister.'

'It's pure farce,' thought Anna, desperately trying not to laugh and hoping that no-one else would do so. They mustn't offend these hospitable people.

At last Roman was able to reply. He bowed politely and said,

'I am greatly honoured and extremely moved by your request and it would make me very happy to see my sister married to such a fine and brave young man. It is with deep regret that I have to tell you that she has been promised to another by our parents. Her fiancé is in the army, fighting for his country and, of course, the engagement cannot be broken.'

'Oh, well done, Roman!' thought Anna

'We are disappointed, but understand. Thank you for listening to us and for the praise you have given to Istam.'

Poor Istam. He had to translate throughout the conversation and was looking very embarrassed. Now he said something to the elder who had spoken and they all rose to go, taking their leave in a dignified fashion, as usual.

Once the guests were out of earshot, everyone relaxed and, laughing, Anna chided Roman, 'Surely I'm worth more than a small flock of sheep. You could have asked them to add some camels.'

Both teams continued to work hard on the bathhouse, keen to finish and earn more money from selling soap. They secretly studied a makeshift map, prepared by Piotr, who had talked to Istam and gleaned information about the surrounding area. They said nothing to the Uzbeks of their plan to leave, not sure of what their reaction would be.

On the morning of 10th January, Roman suddenly collapsed. He lay still, on the floor of the hut, his body swollen. Anna rushed to him.

'His pulse is very weak and uneven,' she reported. Gently, Poitr and George placed him on his bunk. He was still unconscious.

'There's a hospital in Ghizhduvan,' Anna said. 'We must get permission to take him there and beg for some sort of transport. I'll stay with Roman. You two go and see the Chairman.'

An hour later, the camel-drawn cart was ready. Roman was placed on a bed of cotton waste and Anna, Poitr and George climbed up beside him. Anna clutched a big pot of stew because, as she said, 'You never know when it might come in useful.' Roman was lucid now but weak and feverish. It was a slow, harrowing journey. The cart was unsprung and the track full of bumps and troughs. Roman moaned softly once or twice but there was little anyone could do to help. It was early afternoon when they reached Ghizhduvan.

Anna enquired at the small hospital for the doctor. He wasn't there and they were directed to an old people's home nearby. The doctor, a harassed looking Russian in a soiled white coat, gave Roman a perfunctory examination.

'This man is suffering from pellagra,' he said. 'He should be hospitalised immediately but I am afraid that there is no room at all in the local hospital.'

'But what shall we do?' George asked desperately.

'Well,' the doctor said slowly, 'He could stay here at this home. We might just squeeze him in and then I will give him medical care every day and the volunteer nurses will look after his other needs.'

Before they could thank the doctor, he continued, 'I must warn you, however, that medicines and food are in very short supply...' Anna broke in, 'We'll pay for medicines and I'll bring food for my brother. We are very grateful for your help, Doctor.'

But when they saw the dingy room Roman was to share with twenty other patients, who lay on dirty, rag covered beds, they were appalled. The men went out to buy food and blankets for Roman, while Anna stayed with him to explain carefully to him exactly what arrangements had been made.

George and Poitr arrived back two hours later with a loaf of bread and two blankets, purchased at black market prices. They had also managed to buy a couple of kebabs and a few lepyoshki. Together with the pot of stew, they thought this would be food enough for Roman for two days. With twenty roubles, Anna bribed a young Uzbek nurse, who promised to make sure Roman received his food.

Then they left him, their only consolation the fact that the doctor would do his best to effect Roman's recovery.

They were very tired on their return to the kolkhoz but had to give an account of all that had happened, first to their colleagues and then to the Chairman. He listened with concern.

'I am very sad to hear of Roman's illness,' he said. 'I am also sorry that the conditions at the place in which you were forced to leave him are less than ideal. I shall give orders that you, Anna

Grymala Siedlecka be issued with double rations and also with extra meat and milk — for the patient.' Anna thanked the Chairman warmly and he went on, 'I am sorry to say that the camel cart will be available to you only twice a week but you may use one of the small donkeys to carry the supplies, on other days, if you are happy to go to Ghizhduvan on foot.'

'Thank you,' Anna replied gratefully. 'We accept your kind offer.'

Suddenly Anna and her friends were without the confident leadership of Roman. Work output suffered. No-one could concentrate fully because of worries about Roman and Anna was often absent, taking food to him. His progress was good. After six days, Anna was able to report, 'He's feeling much better. The Doctor is pleased with him and thinks he'll be able to return here in about four more days.'

But on the seventh day (January 17th) everything changed.

A commotion outside woke Anna at dawn. There was a thunderous knock on the door. Wrapping a blanket round herself, Anna opened the door to find Istam standing outside, breathless and excited.

'A special messenger has just arrived on horseback,' he cried. 'He brings an order from the NKVD. All Polish men are to report immediately to Ghizhduvan recruiting office, where Representatives from the Polish army are waiting to enlist them.'

'At last!' shouted George. 'At last we are to be allowed to fight for our country!'

'At last!' Anna echoed and the two of them danced with delight around the hut.

Istam hurried away and everyone rapidly pulled on clothes and ran to the kolkhoz office, where Istam's words were confirmed and instructions about transport issued by the flustered Chairman.

'The leader of this group is sick and already in Ghizhduvan,' he told the waiting messenger. 'You can contact him there. His friends will show you where he is staying.'

He handed the list of names of the Polish group to the man, who scanned it quickly then looked up, frowning.

'There's a woman's name here.'

'Yes,' replied the Chairman, indicating Anna. 'Anna Grymala Siedlecka.'

The messenger shook his head and addressed Anna.

'I'm sorry, madam but my instructions are that no women should be included in this enlistment. You must stay here for the time being.'

Anna couldn't believe her ears. She had been through so much to get here. For so long, she had lived in hope of joining the army and fighting for Poland. To be foiled at this stage was more than she could bear.

'I will *not* stay here alone,' she protested hotly. 'I'm as fit for the army as any of these men. At least let me speak to the enlisting officer.' Anna's friends joined in her pleas but the messenger remained adamant.

Anna turned to the Chairman for support but he only smiled and said,

'I once promised your brother that I would look after you if ever the men, only, were called to join the army. I will keep that promise. Now, Anna Grymala Siedlecka, return to your hut straight away and make no more trouble.'

Blinded by tears, Anna rushed from the room and back to the hut. She flung herself on her bed, sobbing with fury and frustration. She wouldn't speak to the others when they first returned to the hut to pack their belongings. Then, when Poitr tried to calm her, she shouted, 'How can you go without me? We have been in everything together. Have I shown weakness? Aren't I worthy of becoming a soldier? You're traitors. You're too frightened to defend me and to make the messenger and Chairman see sense.'

The men were embarrassed by her outburst. George sat down beside her. 'Anna, we have to obey orders. We have to go to enlist. We'll plead your cause at the enlistment office and we'll tell Roman that you're here on your own and ask him to take every action possible to get you out and alongside us.'

Anna felt ashamed of her words and pretending to be reassured by what George said, helped with the packing.

Before leaving, George gave Anna the soap-making recipe.

'As long as you're the only person who knows the whole secret of the soap recipe, your position here will be secure,' he said. 'And you can use it to bargain with, should the need arise.'

The rest of the group gave her gifts as well – a knife, eighty roubles and two bars of soap.

'Will you walk with us to the village square?' asked Poitr.

Anna shook her head. She didn't trust herself to speak. She hugged each of her friends in turn and then stood on the doorstep of the hut, waving until they were out of sight, lost in a blur of tears.

She sat on her bed for a long time after they had gone. She felt abandoned, absolutely alone. The tears came again and at last, exhausted and drained she curled up under the quilt and fell asleep.

She was woken at dusk by Istam and his two sisters.

'We are sorry you are left here without your friends,' the elder said gently. 'Will you come to have supper at our house, please?'

Anna didn't feel like socialising but feared a refusal would give offence so she replied,

'Thank you, I'd be delighted. I need to change into some different clothes first. I shall be ready in a very short while.' The girls went away, saying they would expect Anna soon. She washed, changed and brushed her hair and, feeling a little better, walked to their house. She was greeted warmly by the sisters and their mother, who spoke a little Russian. The food was exotic and Anna, who hadn't eaten all day, was hungry. After supper, the talk turned to the men who had left.

'What will you do?' asked the mother. 'You will be very lonely living on your own.'

'I shall be fine.' answered Anna. 'Tomorrow I'll ask the Chairman if I may take charge of the soap making and train some of the women here to help me.'

But even as she spoke, she knew she wouldn't stay long in the kolkhoz. She was determined to escape and wait, in hiding, until Roman was fit so that they could travel together to join the Polish army.

She refused the offer to stay the night with the girls and, thanking her hostess warmly for her hospitality, took her leave and went back to the empty hut.

'No time for moping,' she told herself. 'I'll have to be very careful if I want to get out of here soon. I'm sure I'll be watched for some time. People will suspect I may try to follow the others. I'll just have to convince everyone that I am resigned to waiting until someone sends for me.'

The Chairman was pleased with Anna's plan for the soap factory.

'I can certainly find you four Uzbek girls to train,' he said.

'I'll teach each of the girls a different part of the process,' explained Anna, remembering Poitr's warning about divulging the recipe. 'I, alone, have the experience to mix the final solution correctly.'

'Indeed,' the Chairman looked impressed.

'I'll blind him with science,' thought Anna suddenly. 'I'll make him believe the process is much more complicated than it is and that I will be here indefinitely to supervise.'

'When can you start production?' asked the Chairman.

'Well…' Anna seemed to consider her reply carefully, 'Now my colleagues have gone, I shall have to re-think the methods of manufacture. I need time to produce the necessary chemicals and will have to change the sequence of the procedure. I think it would be useful to hold a three day induction course for my four new workers, with Istam as translator, if that would be possible.'

The Chairman looked bewildered but clearly respected Anna's scientific and businesslike approach.

'All that is fine, Anna Grzymala Siedlecka,' he said. 'May I suggest that you move in with one of the Uzbek families. It is not good for you to live on your own.'

Anna did not want this. It would interfere with her escape plan so she responded, with a smile.

'That's thoughtful, Chairman, and I am grateful, but I must stay next to the soap factory so that I can mix chemicals and observe the processes at any time of the day or night.'

'Of course, I understand' answered the Chairman – though, clearly, he didn't.

Anna felt pleased as she returned to her hut and set about preparing for the induction course on the morrow.

It was hard going, at first. The girls were eager to learn but could not comprehend how soap could be made from a lump of mutton fat and a pile of wood ash. Istam did his best, but, after an hour, when Anna felt she had made little progress, she had an idea, which delighted the girls and helped them to understand. She drew a series of large cartoons, showing each stage of the process. She stuck them round the walls of the factory. Then each of the girls, in turn, repeated to Anna what was happening in each picture. They were pleased with their progress and thrilled when Anna told them that after a couple of practical sessions, they would be ready to start production.

When they left, Anna felt she had done enough to convince everyone of her intention to stay on in the kolkhoz. Now was the moment to go. She felt a pang of regret at dashing the expectations of her workers... but perhaps they would persist and eventually discover how to make soap for themselves.

She swept the floor of the hut, cleaned the cooking utensils and stacked the folded quilts on the bed. Then she packed her few belongings and the two bars of soap into a bundle with a packet of tea, a handful of dried fruit, a little bag of millet and a dozen small lepyoshka she had baked the previous day. She tucked the eighty roubles inside her shirt. Next she had a supper of soup, lepyoshka and tea and sat down to wait. At ten o'clock she extinguished the kerosene lamp as if she had retired to bed. She sat, in the dark, listening to the girls singing at a party nearby. By midnight all was quiet, except for the sporadic barking of some dogs.

Anna took a last look round the hut, picked up her bundle and opened the door. Checking no-one was about, she crept out. Keeping in the shadow of the tall wall which surrounded the kolkhoz, she made her way to a gap she had noticed several days previously. Her heart was beating loudly and fear made it hard to breathe. She wasn't afraid of her lonely journey across the desert – only of being caught and taken back.

At last she was through the gap and she quickened her pace, eager to get away as fast as possible. It was a chilly night and there was a full moon. Anna suddenly felt tiny and insignificant in the face of the endless, moonlit desert. She calmed herself by finding her half forgotten star in the middle of the Orion constellation.

'My guiding star,' she told herself as she breathed deeply the frosty air and followed the various landmarks she'd picked out when visiting Roman over the last week.

By the time Anna reached Ghizhduvan, the sun was shining and the streets were full of people. She was tired and hungry but wouldn't stop for refreshment. She went straight to the old people's home, to be met with bitter disappointment.

'Your brother made an excellent recovery,' the doctor told her. 'He left two days ago, with his friends and many other Poles. They have gone to the Polish recruiting office in Bukhara.'

Desolate, Anna thanked him and walked away.

'I'm on my own, then,' she thought. Looking up, she saw the railway station in the distance and hurried towards it. It was crowded with passengers, many of them refugees.

'A ticket to Bukhara, please,' Anna said to the ticket clerk.

'There's no direct link to Bukhara,' the man replied. 'The nearest you can get is Kagan, which is about seven kilometres from Bukhara.'

'I can easily walk seven kilometres.' Anna thought, so she said, 'Then I'll take a single ticket to Kagan, please.'

'Can I see your travel permit?'

'Travel permit?'

'Yes, I cannot sell you a ticket if you haven't got a permit.'

In despair, Anna turned away. She noticed a group of Polish people by the station entrance. She longed to speak to them but knew she couldn't spare the time. By now her absence from the kolkhoz would have been noticed. The first place a search party would look was Ghizhduvan... but how could she get away? She hurried out of the station and almost under the wheels of a lorry. The driver swore loudly at her, but it gave her an idea. On her visits to Roman, she had noticed many lorries, loaded with bales of crude cotton and sacks of grain leaving the town and taking the road towards Bukhara. Now she ran up and down the streets, looking for a likely lorry. At last she found one, rather battered, and parked in a side lane. The driver was loading it with cattle cake and a clamour of Uzbeks surrounded it. She heard them haggling with the driver, offering him twenty, then twenty-five roubles for a lift.

'I can do better than that,' she thought and pulled thirty roubles from her precious store, stuffing the rest safely back. She pushed her way through the crowd to the Russian driver.

He was already annoyed by the Uzbek's insistence and, seeing Anna's prison clothes, took her for an urchin and tried to push her away.

'What do you want, you dirty little squirt?' he shouted. Anna had her story ready.

'Please, Tovarishch/Comrade' Anna said meekly, giving a passable imitation of a youth, 'I'm trying to get to Bukhara, where my uncle lives. I was in a labour camp in Siberia until four months ago. Thanks to many kind people, I've managed to reach here. I have only thirty roubles left and would be happy if you would accept them. I have also documents to prove I'm telling the truth. Will you help a poor orphan?'

The driver gave Anna a long look. To her mortification, she felt herself blushing, suspecting he guessed she was lying. But he laughed and said, 'It's only fifteen roubles for a dirty little cheat like you.' He gave her a shove up into the lorry. Greatly relieved, she hoped that none of the Uzbeks had understood the exchange.

The arguments on the ground continued but, finally, eight Uzbeks joined Anna among the sacks of cattle cake. They gave her hostile stares but left her alone. At about midday, the driver was ready to leave.

'Hide among the sacks and keep quiet until we are out of town,' he instructed. 'I'm not licenced to carry passengers.'

Once on the open road, Anna sat with the sun on her face, leaning on her bundle.

'I'm really on my way,' she told herself. 'Tonight or tomorrow morning, I shall enlist and join my friends.'

An hour before sunset, the dusty highway gave way to a cobbled road and the driver stopped, jumped down from his cabin and shouted, 'Everyone down! This is as far as I take you. There's Bukhara. If you're lucky and can run fast, you might get to the city gates before they lock them for the night.'

The Uzbeks scrambled down but Anna, having picked up her bundle, stood up and looked over the top of the driver's cabin, in the direction he had indicated. She stood, transfixed by the sight of one of the oldest cities in Asia.

Bukhara seemed suspended in the air against a darkening sky, encircled by its ancient bronzed walls. Above those rose domes and minarets, shimmering in the slanting rays of the setting sun. All this floated in a dust haze, towards which the straight road ran gleaming like molten copper.

'Hey you, urchin!' shouted the driver. 'Have you taken root up there. I must be off. Get down here now, or I'll come up and throw you down, myself.'

Shaken out of her reverie, Anna jumped down and paid the driver, with a conciliatory grin and dip of her head.

'I'm sorry, Tovarishch. I didn't mean to hold you up. Thank you for your kindness.'

He clapped her on the shoulder and waved her off and then drove away.

Anna walked quickly towards the shining city and entered its gates just before sunset.

Darkness fell suddenly and, feeling apprehensive, Anna walked along several streets before she came to a tchaikhana. A red faced man came over as Anna entered. He eyed her suspiciously.

'I'm looking for some information and for somewhere to stay for the night. Can you help me, please?' she asked.

'Have you got a ticket from the bath house, confirming you have been de-loused?' he demanded rudely.

'I'll get one straight away,' Anna said, red with shame. 'I have money for a bowl of tea. Will you sell me one, please and I'll stand here and drink it?' The man gave an exclamation of disgust.

'Get out, you filthy, flea-bitten urchin!' and he chased her away.

She didn't know what to do next but, seeing a sign to the bath

239

house, she hurried there to find it had just closed until the next day.

Despondently, she wandered about the town, trying one tchaikhana after another. None would serve her with tea, even though she offered to drink it outside on the pavement.

Creeping along the walls of shuttered buildings, she stopped a passer-by and asked him to direct her to the nearest militia station. Without a word, he pointed to an old building at the end of the street and walked quickly away. Tired and desperately thirsty, Anna dragged herself to the door, which was open. She walked into the room, where four militiamen were playing cards and drinking tea, under a dirty shaded light. They stared at her with surprise.

'Yes?' one of them said, shortly.

'Please could you tell me where I can find the Polish envoy?' she asked timidly.

'We're off duty,' answered the soldier. 'Go away and come back tomorrow.' Anna was almost in tears.

'I have nowhere to sleep,' she protested. 'The bath house is shut so I cannot get a de-lousing certificate. I'm on my own and can't even get a bowl of tea, though I have the money for one. Can you help me, please?'

'Get out of here!' shouted a second soldier. 'We don't want any of your hard luck stories here. We're off duty. Get out or we'll throw you out.'

Anna was stunned by their callousness and panic stricken by the idea of a night in the open in this strange and hostile city. She walked out and stood still for a moment.

'I must find shelter,' was her only thought. 'I must find shelter.' She started a frantic search for any sort of sheltered place in which she could hide until morning. A freezing wind was blowing and she had lost all feeling in her hands and feet. She became light-headed with thirst and exhaustion and, without realising how, she found herself up against the city wall. She felt her way along it and, shaking herself back to consciousness, spotted a deep niche about ten feet above the ground. Somehow she managed to clamber up to it, bruising her hands and shins on the way. Then, she curled herself up as tightly as she could and waited for morning. Scalding tears ran down her cheeks but she had not energy enough to brush them away.

After a while, the moon which had highlighted Anna's niche, disappeared. The darkness was absolute. Anna was afraid to sleep in case she should fall out of her hole. She tried to eat the remaining lepioshki, but they crumbled as she held them and mixed with the dust on which she lay. In spite of herself, she dozed and woke with the sun shining in her eyes. She massaged some feeling into her numbed hands and body and then scrambled to the ground and moved stiffly into the city.

She asked for directions to the Polish Representative's Office and arrived there to find it situated in a villa which was surrounded by a high wall. The tall gate was open and Anna walked into the courtyard. She stopped in surprise and dismay, for it was full of desperate, dishevelled people, Poles, Ukrainians, Jews. All humanity seemed to be there, aggressive, shoving towards the closed door of the villa and cursing the Representative for not opening it on time. Anna was propelled forward by the throng and, suddenly, the door opened and three men stepped out. They shouted for calm and order and demanded that the refugees form a queue, to no avail. Fighting broke out as people jostled for position and Anna, certain she would be crushed to death if she stayed, managed, with difficulty to push against the crowd and gain the comparative safety of the street.

She sat down against the wall of the courtyard,
'I'll wait until later and try my luck again, when some of the crowd has been dealt with,' she told herself. She was parched and very hungry. She felt dizzy and weak and dozed fitfully until she woke, with a start, to hear the town clock striking three.
Her little bundle of belongings had disappeared.
Anna couldn't believe anyone could stoop so low as to steal a bundle from a beggar – for that was what she had become. Frantically, she searched around but it was nowhere to be seen and no-one she asked had seen it go.
She sank down again, against the wall and closed her eyes.
'I'll wait to die,' she thought. 'There's no hope.' She drifted into unconsciousness but was roused by a gentle Polish voice.

'Are you ill? Can I do anything to help? Speak to me, please.'

Anna opened her eyes and the face of a man swam into view. He was still speaking.

'I work at the Polish Representative's Office. You obviously need some help. Will you let me help you?'

Anna was unable to speak. She wasn't sure if this was a dream. Then the man put his hands under her arms and lifted her and, supporting her weight, took her through the gate, across the still crowded courtyard and into the villa itself. The main corridor was lined with queues of noisy refugees but the man helped Anna past these into a small office and on to a chair.

'Wait here,' he said and disappeared.

'As if I could do anything else,' Anna thought wryly. A moment later the man returned with a mug of hot, sweet tea and a piece of bread. Anna drank the tea slowly and felt strength flowing into her. She looked at the man over the mug. He was in his thirties, had a kind but careworn face and was wearing a tweed suit which was at least two sizes too big for him.

'Tell me how you come to be here,' he said.

So she told him her story, ending with, '…and now my bundle has been stolen and I have absolutely nothing and I just don't know what to do…' She tailed off miserably.

A young woman put her head round the door.

'Marian…' she began, then, seeing Anna, 'Sorry. I didn't know you were busy' and she withdrew.

Marian looked at Anna.

'You've been through a great deal and first you need somewhere safe to stay and…' he smiled, 'a really good wash. We'll find room for you at my lodgings. Do you think you could manage to walk? It's not far.'

Anna nodded gratefully.

The lodgings turned out to be a two-roomed flat. Apart from Marian, three other Poles were already living there, a father and son and a young Franciscan monk. They smiled and shook Anna's hand as they were introduced and then tactfully withdrew to the other room as Marian set a pan of water on the stove.

'Sit here in the warm while the water heats,' he commanded.

On the scrubbed table, he placed a towel, a small piece of carbolic soap, a teaspoon, a little milk and a tin of Ovaltine.

'Wash and then drink,' he advised and left her.

All at once, Anna felt the tears coursing down her dirty face. The beautiful girl smiled up at her from the Ovaltine label, her sheaf of wheat shining in the sun. Anna remembered so vividly her mother and herself seated, at the table at home, their hands cupped round pottery mugs full of the fragrant milky drink. Shaking the picture from her mind, Anna wrenched the lid from the tin and spooned the malty, sweet crunchy granules into her mouth.

That night she slept deeply, lying on a mattress by the stove, screened from the other occupants of the room by a holey blanket, hung over a piece of string.

The next day, Marian brought her a selection of new clothes to try on. They had been donated by large stores, wanting to clear out unsaleable goods. The dresses were garish and Anna estimated, about twenty five years out of date. Finally she selected a skimpy dress, to wear as an undergarment, a large pair of purple ski trousers and a long sleeved woollen blouse. With relief, she burned her filthy, tattered prison trews but kept the padded jacket and cap. She regarded her boots ruefully. They would have to do, although they were misshapen and worn out. She lined them with fresh paper and cloth and tore into strips an old sheet she found among the clothes. These made fine foot wrappings.

'Now I feel almost elegant,' she laughed as she paraded before Marian.

He smiled at her.

'Tomorrow you must come to the office with me,' he said. 'There are forms you must complete so that you can be declared a free Polish citizen.'

The recognition was instant and mutual. An officer stood in the room through which Anna had to pass after registering as a free Polish citizen the next day. It was Captain Nieczuta, the man who had treated her so unfairly in Farab.

Anna tried to ignore him. She turned away but was forced to stop when he spoke to her.

'Why, it's Anna Grzymata Siedlecka, isn't it?' he said. 'May I be of any assistance to you?'

'No thank you,' Anna replied icily. 'I do not require help.'

She was annoyed when the captain followed her into the courtyard.

'Anna Grzymata Siedlecka I have long hoped for an opportunity to apologise to you,' he insisted. 'After you had gone, I discovered the true nature of the officer who had accused you of immoral behaviour. He was deceitful and a liar. I now know you were the innocent person in that whole affair. Please accept my sincere apology for my treatment of you.'

Something in Anna prevented her from softening towards this man who had caused her such unhappiness. She replied, coldly, 'I accept your apology, Captain but I repeat, I do not need anything from you. Now, please excuse me.' She walked away without a backward glance.

After an open air Mass, two days later, the priest blessed the kneeling crowd of refugees and then made the announcement that Anna had been waiting for.

'The Soviet authorities have agreed to allow recommencement of the recruitment of women into the Polish forces. All women who wish to apply should leave Bukhara as soon as possible and proceed to Guzar, which is about 150 kilometres from here. There they must report to H.Q. of the Polish Army Organisation Centre.'

Anna hurried back to the lodgings and was bundling her few possessions together, ready to leave immediately, when Marian stopped her.

'Tomorrow I'll help you get the correct travel documents,' he said. 'You'll have to travel by lorry, to the railway station at Kagan and then get a train to Guzar. Also we must get some food to last you during your journey, which will take about two days. It's useless to rush off now, unprepared.'

Anna knew that he was right. She put her bundle down and resigned herself to waiting another twenty four hours.

By the next evening all her preparations were complete. As she sat down to a farewell supper with the little household, she turned to Marian.

'I can never thank you enough for what you have done for me but I'd love to know why, out of all the refugees inside and outside the courtyard, you chose to help me.'

Marian laughed.

'I just had to find out what lay beneath that ghastly tear-streaked, mud-caked mask,' he replied. 'And now I know, I hope we'll meet again, under happier circumstances, when we are both wearing the uniforms of the Polish Army.'

On the next morning, February 11th 1942, Anna left Bukhara aboard a lorry bound for Kagan. The ancient walls, towers and pinnacles of the city glowed in the early sunlight, an ivory carving against the pale blue sky. Anna settled herself against her bundle.

'I'm really on my way this time,' she said to herself.

CHAPTER 17

Soldier in Uniform

'Are you stupid, woman?' the irate Uzbek station master shouted at Anna. 'This train is on its way to Tashkent, not Guzar. Or perhaps you are not stupid. Perhaps you are a spy! These travel documents are useless here. You must report to the NKVD. They'll know what to do with you.'

The enormity of her mistake, hit Anna like a blow to the stomach. In all the confusion on Kagan Station and, being unable to find an official to direct her, she had boarded a train travelling in the direction opposite to the way she wanted to go. She had landed in a place called Katta Kurgan – after two whole days on the train.

As panic threatened to overwhelm her, a crowd of passengers arrived and surrounded the station master, diverting his attention. Taking advantage of the noisy argument that ensued, Anna slipped away, unnoticed. She threaded her way through the crowd and hid behind a tool shed at the far end of the platform, her heart pounding. She forced herself to take some deep breaths, to be calm, to think clearly.

The train for Tashkent left the station, amidst shouts and cries. From her hiding place, Anna saw the station master check that the platform was clear, then go into his office and close the door. A few minutes later, she heard him padlock the station gates and walk away. There would be no more trains today. Everything was closed for the night.

Still Anna stood by the shed.

'How can I have been so stupid?' she thought. 'If I'm found by the NKVD, I'll be put on trial for being a spy. I'll end up in prison… No! I won't contemplate that. I've simply got to find somewhere to hide and then slip aboard the first possible train for Guzar.'

She had noticed three empty cattle trucks, coupled together, standing in the shunting yard.

'I'll hide in one of those for the night,' she thought. Darkness was falling as, in the shelter of the shed, she crept slowly towards the trucks. A quick dash across the line and she'd reached them. Hoisting herself up, she climbed inside the nearest one. There was a pile of sacks in the corner. Using a couple as a mattress and three as a cover, she made a bed for herself. She had no food or water left but found a handful of dusty raisins in her pocket. These she chewed slowly, to try to alleviate her sharp hunger pangs.

It took her a long time to relax. She was angry with herself, frustrated and still frightened that she would be caught the next day and handed over to the NKVD.

She must have slept because suddenly it was morning and, peeping through the door of the truck, Anna saw a long freight train on one of the platforms, about a hundred meters away. It was facing west. The way she wanted to go.

She didn't stop to think. Grabbing her bundle, she jumped down. She was sheltered from the station buildings by the trucks and made her way slowly and stealthily through the frosty morning air, towards the freight train, looking for a possible point of entry.

Suddenly she stood stock still. There was the sound of marching feet. It was getting louder. Then, unbelievably, the melody of a Polish song reached her and, finally she could hear the words, in her own beloved tongue:

'*The weeping willows are crying*
And my girl is crying too...'

It was too much for Anna. She broke cover and ran towards the marching column, waving her arms and sobbing.

'Please, please wait! I am Polish too. Please help me!'

The youthful officer at the head of the men gave a sharp order. The soldiers halted and stared at Anna in amazement.

'You need our assistance? How can we help you?' The officer put his hand on Anna's shoulder in a kindly way. She stopped crying.

'Now is the time to be calm and coherent,' she told herself. She took a deep breath and looked up at the sympathetic face.

'I need to get to Guzar to join the Polish army. I set out three days ago from Kagan but, mistakenly, travelled in the wrong direction. The station master threatened to hand me over to the NKVD but I escaped from him and have been hiding in a truck all night. I have no food or water. Please help me.'

'This freight train is military transport. No civilians are allowed to travel in it...' but, seeing the look of despair on Anna's face, the officer continued, '...I'll find the Major and speak up for you. I must warn you, though, he's a stickler for discipline. Still, I doubt if even he would abandon a young Polish girl to the mercy of the NKVD.'

By now, they had reached the train and the soldiers climbed aboard.

'Wait here,' said the officer and he walked on to the platform where a group of Polish officers were chatting. Anna saw the young man salute and speak to a middle aged officer, who looked at her and then walked over, followed by the rest of the group, who regarded her curiously. The Major addressed Anna in a clipped voice.

'I believe, madam that my officer has explained to you that no civilians are allowed to travel on military transport. If I allow you on to the train and the Russians discover you, you and I will both be in very serious trouble.'

Anna swallowed hard, trying to hide her fear but, nevertheless, her voice shook as she replied, 'I've no wish to embarrass you or get you into trouble but my situation is desperate. If you go without me, I shall have to give myself up to the NKVD and I daren't think of the consequences if they refuse to believe my story and arrest me as a spy. My fate is in your hands.'

The Major regarded Anna with a frown and said, suddenly, 'Are you afraid of horses?'

Bewildered, Anna shook her head.

'Gentlemen...' the Major turned to his officers. Before he could complete his sentence the junior officers surrounded Anna, smiling and welcoming her.

'This way, please,' they chorused and she was escorted to a cattle truck at the end of the train. Strong hands helped her into the truck and on to some bales of hay.'

'We're off in a moment,' one of them called to her. 'Stay hidden until we say it's safe to come out.' The door was shut and Anna was alone.

Well, not quite alone for, as her eyes grew accustomed to the gloom, she saw, at the far end of the truck, three horses tethered to a horizontal wooden bar. They seemed unperturbed by their new companion and went on munching as the train lurched forward.

Anna rearranged some bales of hay, to make a cosy nest. It smelled, delightfully of mown grass and herbs. The coal smoke from the engine drifted through the ventilation slots and, trying to forget how hungry she was, Anna fell asleep.

When she woke up, the train was stationary. She was stiff and ravenous and the horses were stamping impatiently. Anna lay hidden until the door was opened and a cheerful voice called, 'It's all right. You can come out of hiding now.' An officer and three soldiers grinned down at her as she struggled to stand. They took the horses out and returned with a large mug of sweet, hot tea and a thick slice of bread. The officer said,

'This is just to keep you going. Proper breakfast will be served to you in about half an hour. Please remember to stay in the truck and to always remain hidden until you're told the coast is clear.'

'I won't forget,' answered Anna. 'Thank you so much for your kindness.' She gulped some of the tea, shivering, her teeth chattering against the side of the mug.

Half an hour later, three of the soldiers returned. One held a bowl of soup and some bread, one a bucket of warm water and a towel. The third carried a Polish cavalry greatcoat, a woollen waistcoat and a pair of thick, outsized gloves.

'Presents from some of us,' he smiled. Anna's eyes filled with tears as she thanked them for their kindness.

Wrapped in the thick coat, Anna enjoyed her breakfast. She washed as well as she could and had just finished when there was a rap on the door and the Major climbed into the truck.

'Are you feeling better?' he asked.

'Very much better, thank you,' Anna answered 'and thank you very much for all you have done and are doing...'

'The Major cut in. 'Don't worry about that,' he said brusquely, 'in times of trouble, we Poles must stick together. Now, tell me the whole of your story. Remind me how you come to be here at this time.'

So Anna told him what had happened to her since the start of the war. When she had finished, he smiled.

'It would be such a pity if you were caught now after all that has befallen you. Be very careful. Stay concealed. Don't attempt to leave this truck until we reach Guzar in two day's time. I'm taking my unit beyond that, to Shahrisyabs but the train will stop at Guzar and it will be my pleasure to hand you over safely to the Polish Army's garrison officer when we arrive there.'

Late that afternoon, Anna was looking through a gap in the planks of the truck. The train slowed as it passed through a station. She read its name and smiled grimly.

'Kagan' and she thought how horrified Marian would be if he knew that, at that moment, she was back where she had started all those hours ago.

On February 16th the train stopped in Guzar. Anna had been well fed by the soldiers, who had visited whenever they could. She had been overwhelmed by their solicitude and kindness and when they crowded round the truck as she left the train, she felt as if she were leaving friends behind.

'Thank you all so much,' she managed to say as she felt tears in her eyes. 'I haven't been happier or better looked after since I left home at the start of the war. My best wishes go with you. I shall pray for you every night.'

'Come Anna, it's time for you to go,' called the Major over the heads of his men. She gave them a last wave and joined the Major. As they walked along the platform together towards the Polish Transport Officer, he said sternly, 'Well young lady, I hope this is an end of your independent globe trotting.' His eyes were twinkling at her as he introduced her to the Transport Officer. Then he shook

Anna's hand and, turning back to the train, called over his shoulder, 'Farewell and good luck.' With that he was gone.

In the waiting room, Anna gave her particulars to an NCO. Several shabby, tired looking women were sitting in the room.

'These ladies are also prospective volunteers,' the officer informed Anna. You will all be served with soup and bread in a few minutes and then you will be transported to temporary billets.'

Half an hour later Anna and the other women were bumping through the streets of Guzar, towards the billets, in a horse drawn cart.

Later Anna had to admit to herself that her first taste of army life was a disappointment. This was what she had longed for, journeyed towards, endured hardships for and what was it?

An inhospitable cold hut, already almost full of sleeping women, a reed mat, two thin cotton blankets and a lumpy pillow. A woman in army uniform and Russian boots, briskly told the recruits that the latrines weren't yet built and they'd have to make do with the rough ground behind the hut.

'No water is available at this time of night,' she informed them. 'Tomorrow you can wash in the irrigation canal which runs nearby. Now find yourself a space and go to sleep in it.'

Anna squeezed herself between two sleeping women. Shivering, she pulled the great coat on top of the blankets, silently thanking the generous soldiers for the gift. Then she tried to sleep.

Reveille sounded at dawn. The new recruits were marched to the army field kitchen and given millet porridge and weak tea. It was starting to snow as they returned to the hut and, chilled, they huddled round the stove until they were called for the evening meal of rice, mutton fat, tea and bread. After they had eaten, the woman they had seen the previous night came into the hut and addressed them.

'You may be wondering why we cannot feed you better,' she began. 'It's because the Soviet authorities won't supply food to Polish civilians, even to those who are waiting to join the army. The soldiers, already on meager rations, donate some of their food to feed you and the hundreds of refugees who were camped around the town. You should report, as soon as possible, to the Polish Army Organisation H.Q., on this site. There you will be interviewed, medically examined and if suitable, allotted to appropriate units. Those not suitable will be sent to the Women's Army Reserve Centre and trained in a variety of skills.'

Early the next morning, Anna, anticipating a speedy enrolment, presented herself at the army H.Q. but the soldier on guard at the door would not let her pass.

'But we were told to come here,' Anna protested.

'Sorry Madam. My orders are to let no-one through unless they have a pass from the small army office over there. It opens at midday.'

Anna looked in the direction he indicated and saw a crowd of women queuing outside a closed door.

She joined them and at last, the door opened and an officer appeared.

'We can issue no passes today, I'm afraid, ladies,' he called above the hubbub of voices. 'We're waiting for a full list of the names and particulars of volunteers. This may take two or three days. Go back to your billets. You must just be patient.' Ignoring the cries of protest, he went inside and closed the door.

Anna stood still as despair and then anger swept over her.

'I have come so far,' she thought 'and been through a lot to join the army, to fight for my country and now I am being prevented by my own people – by stupid red tape.'

Disconsolately, she joined the other women and returned to the cold, inhospitable billet. There they huddled round the stove, only venturing out twice a day for meals. Conditions were worsening. Clothes and beds were damp. The floor was filthy from the mud they could not help bringing in on their shoes. The ground behind the hut had become a stinking quagmire through lack of sanitation and there was an acute shortage of water. Anna developed a hacking cough and sore throat. Influenza and dysentery were rife and lice abounded.

On the fourth day, Anna decided she couldn't wait in idleness any longer. She would go to H.Q. and demand to know why everything was taking so long. Weak and sick, she clutched her greatcoat around her. In spite of a pale sun, the bitter wind penetrated even that. She walked straight past the guard and, steeped in misery and weak with hunger as she was, she didn't, at first, realise that a man was trying to attract her attention.

'Weren't you in Poyma?' A portly, middle aged Polish lieutenant touched Anna's arm. She stopped.

'Yes, I was.' Then she recognised him as a member of one of the lumberjack brigades in the taiga. She hadn't known him well but remembered his name as Alfred.

'Are you ill?' His kind face was concerned as Anna coughed.

'Not badly so,' she answered. 'Just cold and very depressed at having to wait around in terrible conditions to join the army. We can't get any information about why it's taking so long and when things might move forward.' She curbed a desire to cry on this stranger's shoulder and quickly told him about her journey from Asino to Guzar and her fruitless attempts to acquire a permit to see the recruiting officer.

'Come with me. We'll see what can be done.' smiled Alfred.

Half an hour later, Anna walked out of H.Q., a member of the Polish army. Her new friend was waiting for her in the courtyard.

'You have been assigned to a unit called SK 11.' he explained. 'You'll work here, at H.Q. and must report here in the morning. Now we'll go to the stores for your uniform.'

Anna could hardly believe the speed at which everything was happening. They hurried to the store and although there was no proper uniform for her, she proudly donned new underwear, a khaki padded jacket and trousers, thick woollen stockings, a new cap with ear flaps and knee length leather boots.

Without regret, she discarded her old, dirty, damp clothes – all except for the cavalry coat, which she was allowed to keep, once it had been de-loused.

Alfred accompanied Anna back to her billet to collect her belongings and then to the Soviet Army tents, the home of the

P.S.K./Auxiliary Women's Service Volunteers. There he left her, dismissing her thanks with a smile and a wave.

Anna enquired the whereabouts of the Commandant and was directed to a friendly, efficient officer who showed her to her tent and introduced her to some of her tent-mates. It was immediately clear that conditions in this tent were no better than those Anna had left behind. It was unheated and cramped, two raised earth platforms, on which straw palliasses were placed side by side, served as beds. Outside, narrow wooden planks afforded boots little protection from the churned mud. The other women, however, were friendly, chatting about their different duties and explaining to Anna the army routine.

'Which office have you been assigned to?' one of them asked. When Anna replied,

'SK 11,' there was an awkward silence and she was sure that she was not imagining the sudden reserve and change of subject. She had no time to puzzle about this as her group was called and marched to the kitchen for supper and then to a large tent for evening prayers. As she stretched herself on her damp bed that night, looking forward to the challenge of the morrow, she was filled with happiness.

'I am in the army. I am a real Polish soldier in uniform.' She repeated to herself again and again until, at last, she fell asleep.

At H.Q. the next morning, she found her office and was greeted by her Chief, Captain Janusz M., who presented her with an ancient Underwood typewriter and a pile of documents which she was to copy. She was painfully slow, at first, but by the end of a week, her speed had increased and she had settled happily into office life. She made friends with Jadzia, a woman of her own age, who was working at another old typewriter next to Anna. Her cough, though had become worse, her head ached and her body felt heavy. Her Captain sent her to the garrison doctor, who gave her a couple of aspirins and told her to keep warm – which was easier said than done.

Apart from worries about her health, Anna was unhappy in her billet. The other women were polite to her but never friendly. They stopped their conversations when she approached and she was too shy to ask the reason for their apparent dislike of her. One day, she saw Albert on her way back from H.Q.

'Anna,' he called and came over to her. 'How are you? Are you happy in your work?'

'I'm very happy at the office, thank you,' she replied. 'But for some reason the women in my tent have taken a dislike to me. No-one talks to me. I'm sure I haven't done anything to upset them. I just can't understand it.'

'Ah,' the Lieutenant smiled knowingly. 'Did you tell them which office you are working in?'

'Yes, but...'

The Lieutenant laughed loudly and a couple of other officers gathered round to discover the joke.'

'Gentlemen,' Albert intoned. 'Allow me to introduce you to Anna, the latest victim of the stupid misconception of the purpose of our department.'

Anna was baffled by the laughter and knowing looks. The Lieutenant went on to explain.

'SK 11' is the Polish Military Intelligence Department,' he said. 'Those who don't understand what we do, imagine we are spying on them, reporting any misdemeanour.'

'It's happened to us all,' smiled Alfred, another lieutenant, a pleasant man who worked in Anna's office. 'Just assure your tent-mates that what you do is not, in any way connected with them and remain friendly and helpful. They'll come round. They'll get over their suspicion in time.' He went on to explain the duties of the department and Anna was relieved to have the mystery explained. She found that within a few days the women were indeed beginning to relax when she was present and by the end of another week, they had become quite friendly.

Anna's only worry was her deteriorating health. Her cough grew worse and she found herself short of breath and lacking in energy. When she was ordered to join all new volunteers, for a month's basic training, she became seriously concerned. The course was held four kilometres from Guzar and the Commandant was a fearsome woman, a veteran of the First World War. The training was strenuous and relentless and by the end of the first week, Anna lay on her bed and thought about dying.

'It would be a welcome relief,' she muttered to herself. Her body ached, her throat was inflamed and her head pounded.

The next day, Albert visited the camp and sought Anna out.

'How are you?' he asked.

'Please, please rescue me,' Anna begged in a hoarse whisper. 'I don't think I can carry on in this state – or I wouldn't ask.'

'I don't think I can help you,' he replied. 'You see, the Powers That Be have decreed that every volunteer must survive this course, without exception. This is the big test. You must prove you are fit to belong to the Auxiliary Women's Service.'

For two more days, Anna managed to complete the tasks set and then, on the point of collapse, she was pulled up short by a shout from the duty NCO.

'You're to report to the Commandant at once,' he barked. 'At the double.'

Anna had hardly entered the office, when the Commandant, looking up, narrowed her eyes and exclaimed harshly.

'How dare you go behind my back, seeking favours from male officers? I am in charge here. Any problems should be brought to me. I make the decisions.' Before Anna could reply, the officer went on, 'I will not have anyone under my command shirking duties, making excuses…'

She swam before Anna's eyes, the gaunt woman, with her short cropped grey hair and bushy eyebrows. Anna leant against the door frame and summoned all her wits in time to hear '…take you back to camp, where the Medical Officer will examine you. If he finds nothing wrong with you, you will have me to reckon with.' She called the duty NCO.

'Take this recruit to the camp entrance,' she ordered. 'A cart is waiting to transport her.'

Back at camp, the M.O. diagnosed severe tonsillitis and sent Anna to bed.

He visited her daily and her tent-mates ensured she had food and water.

Anna was delighted when she received an unexpected visitor. It was Marek Shapiro.

'I've just arrived here,' he told her. 'I've joined your team at SK 11.'

'That's wonderful! Have you seen Severyn or Roman?' she said eagerly.

'I'm afraid I haven't,' he answered. 'Why don't you write to the Polish Army HQ to enquire about their whereabouts?'

The next day, she wrote the letter and the day after, she was deemed well enough to return to her duties in the office.

CHAPTER 18

The Mosque of Guzar

'The typhus epidemic has hit Guzar. Twenty Polish soldiers have gone down with it already.' It was Alfred who brought this alarming news to the office a few days after Anna's return. 'It's probably been transmitted by the huge influx of Polish refugees,' he went on. 'The quarantine hospital set up in the school is full already.'

'I've heard they are going to use the old mosque in Guzar as a hospital,' added one of the women who worked in the office. 'Part of it is derelict but the rest is all right – just filthy and bare. It will need a superhuman effort to make it habitable and fit to be used as a hospital.'

Anna bent her aching head over her typewriter and tried to concentrate. She had seen the thousands of refugees arriving, exhausted, starving, sick and hoping for help from the Polish Military. Often soldiers would bring in a group of small, orphaned children, who had travelled on their own for hundreds of miles, led by an older sibling. Teams of PSK volunteers and medical staff had organised reception points. Unfortunately the acute shortage of food, medicine and disinfectants made the task of catering for them properly, impossible.

A week later the mosque was receiving its first patients. Alfred had been to look and came back full of praise for the volunteers working there.

'It's on a hill, about 300 metres from the river,' he reported. 'Those amazing women have to carry every drop of water they need up the hill. They're making do with so little bedding and a very few kitchen utensils and, do you know, there is only one latrine bucket for every hundred patients!'

Anna shivered.

'Thank God I survived typhus when I was small,' she thought. 'I don't think you can have it twice. Our office seems immune – no-one here has caught it. Long may it stay that way!'

A few days later, Alfred asked her to stay late in the office to finish some work. She was feeling unwell again, but didn't like to refuse. As she was typing a list of names, she found it more and more difficult to focus on the print. Suddenly sharp pains shot through her head, all became black and she slumped to the floor.

When she regained consciousness, Alfred, Jadzia and the garrison Medical Officer, Dr Jadzia, were bending over her.

'It's pneumonia,' announced the doctor. 'She shouldn't have slept in that damp tent with tonsillitis. She never had a chance to get over it properly. She can't go back there.' Alfred turned away and spoke in a low voice to a couple of the other officers present. Then he turned to the doctor.

'Anna can come back to our lodgings with us. We'll make room for her. You're sure she's not carrying an infection that might spread?'

'Quite sure, at this stage,' replied the M.O.

Later, Anna had no recollection of her journey to the lodgings and little of the next few days, except of a sheet hung across a room, for privacy and a kind women tending to her needs. One evening, when she was feeling a little better, she was propped up, listening to one of Alfred's funny stories, when two Russians burst into the room, one a military doctor and one a militiaman.

The doctor addressed Alfred.

'What is this sick woman doing here? You Poles were given specific instructions that everyone suffering from typhus must be taken to the nearest hospital.'

Alfred stood up.

'This lady is suffering from pneumonia. Who told you she has typhus?'

'That is no business of yours but I'll tell you. It was the landlord and he did the right thing. Now I will examine this patient. I will make the diagnosis and the decision about whether she can stay here.'

And this he proceeded to do, despite protests from Alfred and Anna. After a moment, the man gave a triumphant cry.

'Aha... not typhus, you say? What is this rash then on her chest and abdomen? Let me tell you! It is the tell-tale typhus rash. She cannot stay here but must be moved to the hospital in the mosque at once.'

Anna retained only hazy memories of what followed. Accompanied by Alfred, she was carried to a cart, bumped the short distance to the mosque, then carried on a stretcher and placed in a row of other sufferers in the courtyard. Anna's eyes were wide with fear. She felt sure that once she was taken into this dreadful place, she would never again see the blue sky above her or hear the birds sing. Alfred bent over her and, trying to reassure her, whispered,

'Dear child, don't worry, you'll recover soon. The matron and the good doctors will care for you. Just rest and get well. We'll miss you. Come back to us soon.'

Anna was too weak to answer, but she gripped his hand and let the tears flow down her cheeks.

Soon she was taken into a small room and gently washed. Her black, shoulder length hair was cut and her head shaved. Then she was wrapped in a thin blanket and carried to a larger room to lie on a rush mat, on the floor with twenty other women.

There followed the most frightening fortnight of Anna's life. She hallucinated almost constantly, racked by excruciating pains. She was being tortured by the Gestapo. She was being beaten and burned because she wouldn't betray the whereabouts of General Anders and General Sikorski. When she regained a sort of semi-consciousness, she was convinced that the nurses and doctors were German agents and she agonised on how she could warn the generals of the danger they were in.

One morning, Father Judycki, the garrison chaplain visited.

'Anna,' he said, then hesitated. 'Anna, I think it's time for you to make your confession and take Holy Communion. It will give you peace.'

Anna was semi-conscious and answered,

'I'm sorry, Father, I can't make my confession. If you should be captured by the Nazis and tortured, you may be forced to give away my secret and the generals will die. I'm truly sorry, but there is one thing you could do for me, please. Could you bring me a copy of "The Imitation of Christ" by Thomas a Kempis?'

Surprised, the priest replied,

'I will try, my child, I will try.'

The crisis came at last. Anna woke one night, shivering and cold but lucid. A small lantern flickered in a wall niche. She could see the faithful Alfred, dressed in a doctor's white coat, sitting on the floor by her side, his eyes closed. Suddenly the tiny lantern flame seemed to recede into the distance, Anna became even colder and she knew she was about to die and there was something she had to say before she did.

'Alfred,' she managed in a hoarse whisper, 'Alfred, wake up. I must talk to you.'

Immediately, he was awake and bending close to her.

'What is it, Annechka?'

'Alfred, I'm dying but I'm not afraid. There's just one thing-please, please don't let them bury me in that ditch and cover me with lime. I would like a coffin. Please!'

'You're not dying, Annechka.' His voice shook. 'You will live.'

'Please, Alfred. Please promise...' Anna trailed off, weakly.

'I promise, my poor child. Even if I have to take down the gate of the H.Q., you shall have your coffin...' At that moment, one of the doctors, hearing voices, came into the room.

'Please Doctor, save her. Give her an injection. She's dying,' pleaded Alfred, tears in his eyes.

The doctor took Anna's wrist and said quietly,

'There's nothing more I can do for her. In a matter of minutes, she'll be at peace. Her body's covered with boils, caused by camphor injections. The only other possibility is a calcium injection but that won't help her now. I doubt if I could find a vein, anyway. Let her die in peace. She has suffered enough.'

'He's talking about me,' thought Anna. He says I'll be dead in a couple of minutes and I don't mind... I don't mind.' but Alfred was beseeching the doctor.

'Just try to save her, please. For my sake, just try.'

Anna was just conscious of the tourniquet, the needle, an all enveloping heat and then she knew no more.

She awoke the next morning, without a trace of fever but quite unable to move. She was weak beyond belief and sore all over. But she was alive.

Her slow climb back to health and strength had begun.

At first, she could not turn on her mat and developed bedsores alongside the dreadful boils which covered her body. Her hearing was impaired and she had great difficulty speaking and swallowing. She was coaxed into drinking small amounts of thin soup and spoons full of red wine from a bottle sent by her office colleagues. No visitors were allowed now because of the spread of infection so her contact with the outside world was through short letters sent from the office, particularly from Alfred. These were delivered to her by Dr Tajchner, the garrison medical officer, who told her what was happening in the garrison and the wider world.

As Anna's strength slowly began to return, she lay and marvelled at the selfless devotion of the doctors and nursing staff, who battled for each patient's life in such appalling conditions. Although they must have been exhausted and often sad and disheartened, they never failed to smile and give an encouraging word as they went about their duties and to spend a few minutes of comfort with the dying.

A new doctor joined the medical team at the mosque, Dr Moszkowicz.

'Where's your home town?' he asked Anna one day.

'Warsaw.'

'I'm from Warsaw too.' He grinned delightedly. They were soon talking about life 'back home' and discovered they knew many people in common. After that, he often stopped for a chat. Another favourite visitor was the garrison chaplain, Father Judycki. One day he arrived looking, as usual, more like a dashing cavalry officer than a priest. He wore a battle-dress blouse, jodhpurs and shiny long boots and carried a small book, which he handed to Anna.

'I'm sorry it's taken me so long to track down,' he said with a smile. 'It wasn't easy to get hold of.' It was a pocket copy of the 'Imitation of Christ.'

Four weeks passed. Each day Anna grew a little stronger, although she had not fully regained her hearing and couldn't yet walk. Water was in short supply and she, along with all the other patients, was encrusted with dirt and covered in vermin. She watched, in horror, as fat lice crawled on her bedding and her body.

On a warm spring day in the middle of March, the news Anna had been waiting for came.

'I think you're ready to transfer to the convalescent quarters,' Dr Moszkowicz announced. Dr Tajchner will look after you there. I'll miss our chats. Your transport will arrive early this afternoon.'

'How can I ever thank you and all the staff here bringing me back from the brink of death and caring for me?'

'Just get well, that's all the thanks we need.' was the reply.

Anna was carried into the bath house, bathed and wrapped in a clean towel. Her soiled hospital gown was burnt. She sat, serenely, waiting for her own laundered clothes to be brought to her. A young nurse hurried in, her face red.

'I'm so sorry, Anna. It appears that your clothes have been burnt, in error. I can't find anything for you to wear. You'll have to wait a day or two until we can obtain some garments for you.'

Anna felt sick. She had been looking forward, so much, to leaving the mosque, to breathing fresh air, to leaving behind the stench of sickness and death. Suddenly, she couldn't bear the thought of staying there even one more night. Her eyes filled with tears.

Just then a senior nurse came in, carrying a bundle of clothes.

'I've unearthed these things,' she explained. They're not really very suitable but they are clean and they'll cover you up.'

So it was that Anna left the mosque, wearing a pair of patched man's underpants, a cotton vest, a pair of enormous boots, an outsize army greatcoat and a forage cap. The sun shone as she was carried to the waiting horse drawn cart. She waved to the matron who stood at the top of the mosque.

'Thank you very much for everything,' she called as the cart drew away. 'I'm off to set a new fashion trend... Thank you!'

CHAPTER 19

The last lap to Freedom

'I'm so sorry we have to leave you behind, Anna but *you* know you're just not strong enough to travel yet.' Alfred's arm rested on Anna's shoulder as she sobbed.

'I could try. I might be all right.'

'You wouldn't be. You know that really. Think of all the care you've been given at the mosque and here at this convalescent centre. You can't throw all that away. Also, it wouldn't be fair on your colleagues if they had to nurse you, would it? Dr Tajchner and the new Chief of SK 11 have both promised me that they'll look after you. You can follow us as soon as you are fully fit.'

A few days earlier, Anna had heard that there was to be an evacuation of a large contingent of the Polish Force to Iran but she had not anticipated that almost all of her work colleagues, including Alfred, would be among the first to go. She felt desolate. But Alfred had a surprise in store.

'There's someone I want to introduce you to,' he said and beckoned to a young woman, in civilian clothes, who was standing shyly by the entrance to the tent.

'This is Stefa, Anna. She's your new friend and she'll look after you. I will pray for your swift recovery and I'm sure we'll meet again soon. God bless you and keep you. Farewell.'

With this, he hurried away.

Anna couldn't speak. She turned away from Stefa and the three women with whom she shared the tent and wept. A wound left by the lancing of a big boil on her arm would not heal. Her arm was swollen and throbbing. She allowed herself to sink into depression and despair, falling, eventually into an exhausted sleep.

That night she had a nightmare.

The matron of the mosque stood by her bed.

'Get dressed, you must come back to the mosque with me.'

'I can't walk that far,' Anna protested.

'You must come.' The matron was persistent. 'Dr Moszkowicz is dying of typhus. He is asking for you.'

Anna and the matron hurried over cobblestones, Anna tripping now and again because her shoe laces weren't properly tied.

Then she was in a small hospital room. The doctor, his face waxen, was leaning against the wall, supported by a nurse. Anna took him gently in her arms and lowered him on to a bed. She knelt beside him, holding his hand, until he shut his eyes with a long sigh. Her friend was dead.

Anna woke with a start and cried out. Immediately, Stefa was at her side.

'Are you in pain? Can I get something for you?' she asked.

Anna shook her head and, needing to talk to someone, recounted her dream. She couldn't sleep again that night and Stefa stayed by her until dawn. In the morning the news came. Dr Moszkowicz had died during the night, of typhus.

In a strange way, that was a turning point for Anna. She was extremely sad at the death of the doctor but she knew that he had worked very hard on her account.

'I owe it to his memory to shake myself out of this self pity,' she told herself. 'I must concentrate on getting well. That's what he would want me to do.'

She found a faithful friend in Stefa, who kept the tent spotless. She was short, stocky and very strong.

It was thanks to her perseverance and patience that Anna started to walk again and was soon taking short trips round the camp.

'You spoil me atrociously,' laughed Anna one day, when Stefa brought in a small piece of soap for her, that she had somehow managed to obtain.

Stefa's plain face lit with a smile.

'I promised the Lieutenant I'd do all I could for you,' she said. 'He picked me out from a crowd of refugees and asked me to look after a sick friend of his. I don't want to let him down.'

'How did you come to be here?' asked Anna. And then she heard Stefa's sad story.

'Before the war, I lived with my father and little brother, Jerzy in southern Poland. My mother died just after my brother was born. My father was an alcoholic. He knocked me around when he was drunk. He wouldn't let me go to school. I had to look after the house so I never learned to read or write. One day, I came home to find that my father had hanged himself. Now Jerzy and I were quite alone and destitute. We had to get out of the house, my brother was sick and I couldn't find work. I found a deserted cellar and left Jerzy there alone, during the day while I begged for scraps of food and a few grosze.

Jerzy became very ill. I couldn't do anything to help him and, one night, he died in my arms. I was heartbroken and became ill, myself but I had to go on begging or die.

Not long after this, I was raped. I had nothing to lose, now, so I became a prostitute.

At the start of the war, all the street girls, including me, were rounded up by the Soviet militia and deported to Kazakhastan, where we worked on a state farm until the amnesty. Then I joined a transport of Polish refugees and travelled for months, eventually arriving here, in Guzar, where the Lieutenant found me.' She paused for a moment and then said, sadly,

'So you see, Annechka, I am a bad, ignorant woman. Perhaps now you will want nothing more to do with me.'

Moved by the story, Anna put her arms around the young woman.

'You're not bad, Stefa. You were the victim of circumstances. I'm very glad to know you and you're playing such a big part in helping me to get well. The Lieutenant would be proud of you. As for being ignorant, why don't I teach you to read and write? It'll give us something to do while I wait to be strong enough to go back to work. Would you like that?'

Stefa's hug and smiling face were all the answer Anna needed and so the lessons began. Stefa proved to be bright and eager to learn and was making great headway when Dr Tajchner declared Anna fit and ready to return to the normal sleeping quarters.

'You'll be able to go back to work in about a week, Anna, he said and don't worry, the lessons can still go on,' He looked at Stefa. 'Father Judycki and I have arranged for you to be enlisted in the PSK, if you wish. There's a vacancy in the garrison infirmary that I think you'd fill very well. What do you think?'

Stefa's face was radiant.

'Oh yes please.' she breathed.

New British A.T.S. uniforms had arrived while Anna was ill and she was thrilled to receive a smart new jacket and skirt, poplin blouse, elegant leather shoes, khaki stockings and two sets of proper underwear.

Stefa came for her lesson each evening and was making excellent progress. Anna returned to the office and although she felt out of place at first, because, apart from Jadzia, there had been an almost complete turnover of staff, she was soon absorbed by her work. She still showed signs of her serious illness. She was painfully thin and her hair wouldn't grow, but remained a blue, black stubble. She also suffered from night blindness and fits of dizziness. Above all, she was always ravenous.

At the end of April 1942, the Chief in Anna's office made an announcement.

'Next week, on the 3rd May, Polish National Day, all P.S.K. volunteers are to make an oath of allegiance. The Primate of Poland, Archbishop Gawlina, will celebrate a field Mass at the Women's Army Reserve Centre. Breakfast will be early so that you can meet by H.Q. at 8.45 and march to the Centre.'

It was already hot when they set off. The uniforms proved too warm and the new shoes uncomfortable. They arrived just after 9.30, perspiring profusely. The women formed a rectangle around a field altar. There was no shade and the sun beat down unmercifully.

The girl next to Anna fainted and was carried away, then another went down and another.

'I must hold on! I must take the oath,' Anna said to herself again and again. At 11 o'clock the Archbishop arrived, his golden vestments and mitre blinding in the fierce sun. Anna never remembered how long his sermon was or what it was about. At last she heard the words of the oath of allegiance and joined in, noiselessly, with parched lips. With the final 'Amen' of the oath, Anna fell, face down, into the gritty sand.

'In addition to your normal clerical work, Anna, I'm detailing you to listen to the radio which is going to be installed in the office. This will be done at night time and you will write a report each morning.' said the office Chief. 'A new cadet officer will be joining us next week and he'll share the duty with you.'

Anna was delighted at the prospect.

'Thank you, sir,' she said immediately. 'It will be wonderful to hear the news as it breaks.'

In due course, Stanislaw, the cadet, arrived. His linguistic strengths were German and English while Anna excelled in Russian and French.

'I'm beginning to get some idea of the enormity of this war,' Anna thought after she had been listening to radio reports for a couple of weeks. 'I'm feel quite guilty at being so preoccupied with my immediate survival all this time.'

She had heard that the Soviet authorities were becoming increasingly hostile. Not only had they cancelled all recruitment of Polish civilians who were on Russian soil, they had cut supplies of food to the camp.

The temperature soared to ninety degrees Fahrenheit and Anna, still always hungry and often dizzy, once more feared for her health.

At the end of May, she received a letter from the Army H.Q. in Yangi Yul. She opened it with trembling fingers and a note in Severyn's handwriting fell out. Anna's spirits lifted as she read it eagerly.

'Dearest Annechka,

I cannot tell you how happy I was to hear that you are safe.

I was desperately worried when I discovered your absence on the train and blamed myself for the disaster.

I am now in the Polish Army Camp in Kermine and waiting impatiently, with 1,600 other airmen and sailors, to be sent to Great Britain.

The situation here is grim, with a typhus epidemic raging. Let's hope, that with God's help, we'll survive all the horrors of this war and that you and I will meet again in our beautiful Warsaw.

I am your true friend,

Severyn.'

It was then that Anna noticed a second note in the envelope. It read,

'We regret to inform you that Captain Severyn S. died of typhus at the beginning of March 1942. This letter, addressed to you, was found among his few possessions. We send it to you with our sincere condolences.'

Anna sat very still. She felt numb. Severyn's intelligent face swam before her. She heard his words of advice and encouragement. For so long she'd been sure they'd meet again and now she knew that this could never happen.

'I survived and he didn't,' she whispered and lay back on her bed. She turned her face to the canvas of the tent and cried.

On the following days, she went about all her tasks automatically. She lost her appetite and Dr Tajchner, noticing how ill she looked, called her aside one day.

'I can't seem to get myself going,' Anna confided, in answer to his questions. 'Everything's an effort, I can't sleep even though I'm tired and all the time I've had this great weight of sadness pressing down on me ever since I heard about Severyn's death.'

'Depression,' announced the doctor. 'You're depressed. It's understandable but you can't afford to let it overwhelm you, Annechka.'

'What can I do?' Anna's eyes had filled with tears. She felt hopeless and helpless.

'I prescribe a complete change of surroundings,' he smiled. 'I'll fix it with your chief so that you're able to spend a week helping me in my surgery. I think that will cure you.'

Anna didn't much like the idea and couldn't see how being among a crowd of sick people could possibly help her.

'But I've no medical training at all,' she protested. 'I won't be any good to your patients.'

'Sick people don't just need medicine. They need compassion and understanding. I'm afraid the nurse and I are terribly overworked. We're always working against time. We're really in no position to share our patients' problems. Help me, Annechka. Let them talk to you. Just listen to what they have to say. That's all – just listen, patiently, with all your heart.'

The next day, she presented herself in the courtyard of the small Uzbek dwelling that was Dr Tajchner's billet. A stream, shaded by mulberry trees, ran beside the courtyard and on its banks sat scores of sick soldiers, waiting for attention from the doctor.

Reluctant at first, Anna quickly fell into the routine of helping the doctor and nurse. Without her realising it, her depression and self pity dropped away. She became absorbed in the work. She listened to the personal tragedies and fears of so many and found that a smile, a few words of encouragement or a joke were often as effective as the tonic prescribe by the doctor. Too soon the week was over and Anna returned to SK 11 with renewed vigour and resolution to survive.

Before she left, she spoke to Dr Tajchner.

'Thank you so much for this opportunity,' she said. 'You saw what I needed and gave it to me. I've learned so much this week. When I have some free time, would you allow me to come and help you, please?'

'Please do. We'll always be delighted to see you,' he answered.

So Anna found herself among the doctor's small group of

friends. She felt less isolated and although she still grieved for Severyn, she was more contented than she had been for a long time.

'I think I could be almost happy if only my night blindness would go and my hair would grow,' she thought.

She still lost her sight at dusk and remained virtually blind until the next morning. This seriously impaired her night work in the radio room as she couldn't take notes when listening to transmissions.

As for her hair –

'Ugly and comic,' was her verdict, as she surveyed, in a cracked mirror, the dark stubble which covered her scalp.'

One day, during the midday meal, Dr Tajchner approached Anna and, with a triumphant flourish, produced a bottle and tablespoon from his pocket.

'Open your mouth wide, Annechka,' he ordered as he poured out a spoonful of thick liquid. 'And hold your nose. Swallow at once!' he added as he saw Anna's look of disgust at the taste and the smell. 'Swallow. Do *not* spit it out if you want your hair to grow!' It was cod liver oil. 'I went to a lot of trouble to get this for you,' said the doctor before Anna could say anything. 'Here is the bottle. Take a spoonful every day and, once more you will be able to see at night and your hair will grow.'

The night blindness went in three days and by the time the bottle was empty, Anna's hair was growing.

The summer heat became almost unbearable

'When, oh when are we going to get news about leaving this place and joining up with the rest of the army?' groaned Anna to Stanislaw, one stifling evening. They had been listening to a Moscow-inspired broadcast, in Polish, which was full of criticism for the Polish Government in exile.

'It can't come soon enough.' he replied. 'We won't be really safe until we're off Russian soil. They keep cutting rations, they've closed the Polish Representatives' offices in Moscow and now we keep hearing of NKVD arrests of numerous Polish citizens. And we're supposed to be fighting on the same side!'

'Yes, it's depressing,' said Anna 'but when I was talking to Dr Tajchner and some of his friends, yesterday, they said they're sure General Anders, with the help of the Allied Governments, will be able to persuade the Russians to let us go.'

On 26th July 1942, it became clear that faith in General Anders was justified. An official agreement was reached that the government of the USSR should allow the immediate evacuation of the Polish Army. A couple of days later, the order that the members of the armed forces should prepare to leave reached Guzar, along with notification that General Anders would visit the garrison before the evacuation began.

Anna's spirits soared.

'Just think,' she exclaimed to Dr Tajchner. 'Our General, our own hero, who has been imprisoned, humiliated, incarcerated interrogated and tortured and who has now achieved the impossible – our release from Stalin's clutches – this man is coming to see us.' The doctor smiled at Anna's enthusiasm.

'I couldn't have put it better, myself,' he laughed.

Anna never forgot the sight of General Anders as, leaning on two sticks, he walked slowly between the ranks of soldiers. He was tall, very thin and strikingly handsome. His emaciated face showed signs of his suffering but his dark eyes were piercing, alive, almost hypnotic. He looked into each soldier's eyes and, as Anna said to Jadzia, afterwards,

'He must have known how much we revere him and that each one of us would follow him through hell and high water, to the end of the earth, if he asked us to.'

The following few weeks were hectic. Anna and Jadzia helped to pack documents, army stores and equipment.

She worked enthusiastically alongside her colleagues. Their cheerfulness contrasted with the gloom of the Soviet officials. The Soviet Liaison Officer, a NKVD officer, called Tchaikovski suddenly took to popping into Anna's office at odd times and became quite chummy. One day he approached Anna in the office, with an ingratiating smile.

'Young lady,' he began, 'if you would supply me with a complete list of all the office employees, I'll arrange for everyone named to have an extra supply of cigarettes and sugar.'

Anna laughed out loud, knowing perfectly well that such a list of workers in Polish Intelligence could be used as evidence against every one of them.

'I'm sorry,' she replied. 'you'd have to ask one of the officers but we do have an agreement about bountiful luxuries such as you have offered. The agreement is that we can only accept them if you can offer the same to the rest of the garrison.'

The Officer gave Anna a long look, then, with a thunderous expression, turned and slammed out of the room.

In the first week of August, all Polish military personnel were vaccinated against typhus, typhoid fever, cholera and tetanus and a week later, the evacuation began.

A couple of days before Anna and Jadzia were due to leave, they went to the stores to collect one or two necessary items

'This consignment of ATS uniforms has just arrived from England,' the Quartermaster was telling a group of PSK volunteers. 'Take what you like. We don't want to leave them for the Russians, do we? Give your worn uniforms to the Polish civilians. They are in dire need and then take at least a couple of complete outfits for yourselves. Tell everyone else who wants new clothes to report here as soon as possible.'

Stefa and other members of the PSK left the camp before Anna and the SK 11 staff. Stefa wept as she clung to Anna.

'I'll never forget you, Annechka,' she wailed. 'You have taught me to read and write. How can I ever thank you?'

'No need,' Anna replied as she hugged her. 'Without you, I'd probably still be sitting on a chair. You taught me to walk again.'

It was two days' train journey to Krasnovodsk, the port from which the Polish Army and accompanying civilians, including children, were to sail. The railway station was two kilometres from the port area and as Anna and Jadzia got out of the train, they saw those who had travelled the previous day lying or sitting by the side if the tracks.

'What's happening?' she asked a passing officer. What's the hold-up here?'

'The Soviet Authorities are going to be awkward to the end,' he replied. 'They say we must wait until tomorrow for transport to the docks and, meanwhile, they refuse to supply us with any water or food.'

Exhausted by the heat, the long cramped journey and lack of sustenance, Anna and her companions flopped down among the piles of luggage.

Later that afternoon, several Uzbek women and children appeared from a nearby hamlet. They were carrying loaded baskets containing bottles of water and wine and some overripe melons.

'How much?' asked Anna.

'Water 80 roubles, wine 40 roubles, melon 60 roubles.' The prices were exorbitant but as the Poles had been told they could take no Russian currency out of the country, this seemed as good a way to spend it as any.

'A bottle of water and one of wine, please,' requested Anna. Jadzia, bought water and a melon and she and Anna shared some of what they had and ate the last of their dried bread. Anna put the remaining water and wine into her knapsack and everyone settled down to sleep. Although Anna was tired, sleep would not come. A hum of voices came from all round and the millions of insects buzzed and bit. She sat on a pile of luggage, surveying the men, women and children sprawled among piles of knapsacks, rolled blankets and wooden crates.

'Just like on a battle field but without the blood,' she thought.

The next morning, lorries arrived to collect the heavy luggage and those too sick to walk. Everyone else had to march.

The loaded knapsack was so heavy that Anna and Jadzia had to help each other to lift them on to their backs. Now the extra uniforms became a burden because there was no room in their bags for the greatcoats. They had to wear them over the winter uniforms. Anna trailed at the end of the column, quite sure she would never make the two kilometres. She, and all the women were perspiring, half blinded by the clouds of dust raised by the marchers in front. Anna stumbled, gasping for air. Her lungs felt ready to burst from exertion and her heart beat loud and fast. She dare not stop.

'If I stop for even one second, I'll never get going again,' she gasped to Jadzia.

At last the port buildings came into view and then the blue, enamelled sea.

'Sit and rest,' they were told. 'Food and water will be available very soon, from the camp kitchens. You will also be issued rations to last you the two days you will spend at sea.'

The cool blue water looked tempting. Several people were paddling and splashing their faces. Anna was in the process of removing her boots and socks to join them when a cry went up.

'Look at my feet and legs!'

To the dismay of the bathers, a thick layer of oil covered the sea bed and small lumps of the noxious, black stuff floated just below the surface. It clung to their feet, legs, hands, arms and even their faces. The poor unfortunates had to scrub themselves with dry sand in an attempt to remove it. Anna hastily put her boots back on and did up the laces.

After a meal of soup, bread and tea, Anna and Jadzia watched two of the ships sail from the docks and two more being loaded with equipment. Anna noticed her SK 11 Chief on the quay, talking to a couple of officers.

'Watch the bags for a few minutes,' she said to Jadzia and walked across to see if there were any news about when they would be leaving. She noticed two NKVD officers striding purposefully towards the group. They saluted smartly.

'We wish you to come with us to the port office, please sir,' they said to the Chief, politely. 'There are just a few details we need to clarify with you concerning embarkation.' They saluted again and walked away, the Chief between them.

'I wonder what the blighters want,' exclaimed one of the officers.

'I don't know, but I don't like it,' answered another. 'We all know, from grim experience, that you can never trust the NKVD. Liars and thugs, the lot of them!'

Fifteen minutes later, the Chief returned, red with anger.

'Somehow those so and so sons of bitches have got hold of a list of all SK 11 members,' he spluttered. 'They have suggested – well ordered really, but very politely – that our members should wait until all other Polish units are aboard these two ships. They say that when they have sailed, another, with superior accommodation, especially for us and other HQ staff, will arrive.' He paused for a moment, then went on. 'I don't need to tell you what I think about special transport for the Intelligence Department, arranged by the NKVD! They don't credit us with much of our famous intelligence, do they?'

Anna and the others laughed uneasily. The Chief continued.

'I want you to act very casually. Slowly assemble all your gear and then walk round and tell the rest of your SK 11 colleagues what to do. That is, singly or in twos to wander, apparently aimlessly, towards the ships. Then to mingle with the crowds going aboard and get themselves on one or the other of the vessels. At no time should any of you draw attention to yourselves. Do everything without haste. Good luck.' Silently his office workers nodded. One by one they walked away.

Anna took a leisurely stroll to her luggage and woke Jadzia, who was dozing. She explained what they had to do and they loaded themselves with kitbags and hand baggage.

'Let's go for that one,' said Anna pointing to the ship, named "Zhdanov".'

They mixed with the crowd of soldiers, making their way to the ship, weaving in and out, slipping ahead, unnoticed. They reached the gangplank, to be met by a young and flustered lieutenant, who was trying, in vain, to keep order.

'No girls allowed on this ship,' he groaned. Please go back to your unit and await orders.'

Just then there was a scuffle among the soldiers as some accused others of pushing in.

'Order! Take your turn, there's room for everybody,' he shouted. There was a sudden surge forward and Anna and Jadzia were swept on to the gangplank, clinging to the rope handrail and to each other.

The lieutenant followed them with his eyes and was about to shout to them when Anna summoned all her womanly wiles.

'Please sir, let us aboard. We're in imminent danger because of the nature of the military work we did,' she called across to him, her eyes full of tears. 'We throw ourselves on your mercy. If you don't let us come with you, we may never leave Russian soil!'

The officer looked doubtful.

'I wasn't notified such a request might be made,' he grumbled. 'None of my seniors is nearby, for me to ask. It really isn't proper for two young girls to travel with so many men.'

The conversation was attracting unwelcome attention. Anna was afraid the Soviet crew would notice and take action. Then Jadzia burst into tears at the thought of being turned away and there was an uproar among the soldiers.

'Let them on.'

'Their blood will be on your hands.'

'We won't touch them. They'll be quite safe.'

'It'll be murder if you turn them away.'

In desperation, the lieutenant shouted,

'Go on then. Just get a move on. We're late as it is.'

When the "Zhdanov" left two hours later, Anna and Jadzia were crammed into a tiny space in the corner of the deck, hidden from view by their pile of luggage.

It was a nightmarish two days. Every part of the ship was crowded so that it was impossible to move around freely. Despite a calm sea, many soldiers were seasick. Diarrhoea was prevalent. There were permanently long queues outside the four inadequate, filthy lavatories. These were insubstantial, floorless wooden huts, without doors, each perched precariously on two wooden poles, fixed to the deck, with only the waves beneath.

By the second day, the stench on board was almost unbearable. Dazed by lack of sleep, nausea and heat, Anna felt this hellish voyage would never end. Then, suddenly she heard a cry,

'Land! There's Iran!'

As if by a miracle, new strength surged through her. She stood up and helped Jadzia to her feet. They shouldered their knapsacks and stood still, in their little space, ready.

Now they could see the land. Slowly, oh so slowly, the ship entered the harbour.

'Oh look, Jadzia!' cried Anna. 'What a welcome!'

The quay was crowded with uniformed figures – Polish and English personnel, nurses in blinding white. They were waving, smiling, cheering. Further back were several Red Cross tents and a line of army lorries. As Anna waved, in reply, a feeling of intense joy and peace engulfed her.

As if in a dream, she walked down the gangplank on to dry land. Even though she was weighed down by her luggage, she felt as light as air as she was grasped by eager, helping hands and she spoke out loud the words that were singing inside her head,

'I'm free at last.'

WHAT HAPPENED NEXT

First in Iran and later when she was transferred to Iraq, Anna continued to work for SK 11. Her boss, in Iraq, was none other than Captain Nieczuja Dzierżek, the man with whom she had had so many differences of opinion. Their work took them to Palestine and then to Egypt. At the end of the war their office was moved to Ancona in Italy, where Captain Nieczuja Dzierżek became Commandant, responsible for organising transports for Polish service personnel, many of whom could not return home and needed to be re-settled in a variety of countries. In Ancona, Anna was reunited, for a short time, with her brother. He had just been released from Murnau Concentration Camp in Germany.

Anna and Captain Nieczuja Dzierżek were married, in Ancona, at the beginning of 1946. In November, of the same year Anna, leaving her husband to complete his task, travelled to France, where their daughter was born. She brought the baby to England a couple of weeks later and they travelled to the Polish resettlement camp in Delamere Park, Cheshire. She was soon joined by her husband, who became Camp Commandant and continued his work of re-settling Polish ex-service men and women until the final evacuation and closure of the camp in 1950.

The family, then, moved to Manchester, where Anna studied at the Manchester College of Art. She became a commercial artist and, in 1961, set up her own business as a freelance illustrator, specialising in children's books. She, her husband and their daughter played an important part in the large Polish Community in Manchester.

During the 1960's, Anna's younger sister, Zofia, arrived in Poland with her son. They had been on a collective farm in Siberia since the war and had been prevented from leaving until this time. Anna and her husband arranged for them to travel to England, where they settled.

In the early 70's Anna and family moved to Tooting, South London where Anna continued to work as an illustrator. She visited Poland once during the 70's, for the wedding of Aldona, one of her sister, Justa's, daughters. At last Anna was able to thank Justa, in person, for the two life-saving parcels she had sent so long ago, in 1940. Anna found Poland much changed. She was uncomfortable there and knew that her intelligence operations during the war had made her unpopular with the Communist Government. She never returned to her homeland but remained close to Aldona, who settled in England and then moved to Spain.

Anna became involved with the Polish Institute and General Sikorski Museum in Kensington, for which she worked tirelessly for more than twenty years.

With three other ex-members of the P.S.K. (the Polish equivalent of the British A.T.S.) she produced a book on the history of that organisation. She illustrated several other books on Polish military history.

She was decorated for her military service and for her work in the Polish community.

Anna died on 14th April 1997. She was decorated, posthumously, by the Polish Government, for her outstanding services to the Polish Community.

Captain, now Colonel Nieczuja Dzierżek died in 1998.

POSTSCRIPT

Anna was part of the second evacuation of Polish Forces and Polish civilians, from the USSR to Iran. The evacuation took place during August 1942. Twenty six transports left Krasnovosk during that month, carrying:

2,340	officers
36,701	NCO and other ranks
1,765	PSK / Auxillary Women's Service (Volunteers)
112	army employees (civilians)
2,738	children (pupils at schools organised by the army)
25,500	civilian Polish citizens, including 9,633 small children. All were under the care of the Polish Army.
69,247	**TOTAL**

An army unit of 2,637 officers and men had been left in the USSR, temporarily, to supervise the final evacuation arrangements. They departed in 1942, by land via Ashkabad, to Iran.

The last transport, comprising the children in the Polish orphanage and a small staff, was not allowed to leave the Soviet Union until July 1943. It arrived in Teheran via Meshed.

The total number of Polish soldiers and civilians who left the Soviet Union during the two main evacuations in March and August 1942 was about 114,000.

Left behind

415,800	registered graves
434,300	missing persons
681,400	people to whom USSR refused permission to leave

All these figures are based on original documents, which are held in the archives of the Polish Historical Institute and General Sikorski Museum in London.